GROW YOUR CLINIC

THE 7 DEGREES TO

GROW YOUR CLINIC

AND AMPLIFY YOUR IMPACT AS A CLINIC FOR GOOD®

BEN LYNCH
& THE CLINIC MASTERY TEAM

To the good people of the Clinic Mastery community: thank you for inspiring more health professionals to build Clinics For Good. We hope this book helps you to grow your clinic as sustainably as possible (ASAP) and amplify your impact.

First published in 2022 by Ben Lynch

© Ben Lynch and the team at Clinic Mastery 2022
The moral rights of the author have been asserted

A catalogue entry for this book is available from the National Library of Australia.

ISBN: 978-1-922553-44-7

Project management and text design by Publish Central
Cover design by Pipeline Design

Disclaimer: The material in this publication is of the nature of general comment only, and does not represent professional advice. It is not intended to provide specific guidance for particular circumstances and it should not be relied on as the basis for any decision to take action or not take action on any matter which it covers. Readers should obtain professional advice where appropriate, before making any such decision. To the maximum extent permitted by law, the author and publisher disclaim all responsibility and liability to any person, arising directly or indirectly from any person taking or not taking action based on the information in this publication.

CONTENTS

ABOUT THE AUTHORS

Ben Lynch is a creator and big picture thinker. His genius is being able to distil complex systems into easy-to-use frameworks so that health professionals can experience more meaningful work. As a podiatrist, Ben understood that a common thread connected all health professionals: wanting to help more people. As a result, Ben co-founded Clinic Mastery in 2015 alongside Daniel Gibbs and Shane Davis before Jack O'Brien joined the director team in 2017. Their mission became helping more clinic owners lead inspired teams to transform client experiences so that they could grow their clinic as sustainably as possible and amplify their impact as part of the Clinics For Good® movement.

The Clinic Mastery team quickly grew beyond the co-founders to a selection of passionate, purpose-driven and successful clients of our Business Academy. Those early clients who had a desire to educate and contribute to the stories of other clinic owners joined the team as a way to amplify their impact in creating more Clinics For Good®. Their contribution to the Clinic Mastery community has enabled the brand to evolve beyond any one person and remains a core driver in allowing us to help more people through cultivating a collaboration of different perspectives, professions, experiences and geniuses. The team has contributed in direct ways through their edits and through indirect support by providing their insights, stories and expertise from resources built over time that have contributed to this book.

INTRODUCTION

The ones who are crazy enough to think that
they can change the world are the ones who do.

Steve Jobs

Aligning with good people

Why do you do what you do? When we ask health professionals
this question, at the core of every response is a version of, 'I love
helping people'. Whether that means connecting families at the
dinner table through speech therapy, helping everyday athletes
achieve a personal best after injury using physical therapy or
helping those with mental health challenges through psychology
to better integrate their work and life, health professionals just
love helping people live a better life.

For many health professionals, showing how much they care
is often a driving force for going into private practice, where
there's often greater scope for more personalised and progressive delivery of care. It's often also for the same reason that they
decide to start their own business. For most health professionals,
running their own clinic gives them abundant opportunities to
help more people, help them more often and add more value
to their lives – through having greater agency and autonomy to
design great healthcare experiences to facilitate meaningful outcomes for patients.

Indeed, when health professionals share their journey into being a private practice owner, they usually mention one or more of the following as contributing to their decision:

- They saw no opportunities at their current role (and perhaps felt they weren't being listened to).
- They didn't see any pathways for progress in their current practice.
- They had a vision or an inspiration for what the practice could be like.
- They wanted to explore the commercial and creative opportunities for offering evidence-based practices with a modern healthcare experience.
- They didn't feel they had appropriate support, mentoring or guidance from those more senior in the practice.

If you're reading this book you likely run your own clinic, and perhaps one (or more) of these reasons sounds familiar to you. Clinics are a real force for good in this world and no doubt you started your business to do more than just breakeven; you started because you wanted to make the world a better place, and live in alignment with your mission by becoming what we call a Clinic For Good.

In an attempt to do work that matters for people who care and change the world by starting a private practice, however, we often see clinic owners wrestle with burnout, as the day-to-day demands of business overwhelm their ability to bring to life the vision they had at the start.

Perhaps this is you. Perhaps your challenge has been finding the support, guidance and connection you need from a community of good people, to help you navigate the journey of being a health professional and business owner. Perhaps the options you have been able to find have only reinforced your sense of overwhelm and burnout by emphasising accelerated growth, and making money the goal.

> The purpose of a car is not to buy gas.
> The purpose of a company is not to make money.
> The purpose of a car is to go somewhere and
> fuel helps you get there.
> The purpose of a company is to accomplish
> something, to advance a greater cause.
>
> Simon Sinek

To grow your clinic sustainably, it's important to identify and amplify the meaning behind why you do what you do for yourself and all members of your team.

Infusing meaning is central to aligning with Clinics For Good, a movement of health professionals playing a bigger game and amplifying their impact through collaboration and conscious business practices.

Here's why we think finding your 'why' is so important:

- Infusing your 'why' into what you do will create more meaningful work for you and give you (and your team) greater fulfilment.
- Purposefully designing your business to make an impact attracts like-minded partners, team members and clients.
- Clients are more socially conscious in the market today, creating an attraction advantage that positions you as a business to trust.

Knowing what to do

Being a clinic owner can be tough. Typically, health professionals go to university to study health because they had a passion for helping people, for the human body, or both. No doubt you were the same. As your journey progressed, you likely found yourself in a variety of different settings and environments working as a health professional, and perhaps then the opportunity to purchase or start a clinic came up. This is a natural progression. Unfortunately, our university and tertiary education institutions leave us health professionals under-prepared for the realities of the private practice environment.

A university degree for health professionals can't cover every-thing. By necessity, degrees have to focus on the healthcare aspects – rather than potential business aspects – of getting students ready to start seeing patients. Typically, the education provided doesn't cover being in private practice. So many professionals graduate with a lack of preparedness around time management, mindsets and systems around money and fees, marketing yourself to attract more clients and human resources to manage a growing team. And this just scratches the surface of what it means to be a practitioner – let alone a business owner.

You also have to be on top of leading a team, handling a payroll and the ensuing salary and wage discussions, taking care of substan-tial overheads and tax obligations, and working out cashflow issues that arise when third parties pay on their terms (not yours). And you have the constant pressure of ensuring a flow of new clients to satisfy your team members – who may or may not treat them in the same way that you would, or nurture them to continue to provide value over the long term. No wonder you can start to feel overwhelmed!

However, despite all these pressures, I am confident a deep desire still exists in all of us – we want to help people. In our experience of working with thousands of clinic owners, that is a sentiment that continues to ring true, regardless of the journey or path towards clinic ownership.

Here is what else we know to be true about clinic owners. We have all come to the realisation that, despite our desire to help more people, we are often limited by the number of patients (or clients) that we can physically see each day. Our impact is capped by our capacity to fit clients into our diaries. And so we recruit and hire other team members to allow us, by extension, to be able to help more people.

This is why we fundamentally believe clinic ownership to be a noble pursuit. For sure, private practice comes with commercial realities, and these are multifactorial. But we know that inherently, intrinsically, clinic owners do good work, for people who matter. In fact, we believe that private practice health clinics play a huge, and vital, role in communities globally.

Health professionals turned clinic owners often see it as their contribution to the world – and perhaps duty – to create, develop and grow a clinic that is able to help more people.

Think about it like this: if we are a part of a health industry that really cares to make a difference, if we have skills, knowledge and expertise that can help so many individuals to get out of pain, manage their disability, get on a pathway towards wellness, and rediscover their ability to achieve their meaningful goals and dreams as part of the human experience – we have a responsibility to deploy our skills, talents, knowledge and experiences to be able to help those people.

Escaping overwhelm and burnout

Of course, the pressures of owning your own clinic cannot be ignored. The rates of overwhelm and burnout in health professionals, and specifically in clinic owners, are at an all-time high. Certainly in an age of social media, comparing your reality with another clinic's highlight reel means you can easily fall into the trap of anxiety and feelings of inadequacy.

Legitimate health and medical perspectives are available when it comes to burnout and overwhelm - you should seek support from your own healthcare team if you're finding it hard to manage. However, we've also become aware of some things through observation and experience. Having to start from scratch and recreate the wheel to get a clinic off the ground is a tall order. When you consider that you likely didn't learn the context, skills or capacities required to run a business when you were studying, having unrealistic expectations is simply unfair. Couple this with an often unconscious lack of holistic self-awareness and absence of conscious personal development, you might have found yourself in a place of simply being out of your depth when it comes to having the capacity to deal with the rigours and weight of clinic ownership.

However, it doesn't have to be this way. A tried, tested and proven framework to growing your clinic is available, in the following Degrees in this book. The need to reinvent the wheel is a myth, often perpetuated by limiting beliefs or even pride. So many clinic owners have gone before you (and are still blazing a trail) who are abundant and open-minded enough to show others the way; you can piggyback off their hard work and knowledge (and mistakes) and make the progress you desire. Business is a skill that can be taught and learnt, and you can choose to do that in an effective or ineffective manner. Sometimes, this requires a solid dose of humility and swallowing your pride, and having the self-awareness to be able to see your blind spots and find the right mentor to guide you through the coming seasons.

You have a wonderful responsibility

Here's our charge to you: you have a responsibility, and an opportunity, to grow your clinic. Growth may not come easily – you might not know what to do because you haven't been taught how to do it as part of your training or study – but you can learn it. We will guide you through our 7 Degrees to Grow Your Clinic. We know that, in each degree, your *level* of mastery may be different – and that's okay. In our experience of working with thousands of health professionals across the world, a few things are true:

· Passion, hunger, devotion and commitment are the fuel to help you achieve almost anything.
· The majority of skills related to being a business owner are transferrable, and can be learnt.
· You've likely invested at least three years and $30,000 on learning to be a health professional. Don't expect it to be any different for learning the skill of becoming a business owner (even if you have been doing it already for years, or decades!).

A commitment to the process, and the journey, will see you achieve your desired outcomes. We hope that this book becomes a guiding light for you, one part of a lifelong learning process, and helps you to identify your opportunities and what you can do to grow your clinic with a higher degree of mastery (ongoing improvement).

Let us be clear, this book is simply a call to action to grow your clinic in a way that is meaningful to you and makes a positive impact on the causes and community that you care so much about. It doesn't provide a definitive blueprint to follow or 'cookie cutter' clinic to create. Your focus should be creating a clinic with the greatest expression of the client care experience that's evidence based, and meaningful for you, your clients, your team and the broader community. Our call to action to grow is all encompassing – from finances, to personal growth, team development, client experience and more. It's about doing your life's best work and using your clinic as a canvas to paint a picture of a better healthcare ecosystem.

'Open your aperture'

As healthcare professionals, we can learn a lot from our own industry and peers – for example, from attending conferences, learning at workshops and connecting in social groups. Psychologists commonly think the same way as other psychologists. Physiotherapists commonly face the same problems as other physiotherapists. And speech pathologists commonly need to navigate the same challenges as other speech pathologists. The same is true for all other professions. You can find great support within your own industry – but you shouldn't stop there. Just like opening the aperture of a camera in low light allows you to capture more colour, depth and richness in an image, opening your aperture to take in more than simply your own industry allows you to capture more insight and inspiration.

Open your aperture to see how other disciplines work within healthcare – for example, a psychologist can learn from a physiotherapist about navigating diary utilisation of clinic therapists. A speech pathologist can learn from a psychologist about navigating burnout in the clinic team. A podiatrist can learn from an occupational therapist about patient compliance in home exercises and activities. These are just some of the insights that become obvious when you see a community of healthcare professionals interact.

Open your aperture further to learn from professions beyond healthcare – for example, to learn from the restaurant and cafe industry about creating welcoming experiences and memorable customer service. Or learn from the hotel and airline industries about making people feel comfortable in a foreign environment. These are some of the many potential insights and starting points for discovery that will help you bring a richness to the journey of growing your clinic and allow you an abundance of inspiration to create meaningful and memorable client experiences. All you need to do is open your aperture. Ask questions, take notes, document your own experiences, join different groups and learn from beyond your industry.

Opening your aperture means seeking to understand an alternative point of view and then using your beliefs, values, paradigms and methodologies (in other words, your filter) to process this point of view and use it to guide your next action points. Not everything you see, hear or experience (even from the people you follow) is going to resonate. However, you always have an opportunity to learn from different viewpoints – and gain from them by evolving how you do business.

Because we encourage looking beyond the healthcare industry for inspiration and believe innovation can come from anywhere, you'll find a mix of healthcare stories and those from other industries in this book.

So open your aperture – and advance healthcare in a way that brings you joy and differentiates you so you attract more of your ideal people to work with, as part of your team, clients and partners.

> The best time to plant a tree was 20 years ago.
> The second best time is today.
>
> Chinese proverb

Building personal mastery

As we outline in this book, growing your clinic in a way that is meaningful to you, sustainable for everyone and makes a positive impact in your community involves continual improvement across the 7 Degrees. We refer to these improvements as levels of mastery. Self-awareness and personal mastery is such a vital key in navigating your growth experience. Self-awareness means really knowing yourself, how you learn and operate, and knowing how to embrace your inner genius to create more workflow and be the most resourceful, best version of you. This all contributes to your experience and personal mastery. Regardless of what has got you to where you are now, you always have the potential to grow and further improve. Our Personal Mastery Degree (the first of our 7 Degrees to Grow Your Clinic) will help show you how this can work. As you do build personal mastery, you'll find yourself gradually identifying your underlying strengths and weaknesses, and how you can best operate in your workflow – and lead others to find their workflow.

Here's the key: knowing what to do and doing what you know. You cannot begin if you first do not know what to focus on and where your strengths lie. You've invested tens of thousands of dollars and years into your clinical education – and you should also do the same for your business, leadership and personal education. Taking a deep dive and committing to learning the 7 Degrees to Grow Your Clinic throughout this book is an important next step in experiencing meaningful and measurable growth. Doing what you know comes later (and we cover this later in the book). Take the time now to prioritise working *on* yourself and working *on* your business by immersing yourself in the right information and getting around the right people – the ones who will challenge you to think big and support you to amplify your impact. We have seen this process work countless times, and we are excited to see and hear about your progress.

We have used the word 'mastery' because our process is about continued improvement. Just because you're at this *level* of mastery today doesn't mean you should rest on your laurels – the environment and conditions we're exposed to are always changing, and so you should be constantly readjusting. Focus on taking action on what you know.

Our hope is that by engaging with us through this book, you will find some distinctions that help you know what to do and, more importantly, once you progress, do what you know so that you grow your clinic as sustainably as possible.

Build assets along the way

Your clinic is a business. A business is an asset. And an asset is something that creates and yields value for those who engage with it. In your clinic, that value comes in the form of delivering meaningful health outcomes for your community, providing career and personal development opportunities for your team, creating income and impact for your family, and providing many other positive experiences for everyone who engages with your clinic (such as partners and suppliers). When you start a clinic, you are choosing to invest in a small business as a way of creating something of value (that is, an asset) so that you can amplify your impact.

Importantly, your clinic is not one asset. Instead, your clinic is many internal assets that combine to create and deliver value. These internal assets are valuable on their own, but combined together they help grow your clinic to be a preferred place to work, the top of mind choice for healthcare, a vehicle for change in your community and a rewarding experience that makes the journey sustainable even in the face of adversity.

These assets create structure, accountability and consistency; they guide workflows, generate cashflow, guide decision-making, foster personal connection, expand your network, boost your brand and so much more. At their core, these assets create value and yield value by delivering meaningful outcomes – whether that is for your clients, team, partners, suppliers, yourself or your community.

Throughout the book, you can find references to examples of assets you can create and use to help grow your clinic. You can also access real-world assets by following the QR codes provided throughout the book in the 'Assets in action' breakout boxes (see 'Milestones of growing Clinics For Good' for more on these boxes).

Make it sustainable

Anyone can rapidly accelerate the growth of their clinic, but at what cost? How might growth affect the sustainability of your clinic financially, the connection of your team, your energy levels and health, the quality of your systems and the sustainability of your results? Looking outside your clinic, how might growth affect your lifestyle and relationships?

It's likely you're planning on being in business for many years to come and, even if you're not, I'm sure you'd like to see your legacy and the clinic sustainably continue into the future. You want to build a good business, something that's built to last and something that does good for your local and global community. You want a clinic that grows meaningfully and is sustainable.

Finding your own way

The knowledge provided in this book has formed from growing clinics and seeing the work of thousands of health professionals. What we're providing here is not the only way. It's one way, and it continues to evolve. This is an account of stories and lessons that have guided meaningful growth. You can take the wisdom from this book and apply it to your own situation – your own clinic, your team, and your vision of the future. We simply ask that you run it through your own filter to apply it in a way that's meaningful for you.

How good are you at this?

It's likely you've learnt many of the lessons detailed in this book already.

This book includes concepts you already know. Guaranteed. Many of the business principles we share are tried and true, even when applied in private practice. However, are you *doing* what you know? Better still, how good are you at the task you've taken on? Coming from this perspective is central to creating a high-performing clinic, and ensuring its growth is continued and sustainable. This perspective comes from a place of humility and lifelong commitment to mastery. To be better every day. So, even as you read familiar text about a familiar concept, ask yourself, 'How good am I at this?'

Have we and others in the Clinic Mastery community made mistakes? You bet. But we got back up and we continued to learn how to be better. Through our own experiences and those of the clinic owners we've worked with, we've recognised some patterns for what works and gained lessons from the things that haven't. As health professionals, we love helping people live a better quality of life. We hope that the ideas, principles and stories in this book allow you to find more meaning, joy, success and impact for yourself, your team, your clients and your broader community.

MILESTONES OF GROWING CLINICS FOR GOOD

You're mad. Bonkers.
Completely off your head.
But I'll tell you a secret.
All the best people are.

From Tim Burton's *Alice in Wonderland* (2010)

Respecting the nature of business

Starting a business is a bit mad. The failure rates are high and, even if you're 'succeeding', it takes its toll on you – including some sleepless nights, regular worry about who might leave the team, a healthy dose of constant chatter in your mind about what needs to be added to your to-do list and some more pronounced wrinkles. (Starting a business is certainly not the anti-ageing formula you might be looking for …) And yet, we still do it, even though at some stage we've all no doubt said to ourselves, 'I didn't get taught how to run a business while studying healthcare at university!'

That's alright, because how do you really learn anything? You learn through experience, by first practising the fundamentals in isolation and then bringing it all together in a holistic framework that results in good outcomes.

As a healthcare professional, you're an intelligent person. You don't get to practise without a license, and to get that level of expertise requires serious commitment and investment to learning. You likely had to 'qualify' to enter your field of study (through your high school results), and then invest at least three years and $30,000 just to be eligible as a health professional, let alone be any 'good' at it. To develop into a quality health professional usually then takes quality mentorship, hundreds of hours in post-degree courses, many mistakes, a lot of hunger and bucket loads of humility.

On the other hand, starting a business and opening a clinic can often be done a lot quicker and for a lot less money. Then, usually after a honeymoon period – once the excitement settles and the reality of bills, overheads and a variety of added demands hits – health professionals turned business owners often realise running a business also requires a serious commitment. They need to invest – again – in applied learning, quality mentorship, hundreds of hours in post-degree courses, many mistakes, and, yes, a lot of hunger and bucket loads of humility. It can feel like being in the first year of uni all over again!

So your first step as a clinic owner is to respect the nature of business – it's the only way for you to truly grow yourself and your clinic sustainably.

7 Degrees are your real-world university learning

You didn't learn how to run and grow your clinic at uni, so in the following Degrees we've codified everything we can to break down the 'degrees' you need to qualify in to be successful as a health professional in business. This framework represents the real-world 7 Degrees of Clinic Mastery you need to sustainably grow your clinic and craft a well-rounded business and life.

Degree of difficulty

The first time I (Ben) learnt about the varying types of ski slopes was when travelling to Switzerland in 2015. Being a complete skiing novice, I thought just one type of slope existed – the ski slope. Of course, it turns out you can choose from several types of slopes, and each has a rating indicating its degree of difficulty – meaning a different level of skill is needed to be able to safely ski each one. I had a choice of slopes rated Blue, Green, Black Diamond and one scary, thrill-seeking, 'hope your life insurance covers you' slope called the Double Black Diamond.

I was told trying to ski a slope beyond your skill set could lead to real harm to yourself and others. I needed to get the fundamentals down pat first before progressing to the other more difficult slopes. In fact, I had no chance of getting to the more advanced slopes without months of advanced training and practice … probably alongside the mentorship from a ninja ski master.

A good parallel exists here with being able to navigate the different degrees of difficulty on the slopes of business.

The temptation is to grow your clinic as quickly as possible, and perhaps implement more advanced strategies before grounding your growth in the fundamentals.

We commonly hear clinic owners say one or more of the following:

- They've tried something but it didn't work for them.
- What they tried worked for a while but the growth or success wasn't sustained.
- Any changes they attempted only increased the sense of chaos and overwhelm with so many other things to manage.

Business is always going to present challenges – not every slope is perfectly smooth and flat. However, knowing the stage of business you're in helps you know what you need to focus on as you navigate the degrees of difficulty in growing your clinic.

The key point is to establish your fundamentals as you grow and respect that, as you progress, you'll always face new challenges and difficulties – and awesome new slopes to experience.

You'll also have the ride of your life.

Milestones of growing Clinics For Good

At the core of building Clinics For Good are two central intentions. The first is to build a good business – something that is robust, resilient and gets results for team members, clients and yourself. The second intention is that your business does good – by contributing to the causes that matter to you, and allowing you to amplify your impact for good.

Through our own experience and having walked alongside many clinic owners in building Clinics For Good, we've identified and characterised different milestones. These milestones are reflective of the common narratives, challenges, opportunities and strategies that a clinic owner will be presented with as they progress and grow.

Within each of the stages, these specific milestones characterise when you enter the stage, when you hit a maturity or stability point and then when you're about to transition into the next stage.

Comparison is the thief of joy.

Attributed to Theodore Roosevelt
(26th president of the United States) and others

Age for stage

A paediatrics class at university introduced me to a concept called 'age for stage'. We learned about what stage of development a child should be at for any given age – for example, what was the general age range for a child to crawl, sit or walk. These specific stages were called milestones, and the meeting (or otherwise) of these milestones helped identify if a child was advanced, on track or delayed in their development. Tracking these milestones, therefore, then guided any required treatment or intervention.

This useful concept can be applied in clinic ownership.

Just like you wouldn't expect a baby at three months of age to be able to walk, or a two year old to speak in full sentences, you need to appreciate the age and stage of your business so you know what the next steps are for sustainable development. You can understand where your business is at now, and what you should be aiming for. If you're an early stage clinic, you likely don't have your business operations systemised into a central intranet hub. However, if you've been in business for over three years, we would expect you to have standardised operations procedures for running the clinic in a centralised, mobile and global intranet hub. You must understand where you are at in your business's development so that you can grow your clinic in a sustainable and realistic way.

> Compare yourself to who you were yesterday,
> not to who someone else is today.
> You need to be aiming for something;
> you need a hierarchy of improvement.
>
> Dr Jordan Peterson (professor of psychology
> and clinical psychologist)

Knowing the 'age for stage' in your clinic ownership journey can help you:

- **Compare like with like:** A relevant peer comparison will help you understand how you're advancing. So many clinic owners unfairly and inaccurately compare their current business with that of a variety of their colleagues, even though they have no understanding on what stage of business they are comparing with.
- **Focus on fundamentals:** Getting the basics right for your stage allows substantial growth and development into the future.
- **Do the right thing at the right time:** To minimise the overwhelm, you need to list tasks in order of priority, and implement the changes correctly and thoroughly. Knowing what's needed for right now means you can operate by design not default, and realise the opportunities to transform your

clinic into the business asset that you deserve for your hard work and to bring your vision to life.

· **Create sustainable change:** Knowing your level of mastery in each of the functional areas of business means you can make the right decision and take the appropriate action at the right time, based on your circumstances, not what you think you 'should' do or what you see others doing. This leads to changes that are sustainable, because you're allowing the right amount of time, space and resources to learn, do, track, review and innovate.

For the reasons just listed and many more, knowing the 'age for stage' in your clinic ownership journey can take a lot (although not all) of the uncertainty out of what to do and when. This is why the 'age for stage' concept has guided and inspired the creation of our 7 Degrees framework.

Settle the symptoms and correct the cause (assess, diagnose, treat)

Your clinic is similar to the human body. Many vital systems need to work together for your health – and the health of your business – to thrive. When the underlying systems are not working as well as they should, you become out of balance and symptoms arise.

Looking for a bandaid approach to settle the symptoms may seem like the easy option, because life is busy and business moves fast! However, addressing the underlying problems is what's really needed – and having the 7 Degrees framework to assess your clinic means you can correct the cause to enjoy more balance.

As a health professional, you learn about different conditions, their underlying causes and their resulting symptoms so you can sustainably solve the problem for a patient. Simply put, your ideal approach is to settle the symptoms and correct the causes to produce sustainable change.

Often this treatment plan takes weeks, maybe months to complete.

A great parallel exists here in growing your clinic.

Symptoms might present in your business, indicating an under-lying issue – for example:

- tasks being missed
- gaps in the appointment diary
- patient complaints about their experience
- team member conflict
- lack of money in the bank to pay the team and bills
- appointments not running on time
- the financials of the business not being under control.

Often, many symptoms (also known as 'spot fires') present all at once, and focusing on just trying to settle the symptoms with short-term solutions seems to be the best option. For example, you may try to:

- throw more money at the problem or hire more people
- fix it yourself instead of delegating or creating a system
- fix the immediate problem in front of you without finding the cause.

These responses are understandable, and we all try them. Sometimes, there doesn't seem to be enough time to critically think, plan, prepare and implement something more substantial to correct the causes. If you've 'been here before', perhaps it's time to slow down and correct the causes for sustainable change.

To be able to create the ideal outcome for your patient, you need to complete an assessment, create a diagnosis and then devise a treatment plan. This is also a useful framework to help you grow your clinic. Start by assessing your clinic, discovering the problems (or opportunities), and then transform your clinic, remembering that a one-size treatment plan doesn't fit all.

One size doesn't fit all

As health professionals, we might laugh to ourselves when a patient says they've googled their condition and trialled possible treatments – without an assessment or diagnosis to guide their treatment first.

However, we often do a similar thing in business: we see a colleague or competitor do something and we try to copy it without first having determined if it's the right thing for us or without knowing all the other contextual factors that might support it to actually work.

You do you

Comparing yourself to other clinics is easy. But it's also unfair. You don't know the challenges or dynamics going on in another clinic. It's okay to be inspired by others, and to be inspired to create or refine what you do by other clinics. However, you do you.

You're not better than. You're not less than. You are in the right place, right now, for what's about to come if you do you.

Learn from other clinics, ask questions, seek guidance and pay it forward when it's your turn. Abundance creates abundance, especially when you do you. You'll make growing your clinic an enjoyable and meaningful experience – and a profitable and sustainable one when you do you.

7 DEGREES TO GROW YOUR CLINIC

Embrace a holistic approach to integrating business and life to create a well-rounded experience.

Ben Lynch

Crafting a well-rounded business and life

Assessing your clinic provides a clear roadmap for navigating the next stage of growth. Our 7 Degrees model represents the anatomy of your clinic as a business. You need to understand the anatomy of your business and how each system interacts with one another before diving into the pathologies of business and the treatments to help build a robust clinic.

We commonly hear clinic owners say they feel like they're juggling many balls at once or wearing many different hats when running a business. Our 7 Degrees model is the structured framework that represents those balls or hats. Each Degree represents a functional area of business that you need to work on if you're looking to grow your clinic in a sustainable way over the long run.

We've worked with clinic owners before they've opened their doors for business to those generating $10 million (and above) revenue per year with investors and 150-plus team members – and everyone in between. We help clinic owners to start up, grow up, scale up and exit out of their clinics. Our 7 Degrees approach, shown in the following figure, works for all of them.

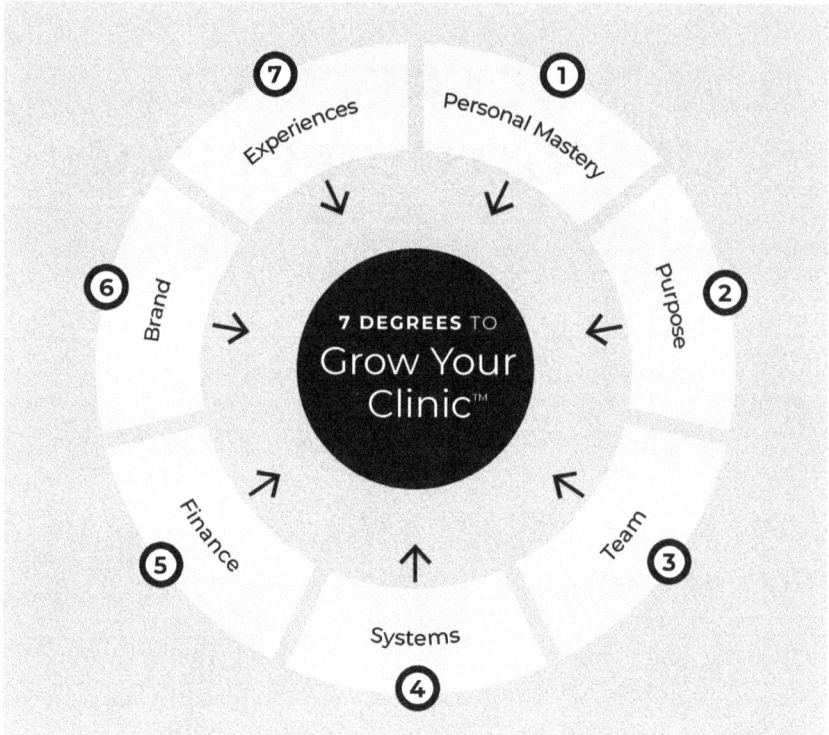

Mastery in each of these Degrees is not a one-off thing; instead, you will fluctuate in your level of mastery and will need to continually improve. We've called them 'Degrees' for a reason – not only do they represent the real world university 'degrees' (functional business units) you need to understand and influence to grow your clinic, the Degrees also serve as a unit of measurement to understand how good are you doing at any given time. Nothing is ever fixed, so your degree of mastery will fluctuate based on many internal and external factors including your stage of business, new philosophies, methodologies, technologies and so on. Therefore it's about playing the infinite game and embracing ongoing improvement.

The following sections take a closer look at each of the Degrees.

- **Degree 1: Personal mastery**
  Objective: Your best self

  You'll enjoy more success and greater fulfilment when you commit to your own journey of self-awareness, sustainability and mastery.

- **Degree 2: Purpose**
  Objective: Amplify your impact

  To have a bigger impact, you need to clarify where you're going, who you'll be along the way and how you'll get there.

- **Degree 3: Team**
  Objective: Lead inspired teams

  You need to attract, train and nurture quality team members so you can help more people.

- **Degree 4: Systems**
  Objective: Reduce reliance on you

  You need quality systems and structures to reduce the reliance of your business on you or any key person.

- **Degree 5: Finance**
  Objective: Grow profitably and sustainably

  Understanding your numbers helps you to make better decisions and reap the financial rewards of owning your clinic.

- **Degree 6: Brand**
  Objective: Attract ideal people

  You can create a framework that supports a consistent stream of ideal new patients, team members and partners.

- **Degree 7: Experiences**
  Objective: Create raving fans

  You need to create raving fans by delivering personalised, engaging and memorable experiences for better health outcomes.

Within each Degree are three core elements (strategic), and within each of these elements are three key focuses (operational) that you can implement to grow your clinic. We've included a Venn diagram with each Degree to capture and communicate these elements and key focuses.

In the following Degrees, you can read about the principles behind each element and each key focus, along with the practices to action so that you can make sustainable changes in your clinic.

Bonus elements

Insights + Intelligence + Implementation

Along with a breakdown of each Degree and its core elements and key focuses, we've also provided some bonus elements to help you relate the provided information to your particular experience and put the ideas into practice in your clinic.

The following sections highlight these bonus elements included throughout the book.

- **Relatable experience**

  Insights

  The 'Relatable experience' boxes provide real-world stories from the good people of the Clinic Mastery community. These people have also navigated the highs and lows of being a health professional in business and can provide insights to use in your own journey.

- **Mentor session notes**

  Intelligence

  The 'Mentor session notes' boxes provide frameworks for simplifying your growth approach by providing you with some intelligent solutions to frequently asked questions about growing your clinic.

- **Activity to amplify**

  Implementation

  The 'Activity to amplify' boxes provide something for you to use as a reflection or guided implementation of a particular system that you can use to grow your clinic. This allows you to tailor the activity for yourself and your business.

- **High-impact action**

  Implementation

  In the 'High-impact action' boxes, you can find clear ways to make meaningful, substantial or sustainable progress in growing your clinic. These are the actions you should prioritise to help you create a momentum of progress.

- **Tools and techniques**

  Implementation

  The 'Tools and techniques' boxes provide useful ways to fast-track results, automate processes and leverage your time for greater consistency. These are the sometimes subtle yet usually significant resources to use in order to create sustainability in your growth.

Assets in action

Implementation

In the 'Assets in action' boxes, you can find something that adds value to your clinic now and into the future. Included here are resources, strategies, intellectual property, policies, procedures and many other things that make your clinic more robust. By implementing these assets, you can help grow your clinic sustainably by creating repeatability, consistency and structure.

DEGREE 1:
PERSONAL MASTERY
Your best self

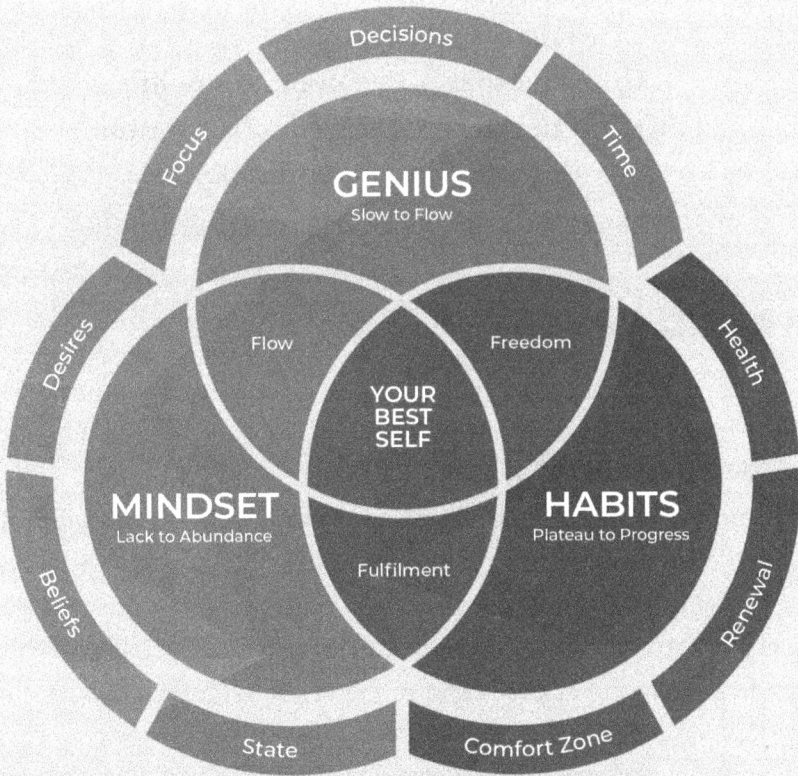

Core element: Mindset

Perhaps you know the old adage, 'Your business can't outgrow your own personal growth'. Mindset is about shifting from lack to abundance. And, as author and coach Anthony Robbins highlights, what stunts growth is rarely a lack of *resources* but a lack of *resourcefulness*. In other words, you need to go beyond scarcity and think more creatively, and be generous and abundantly minded so that you show up as a better version of yourself every day.

Key focus: State

Principle: Progress over perfection

> All of the things I've done in my life that I'm proud of have been done on the threshold of immense fear.
>
> Megan Washington (musician and songwriter)

It doesn't get easier; we get better

Running your clinic doesn't get easier, especially as you grow. You have more to manage, more that seeks your attention, and more things that are out of your direct control.

Anthony Robbins said, 'Every problem is a gift – without problems we would not grow'. Being conscious of your past experiences in growing your clinic is valuable because they can create a perspective through which you see certain aspects and principles that guide your actions. These experiences can also create a bias towards certain approaches that can be both empowering or disempowering. Ensure you learn the lessons from these experiences, but also ensure any lessons are not too limiting. For example, perhaps your past experiences have led you to believe business partnerships don't work. Another way of looking at this is that to make a partnership work well, you now know you need quality agreements from the start and a rhythm of connection and communication.

Relatable experience

Lisa, owner of a multidisciplinary musculoskeletal clinic, reflected on a subtle, yet significant shift in her state. 'Like all of us, my to-do list hasn't shrunk at all (it has actually grown) but I feel much less overwhelmed and more in control of my time. I feel excited and grateful by the things I get to do and the future of our clinic's journey. I have realised that I need to love this journey no matter what stage I am in, so I am re-framing my mindset to help serve me better.'

Conditions are always perfect

Trevor Hendy has won several world Ironman championships, joined the Sport Australia Hall of Fame, and received an Order of Australia for his services to the community and the sport of surf lifesaving.

As much as Trevor has become known for his success, he's become just as well known for his approach – captured by the saying that was commonly associated with him: 'conditions are always perfect'. In other words, if you focus too much on the external and not your internal state or statements, you run the risk of distraction and burnout.

Similar to being an elite athlete, growing your clinic presents many obstacles that can lead to moments of adversity. Some of these factors are out of your control or influence, which has the potential to weigh you down and discourage you from starting or continuing. Instead, you need to focus on your internal conditions and what you can control. Regardless of your circumstances, conditions are always perfect to grow your clinic – you simply need to tap into a more resourceful state to capture the momentum you need to make progress.

IFTTT

No, it's not a typing error. The acronym IFTTT stands for If This, Then That. It's a form of conditional logic (or sequence of steps) that designers of software and systems use.

IFTTT is a very simple way to describe how you might create automations in software and systems. The automation works like this: If This [event occurs], Then That [action will be triggered].

However, when it comes to your own logic (or sequence of thoughts) as a clinic owner, IFTTT can become a cognitive error – and an error that can make being a clinic owner exhausting. The exhaustion comes from the IFTTT sequence being a repeating pattern:

> *If This* happens, *Then That* will …
>
> *If This* month we can make more money, *Then That* will make me less stressed.
>
> *If This* busy next six-week period can go to plan, *Then That* will allow me to think more clearly about the important things.
>
> *If This* prospective team member joins us, *Then That* will give me more time.
>
> *If This* campaign fills the diary with clients, *Then That* will take the consulting pressure off me.
>
> *If This* waitlist of clients can be serviced, *Then That* will be a huge burden off of my shoulders.
>
> *If This* series of lockdowns ends, *Then That* will make business easier.

Be mindful of the unhelpful thinking styles you might be running. Your IFTTT may well be true. The challenge with IFTTT, however, is that your next IFTTT will come shortly after any goal you achieve.

With too many of these IFTTT conditional situations back to back, your sustainability and resilience will be continually tested because you're rarely in the moment. Your joy, happiness and fulfilment are always conditional on something, or someone else, someday in the future. That's exhausting.

Here's a practical (although not comprehensive) list of actions to consider to break away from IFTTT thinking:

- Get a psychologist and/or coach as part of your support team. Being in business is a challenging beast. Having someone by your side to guide you through can be just the support you need to navigate the turbulence of business.
- Get in the moment with mindfulness, gratitude and perspective to enjoy the journey now, rather than making happiness and fulfilment conditional on something else later. Meditate or journal.
- Focus on what's within your control, what's within your influence and what you just need to accept.

IFTTT thinking can be driven by the need for things to be perfect to ensure success. This often results in no change being made as you become stuck in the same place.

Relatable experience

Jess, owner of a musculoskeletal clinic, shared a milestone achieved by one of her team members following a recent retreat. Jess's team member reflected on the experience and shared that the team retreat came at the perfect time – because they had been coasting. He felt they'd all been acting like passengers in their own lives. They had been running the IFTTT thinking process – waiting on things to happen before making the next step in their career or life. Over the weekend, in the days following the retreat, the team member sent a message of gratitude and celebration – he had asked his partner to marry him and she had said yes! The message signed off with 'Thank you for the opportunity, inspiration and accountability to my desire statement'.

Key focus: Beliefs

Principle: Check in with yourself

> **Think you can, think you can't;**
> **either way you'll be right.**
>
> Henry Ford

Who's captaining this ship?

Daniel, owner of a multidisciplinary musculoskeletal clinic, realised he thought his clinic changing was what would then change his life and the lives of those in his team. What was needed was the opposite: 'What I didn't expect was that working on myself would help my clinic change at the speed it has done'.

As Holocaust survivor and author of *Man's Search for Meaning* Viktor Frankl wrote, 'When we are no longer able to change a situation, we are challenged to change ourselves'. Daniel realised he had been passive in the journey of growing himself and his clinic. He'd started many attempts at introducing cultural change, systems improvement and financial growth, but many attempts had failed. The same cycles were repeating and so were the same belief cycles – until he became aware and stepped up to captain the ship.

Daniel reflected on the three biggest shifts that unlocked his awesome progress in growing his clinic:

1. Identifying personal values and considering these values before making every decision.
2. Creating a process for regular self-reflection.
3. Understanding the relationship between time and identity.
   (I am not who I used to be and I am not going to stay the same. I am always changing. Life is always changing.)

Daniel now feels he has a compass for where he now is, and where his clinic is heading.

Beliefs are precursors to results

You must first have the right mindset state to formulate the right beliefs before you can act accordingly. Growth and strong results start from empowering beliefs. You know this to be true in your treatment of clients – first exploring their beliefs about health and wellness allows their results to then be much more sustainable. Daniel first shifted his beliefs, and then his results also shifted. Over the course of 12 months Daniel:

- hired five new practitioners across four disciplines
- expanded the clinic to double the number of consulting rooms and built a rehabilitation gym
- added psychology and dietetics services to the existing service offering of podiatry, physiotherapy and remedial massage therapy
- rebranded and reinvented their website
- terminated a contractor team member
- changed their practice management software to one that was more user-friendly – meaning notes, letters and bookings were completed with ease and billings were processed on time
- introduced new tech (including Slack, Asana, Google across all relevant options and Cliniq Apps), streamlining systems and communications for a more connected team

- created clarity with the financial numbers and started working with an amazing proactive accountant to know exactly the position of the business (after the previous accountant left them with an 'unexpected tax bill')
- switched to a more progressive, cloud-based accounting software that was also more user-friendly and supportive of better financial reporting
- increased annual revenue by 122 per cent from Q1 to Q4 in the same year
- established a meaningful relationship with referrers, clients, employees and community.

See Daniel's 'Relatable experience' box later in this Degree for more on his journey.

How good is this?!

Choosing to start your clinic means choosing to be able to experience the creative and commercial opportunities in delivering progressive, evidence-based, experience-led healthcare. You don't have to cut through red tape, bureaucracy and board approvals before making simple decisions. Instead, you just have creative freedom to design and express on a blank canvas the way you see healthcare.

How good is it that you get to think of an idea in the shower or on the commute to the clinic, and then bring it to life within hours, days, weeks or months? Once implemented, you can then get paid for it, be proud of it and see the impact of it – all pretty awesome. You have the ability to learn, think, do, achieve. It's an amazing opportunity, once you believe with conviction that it can be done.

Rise of the do-it-yourself (DIY) mindset

You don't need to do it all yourself when it comes to your clinic. Doing it yourself might make for a more entertaining story later on, but the reality is it's foolish in the context of your clinic.

Growing your clinic involves many fundamentals and characteristic milestones that with the right guidance can be made simpler and more enjoyable, and yield less stress and overwhelm. Business has enough knocks without you trying to do it all yourself in areas that have already been mastered. You should focus on playing to your genius and area of expertise, and leveraging your time productively.

Immersing yourself into various communities, investing in different advisors and engaging with progressive peers can teach you a lot. If you're part of the 'do it yourself' crowd, however, you'll no doubt hear an abundance of beliefs that are self-perpetuating prophecies about their experience. For example:

- Making lots of money as a health professional means you must be doing something unethical.
- You'll always face a shortage of good-quality therapists to join your team.
- Business is lonely and you've got to figure it out yourself.
- Your employees can never do the job as well as you.
- Your team would never adopt these new ideas or practices.
- You have to work hard to 'make it'.
- Business partnerships don't work.

These beliefs are underpinned by that thought highlighted by Anthony Robbins that your problems are rarely based on a lack of resources; they're often due to a lack of resourcefulness. Check in with yourself to see what beliefs you might have that could be limiting your ability to be resourceful in finding solutions to those challenges in growing your clinic.

Regardless of what's going on, you always need someone who's keeping you accountable to your actions and giving you directions and mentoring as you grow. In other words, you need a mentor, board of advisors or mastermind – and you no doubt already understand the importance of mentoring and how it works. You wouldn't expect your therapists, for example, to grow without supervision or structured mentoring. In the same way, it's important that as you grow your clinic, you are levelling up to a version of yourself that is capable of continuing to grow it. As you grow, you will face new and different problems and challenges that are characteristic for that stage of growth. And so you're required to develop your characteristics, beliefs and skills as a business owner to navigate those stages. The trap is in thinking that the version of you who has grown your clinic to this point is the same you that can grow it further. However, the old you can be holding on to certain mindsets, approaches and limiting beliefs that are a reflection of you from months or years ago, and this can cause a sabotage loop. With our clients, we've observed that a business not being able to get past a certain threshold – such as number of team members or revenue size – is often due to the owner not being able to grow their own character (whether that be their state or resourcefulness, beliefs or skills) beyond their present stage to effectively progress into the next business stage.

Key focus: Desires

Principle: Meaningful growth matters

> ### Growth for the sake of growth is the ideology of the cancer cell.
>
> Edward Abbey (writer and environmental activist)

Personal desire statement

Before we dive into the key elements that define an organisation's purpose and allow a business to play a bigger game, we must first look within ourselves. It is a cliché, but it is often said that if you aim for nothing, you'll hit it every time. Think about the analogy of going on a journey or a trip – unless you know the destination, making sure you're heading in the right direction and making the right decisions is impossible.

Far too often we see clinic owners who are vague in their clarity around their vision of the future and what they want from their clinic – and, by extension, their life. Having the self-awareness to know what you want and how you operate, as well as the power of goal setting and deciding your intentions, is incredibly powerful.

As owner of Pro Feet Podiatry (and co-founder of Clinic Mastery) Shane Davis often says, 'Most people spend more time planning their wedding than they do their life or their business'.

We like to use a personal desire statement as a tool for you to articulate how you would like your life to look, across multiple areas, and at defined points in time in the future. The statement needs to be worded in the present tense for that future time, and allows you to feel what it will be like when your current desires become your future reality. You can use any form of domain or spheres of life criteria to begin to flesh out your personal desire statement and determine your areas to focus on – for example:

- health and wellness
- psychology and mental wellness
- love and relationships
- productivity and performance
- career and business
- wealth and lifestyle
- leadership and impact.

The 'present tense' language is a vital component of your personal desire statement. The intention is that you regularly review your statement (weekly or fortnightly) and update your statement (monthly or quarterly), so you want to be able to feel the emotion associated with the accomplishment of your goals. Rather than saying, 'I want to live in a nice house', for example, a desire statement should include something like the following:

I am so grateful to have purchased and be living in our dream family home in Henley Beach – a recently renovated

Californian bungalow home on a 800m² block with four bedrooms, two-car garage, cinema room, home office and 30m² swimming pool with spa, 200 metres from the beach and 500 metres to the kids' primary school.

It's important to include as much detail as possible to make the statement vivid and real. In something like the preceding example, the greater detail also helps determine the required budget – allowing you to then work backwards from that target to determine your actions today. Exploring why this specific desire matters is also important, along with what's the meaning behind it for you. In the preceding example, the meaning could be that you're looking to start a family and you want the kids to go to the school that you went to – so proximity is important. Or it might be that you don't want the beach to be something you do twice a year on holidays but, instead, part of your daily living because it brings you joy, calmness and promotes healthy living choices. Make your desire statement specific and meaningful to you.

Your version of success

When we ask clinic owners to share their version of 'success', it's always great to see some similarities, and many differences.

Your version of success is unique to you. That's why you don't need to grow your clinic to a particular size or status – for example, $1 million annual revenue. You will have to hit certain financial targets to allow you to grow and stay afloat, but that does not mean your version of success necessarily has to be based on financial goals. Maybe you want to take every Friday off, or have six weeks of vacation time every year, or open three new locations. Most commonly, underneath the first few responses to 'What does meaningful growth look like for you?' the clinic owners we speak with get to sharing their desire for impact and legacy. They want to create a clinic that can have a positive impact on the causes that matter to them, their local community, their clients and team and, of course, their family. That impact looks like a variety of different outcomes, of course – and that's why it's important to explore for yourself what your version of success is. What does meaningful growth look like for you?

Action matches ambition

One of our clients – John – contacted us to ask for financial support with his membership of our Clinic Mastery Business Academy. At the start of the conversation I asked John to first take a moment to reflect, saying, 'If you were to rate your level of implementation out of 10, where 10 is "I'm following through and taking massive action" and 1 is "I'm doing sweet nothing", where would you rate yourself?'

John paused, cleared his throat, and said, 'Probably a 4 out of 10'. I thanked him for his honesty – because now we could delve a little deeper into why John's finances were so tight.

At times you need to be able to change pace, and perhaps seek more renewal or rest time. At those times, your implementation levels are going to be reflective of your level of effort and engagement. However I could see from John's social media that he was doing a lot of socialising – and it didn't look like the kind of work that was needed for growing a clinic or, more importantly, that was required to achieve the meaningful goals he'd set for himself.

One of our core values is keep it real, so I asked, 'Do you think 4/10 reflects your ambition?' John's answer was no. I told him I was happy to help him out with his membership, but perhaps the reason he needed this support was because he needed to take some ownership and follow through on the things he said he was going to do.

Support is always available, whether that be from your network, team, clients, advisors or friends. However, you need to also show up with your actions in a way that aligns with your ambitions for meaningful growth.

Core element: Genius

Genius is about transitioning from slow to flow. And flow comes when you're focusing more of your time in the zone where you're gifted, highly engaged and most effective in your work.

Key focus: Focus

Principle: Play to your genius

> **Everybody is a genius. But if you judge a fish by its ability to climb a tree, it will live its whole life believing that it is stupid.**
>
> Anonymous (commonly misattributed to Albert Einstein)

Your zone of genius

We all suck at plenty of things, and we're only average with a number of things. However, we also know we're awesome at doing a select few things. Hearing the preceding quote about five years ago catalysed a few thoughts for us – and, more importantly, a few actions …

You need a hint of self-reflection, a dash of learning and a pinch of quality feedback from others to help clarify your 'genius'. And we believe your idea, and belief in, your own genius is continually clarified over time.

Capturing your genius and writing it down so that it can be kept front and centre is an important part of being able to simplify your work, delegate effectively, access more flow in your role and get better outcomes.

Another way to look at this is to consider the concepts (taken from the world of software development) of impact and ease. Essentially, considering what impact your action will have and how easy it is for you to take that action helps you sort the high-value from the low-value tasks, and identify the items that only you can and should do for maximum impact.

Otherwise – and we all do this – you can easily start to beat yourself up about the fact you're not 'making progress', you 'don't understand it' and feel 'stupid'.

So, if you can do one thing really well, it's your genius – what is it?

Immersing yourself

Clinic Mastery member Cathy was excited to be able to take off an entire week from her consulting schedule to work on her clinic. Six months later, Cathy reflected on the value of immersing herself and playing in her genius zone. Cathy had:

- Realised her massive mindset shift from six months ago when, after an employee quit, she didn't panic, or get stressed or anxious. Instead, she took a breath and thought, *This is good*.
- Achieved her biggest week ever in terms of finances, even with her reducing her clinical consulting hours. So the clinic had booked in more patients but Cathy wasn't the one seeing them!
- Ensured her systems were working, and rebooking rates for client care continuity were up.
- Started a clinic walking group on Saturday mornings (following a team member's suggestion).
- Realised if this momentum stays on track she will need either a new team member in the second half of the year or a final year intern, or perhaps even both.
- Overseen team members taking on the training of other team members.
- Witnessed momentum building in the team.

When you immerse yourself in your genius and prioritise tasks to focus on, consider three areas and ask yourself the following:

- **Impact:** What will be the impact or outcome of this task or action (make it measurable)?
- **Meaning:** Why do it – what will the result mean?
- **Action:** What is the massive action that only you can do?

Activity to amplify

Video journal questions

Answer the following questions in a private video journal once per month to capture your story as you grow your clinic and yourself. Using video allows you to hear your tone of voice as well as your words and see your physical state. This gives more colour and context to what you're documenting rather than simply writing in a journal.

Include the following in your video journal:

- Today's date. (It helps when you watch back to know when it was!)
- What's top of mind.
- What you're excited about and what's on the horizon.
- What you're concerned about and any challenges you're facing.
- What you're currently working on.
- How's business looking – share some stats.
- What you're doing well at the moment as a team or personally.
- What you could be better at currently as a team or personally.
- What's in your genius zone – what are you really good at doing and being?
- Ideas on how you can play more in your genius zone in the next four weeks.
- What is one big ideal outcome that you're looking to achieve four weeks from now?

Do this exercise once per month and document your years in business. Use your previous entries to look back at how far you've come personally, professionally and as a practice.

Key focus: Decisions

Principle: Document your decision-making criteria

Change is inevitable. Growth is optional.

John Maxwell (leadership expert)

Don't major on minor things

You make hundreds of decisions every day that move you toward your vision. Making these decisions is much easier when you have clarity of your core purpose and have painted a picture for yourself (discussed further in Degree 2: Purpose). The ease doesn't come from having guarantees about the short-term outcomes of those decisions; rather, it comes from having a filter through which to assess each decision with conviction on whether you're moving in the right direction. And remembering that indecision is still a decision – to do nothing.

As a leader, one of the greatest characteristics you can express is your ability to make quick, meaningful decisions. Examples of the types of areas where you'll be faced with decisions in your clinic, grouped by their impact, are:

- High-impact decisions:
  - Business partners
  - Team hiring
  - Location expansion
  - Specific niche for the business

- Medium-impact decisions:
  - Website design
  - Practice management software
  - Investing in new technology or equipment
  - Clinic design and layout
  - Signage
  - Advertising
  - Opening hours

- Low-impact decisions
  - Design of business card
  - Types of computers
  - Office furniture
  - Uniform

Growing your clinic requires you to make quality decisions backed with consistent action. In order to grow your clinic sustainably, it's important to get better at making more meaningful decisions, more quickly. When you know how to make progress and pick yourself up in the face of a wrong (or bad) decision, you'll find freedom in testing many different things that work and don't work in your journey towards building a Clinic For Good.

Avoid trying to make 'correct' decisions. In a desire to feel confident and absolutely certain we can paralyse ourselves with analysis of all the contributing factors to a decision. And sometimes all the information isn't available in a timely manner. It's better to focus on the criteria for clear decision-making so that you can easily adjust and course correct along the way. Be humble enough to be wrong, smart enough to accept it when it happens and hungry enough to keep making progress even in the face of uncertainty.

Hindsight is 20/20 vision

You've probably made a bad decision before (once or twice). We all have, we're human. The bad decision could have been about who you hired, or who you didn't fire soon enough. And you're going to make more wrong decisions in the future, and so will your team. The value of hindsight is learning from those decisions so you don't repeat them, and learning to minimise the frequency of poor decisions and lessen their impact or damage. Remember, progress comes from learning so be committed to fail forward and make mistakes. The key action is to document your lessons of decision-making in the form of principles so that as you grow, you're able to delegate with confidence and decision-making consistency.

Share this document of principles with your team so that they can contribute to it and use it in their decision-making.

Moving on from overwhelm

Amid the experience of feeling overwhelmed at various points of growing your clinic, you have the decision to choose where your focus goes. Overwhelm is a state you reach when you're faced with too many decisions or distractions all at once, and can make even deciding what to leave and what to tackle straightaway difficult. Much of the overwhelm comes from thinking about factors that are outside of your control, so narrowing your focus back to what you can control is key to feeling like you've 'got this'. One thing you can control is your decision to do one thing – to make the next right (or right for now) decision. Quick, meaningful decisions create momentum, and this is the best way to get out of over-whelm. Focus on the decision that you can make with relative ease and that will be impactful once acted upon.

Relatable experience

Annie Strauch, director of Performance Medicine and Clinic Mastery mentor, shared a subtle, yet significant shift she identi-fied. This shift relates to a distinction around our language and how it relates to our decisions. Annie was mentoring Bec, a clinic owner, and they were talking about the stress that comes from juggling kids, business and life. Bec was feeling overwhelmed with all the roles she had to play – including therapist, leader, mentor, wife, mother and business owner. Bec said she wasn't able to find the time to work on her business and, among her reasons why, she said, 'I have to pick up the kids from school'.

Consciously or subconsciously, the decision to pick up the kids from school had become a 'chore'. Annie shared another perspective with Bec: some parents would love to be able to finish work at 3 pm to pick up the kids from school (or any other version of this). The distinction that Bec could make was that instead of 'have to', she 'gets to'. ('I get to pick up the kids from school.')

This simple shift in your language provides an opportunity or at least an option to shift how you approach or focus the outcome of your decision. What you may take for granted, someone else likely wishes they had. This shift also takes you to a place of gratitude. It's not always easy to do, but give it a try. Ask yourself when faced with a challenging decision, do you 'have to' do this or do you 'get to' do this?

Pressure is a privilege

Legendary tennis player Billie Jean King famously said, 'Pressure is a privilege'. Billie won 39 Grand Slam titles in the late 1960s and early 1970s, and is one of the most successful tennis players to have ever played the game. Billie's success meant that so many believed and expected her to win every time she played. That sort of expectation might have weighed heavily on some, but Billie took this pressure as a privilege. The pressure was on her because she was facing an opportunity to do something great – and important and meaningful. It was, therefore, a privilege.

For you as a clinic owner, pressure is also a privilege and it comes in many forms on a regular basis. You face the pressure to make the right strategic decisions about who to hire, what's the right location for your first or next clinic site, what technology you should invest in, how to manage competing priorities when someone has resigned and you need to run a sustainable and profitable business, and how to be a good person, professional and practice leader. Pressure is all around. It's also a privilege because you're able to effect change. You're able to make a meaningful contribution to the lives of the people you work with – from your clients and team members, to your partners and members of your community. Of course pressure can feel like a burden to carry, and it's at those times when it's important to reflect on the privilege you have to make a difference and be a force for good.

Relatable experience

Daniel Monteleone, founder and clinician at Proactive Health and Movement, shared the following in Clinic Mastery's Business Academy private forum.

Own your business; don't be owned by your business!

What does it mean to truly own a business? Let's get a bit business-y for a moment. If you're building an asset, traditionally you look at return on investment combined with the least reliance on you to create that return.

This win story starts as a loss.

Before my journey with Clinic Mastery, I struggled with confidence in managing members of our team who have different roles to my background.

At a mastermind session in Sydney, Ben asked me a question: 'Who is steering the ship?' And then he answered for me: 'You need to steer the ship.' I thought to myself, *Ah crap! He's right!*

After this reality check I made the decision to take more responsibility and to take the business down a deliberate path of improvement and purpose. All the while, I was fully aware I still had my L plates on when it came to 'business' and managing people.

Over the last month, I have been challenged by three separate members of my team in relation to:

· increased accountability
· changes to procedure
· and the big one: the need for and effectiveness of
  mentoring sessions.

There have been tears, some surprising behaviour and a lack of ownership. The support I have offered through meetings has been viewed as micromanagement, unnecessary and telling people who they should be rather than letting them be who they are.

Thankfully, I have had my coach Andrew Zacharia [another member of the Clinic Mastery team], this community and some other great people in my life to guide me.

I can now reflect on how the lack of skill and communication on my part in the past has allowed for unclear expectations and ultimately led to this outcome. And so, I've put in a lot of time over the last month with each of the three team members individually. We've had meetings over dinner, walks and talks, and thrown in some informal mentoring throughout the week.

I'm pleased to say that I've seen a positive outcome in every situation and with every relationship. I think finally everyone has realised the real purpose behind all the change has been to help our clients, to help our business, and to help them!

The change I have seen in these people is actually hard to believe or describe. But the results are clear:

- Accountability is up.
- Culture and relationships are up.
- Patient visit average (care continuity) and client outcomes are up!

Upon reflection and after seeing a social media post that triggered my thought process further, I have come to realise I can see a pattern here that has me fascinated:

Mental breakdown (including stress, retreat and frustration) comes before mental breakthrough (ownership, responsibility and capability).

I can look back at the start of my Clinic Mastery journey and realise I have been through the same thing!

Failing at getting my head around the various platforms, weekly meetings, reducing my consulting time, actually committing to achieving something week to week was my mental breakdown (where I experienced stress, retreat and frustration).

My breakdown allowed me to reflect, reconsider and have another go – to then achieve the mental breakthrough.

Now, I can look forward to the next mental breakdown! The next challenge. The next level up.

In other words, I'm talking about load and capacity – which is no different from a pain or performance-related management plan.

Have you had the same revelation with yourself?

Have you noticed this pattern of behaviour with your team?

Key focus: Time

Principle: Create a workflow not a workload

> In every job that must be done, there is an element of fun. You find the fun and snap!
> The job's a game.

'A Spoonful of Sugar' from *Mary Poppins* (1964)

Workflow versus workload

Workload feels like resistance and inertia. *Workflow*, on the other hand, feels like rhythm and results. It's obvious which one we'd love to have every moment of every day – workflow, of course. So how does it evade us so often? Perhaps it's related to priorities, self-awareness, mental clarity and vision for the future. Perhaps it feels like a workload for a number of reasons. One thing's important: our language and inner voice guide how we feel about the work ahead of us. Workload feels heavy – it feels stationary on the desk, requiring a lot of energy to move – so procrastination becomes easy.

Think of your projects and priorities like a river, like water: they're meant to flow to create momentum and energy. With this attitude, you develop workflow rather than a workload. You've got to keep the 'work' moving – whether that be through prioritising progress over perfection and just getting started, or delegating to someone else. Perhaps you can engage some help from advisors or mentors, or hire new team members. Create the structure in your day and team for the work to flow and watch your clinic grow.

Have you built a business or built a job?

Darron is a physiotherapist and clinic owner of a multidisciplinary clinic. He started his clinic in the late 1990s, with one major clinic site and a huge renovation (at a cost of more than 250,000).

David had developed a great reputation in his special area of clinical interest, building massive demand for his work. After establishing his clinic, he was still consulting 60 hours a week and had dug a *very deep* hole for himself. He realised he had created a massive job for himself but not a business. Being so focused on consulting had resulted in him not dedicating enough time (and not having any spare time to dedicate) to work on other aspects of his practice, including developing a high-performing team.

But after 11 months of working *on* himself and his clinic, he was down to consulting only 29 hours a week – under half of what he was doing before. Even at this stage, Darron said the process had been life-changing. In that time he'd:

- hired three physios
- defined the patient journey
- gone from paper to cloud computing
- changed practice management software
- created a 100-day team onboarding process
- achieved a massive decrease in stress and a huge lift in enjoyment.

In the months following, with further time to build the team and systems, Darron transitioned through the final stages of reclaiming time. Darron reflected, 'I can't believe that in 20 months, I've been able to go to zero. I'm having a brilliant time travelling by train in Europe with my family and seeing some magnificent scenery with my wife and two sons. This is priceless'.

'I don't have time'

We all have the same 24 hours in a day. Where you are now is the product of your decisions and actions. Feeling like you don't have enough time is really about needing to prioritise your time and have the confidence to take action on what you're working on. No-one said this would be easy. Success isn't easy.

You can achieve more in one hour of inspired time than in a week of being reactive to the problems of the day. How much is it costing you to stay where you are – not just financially, but also in terms of your happiness and lost time?

If you're lacking time, you're lacking priorities for what's important and what's needed to achieve your meaningful outcomes. Once you have these priorities, you can delegate, eliminate, automate or dominate the tasks in your responsibility so you simplify your workflow for greatest impact.

Keys to effective time-blocking

Time-blocking is about focusing your energy by optimising your day or diary for facilitating more workflow. As you grow your clinic, your roles and responsibilities will change and, therefore, the structure of your day and diary will also change. It's important to continually adjust your approach to time-blocking as your role changes. Many different methods for effectively time-blocking are available, so be sure to try a few to find what helps you experience the best workflow.

In essence, you need to create blocks of time in your diary to focus your energy on working on important tasks. The reality is we're always tweaking our approach to time-blocking to find new and better ways. So rather than thinking, *I've tried and this doesn't work*, or *I haven't found how to do it for long periods of time*, take what does work and keep testing new ways. Rather than cover all methods here, we explore some important considerations about the connecting elements that bind all methodologies together – keeping things simple.

When considering how you time-block your diary a valuable resource can help guide you to be more effective – your consulting diary. You need to put in your diary time for dealing with many problems (clients) every week. Of course, the clients aren't 'problems', but they present with problems (health concerns). With time-blocking, you're able to see 20, 50 or even 100 clients (problems) in a week. How can you see so many clients (and solve so many problems) and run on time most of the time? It comes down to allocating specific times to specific problems: you might see routine follow-up clients on one morning, for example, and new clients in the afternoon.

You can take this time-blocking technique further and stop using 'admin' time as business time. Specifying a time being for 'admin' is way too broad, and doesn't provide enough focus. Admin time usually starts with you going through your emails. Once you see one that really needs your attention, you jump to working on something related to that.

Time-blocking for specific clinic owner tasks helps you get focused. The key is to know where each task fits so that you can create a well-rounded and sustainable solution. You must consider the following:

- **Where** – are you physically? Is the environment conducive to productive, distraction-free or collaborative work?
- **Who** – are you with or without? Are the people around you helping or hindering?
- **When** – in your day and within your week is best suited to your flow or focusing on the task? Is the timing of this focus right for when it is scheduled?
- **What** – is the best amount of time to allocate to this task? (Remember Parkinson's law which says that the work expands so as to fill the time available for its completion.)
- **Why** – is this task important? (Consider its connection to your purpose or painted picture for your business. See Degree 2: Purpose for more on your painted picture.)

- **How** – will this task be completed? (Have a checklist for different themes of tasks for repeatability.)

Coming off the tools

Darron's reflection as he was reducing his consulting work was that being a therapist was all he'd ever wanted to be. It's what he had done for two decades. He wondered how he would cope not treating patients – and not getting the 'warm and fuzzies' when he got to improve the quality of their lives. Again, this speaks to the heart of why we do what we do as health professionals – we love helping people.

The goal is not to stop helping people. You should put yourself in a position where your decision to consult with patients comes from your desire to do so, not because your clinic needs it! It's about removing yourself as the bottleneck for growth. As you make this decision, you're able to help more people through the training and mentoring of your growing team so that they add more value to the community.

You don't need to rush – though we've noticed you can always do it sooner than you think. You will likely experience a short-term hit to your revenue and profitability; however, when you come through to the other side you'll likely experience increases beyond your previous highs in both of those areas.

Your reasons for making the transition are highly personal. You may simply want to gain some freedom from the day-to-day grind, or build value into your business before selling it. You may feel passionate about teaching and mentoring your team and need more time to do that. Or you may want to be able to take an extended break, spend more time with family or have space for chasing other opportunities. You may find it easy to 'come off the tools' or find it supremely difficult. However, the reward is huge, and the key to success is to have a clear conviction to see it through. Follow the process carefully (see the following 'Assets in action' box), and surround yourself with people who will support you along the way.

You can always return to consulting later – but it will be on your terms, with the people you want to see, in a business that operates without you, where you have a choice to do what you love doing.

Assets in action

Director and co-founder of Clinic Mastery Daniel Gibbs created the following framework to help clinic owners to reduce their consulting hours (on their terms) and achieve their version of success.

Coming off the tools

If you've made a decision that 'coming off the tools' (no longer consulting clients at all) is something you need to do, the following action plan can help you achieve it.

Step 1: Write your new job description

Identify exactly what your position description will be once you are no longer seeing clients. This will help to reinforce your outcome, provide your team with clarity as to your role, and also give you motivation to see it through.

Your new role will see you take on new responsibilities but also hand over a number of responsibilities to others, so you may also like to create a new organisational structure and look at the position descriptions for other key team members at the same time.

While it can be confronting to list all the tasks you feel you're not accomplishing to the best of your ability right now, it can be very motivating to see that there will be a time soon when you can focus entirely on working on your business, rather than in it.

Step 2: Nominate your final date for consulting, and absolutely commit to that date

Perhaps you have a date in mind that coincides with an upcoming life event such as moving house, taking extended leave or preparing for an addition to the family. Or you may like to nominate a date that coincides with a calendar event, such as the end of the financial year, or Christmas.

The reason you need to absolutely commit to that date is because over the course of your journey coming off the tools you will be pulled in various directions, and tempted to continue consulting for a number of reasons.

You need to decide that even in the face of major disruption to your business, and potential loss of money, clients or even team members, you will not budge on this date. It will become an anchor of stability within rapid change, and motivate you to keep going through tough times.

It doesn't matter if this date is three months, six months or one year from now; the commitment and the process to get there is the same.

Step 3: Prepare your appointment book for your final date

Complete the following steps to prepare your appointment book:

1. **Rule out your diary after your final date:** Make it clear to yourself and your team that no-one can book an appointment with you after this date.

2. **Schedule a gradual reduction of available consulting sessions before this date:** Create time to develop the systems needed for your business to survive without you, and to engage and motivate your team to be aligned and focused on the outcome of the entire process by systematically removing either half days or full days from your appointment diary between now and your final consulting date. This will have the added benefit of making your appointment availability more scarce, enabling you to manage the transition for some of your clients to start seeing other practitioners in your clinic.

3. **Communicate you are now no longer accepting new clients:** Your focus is on managing a transition for your existing clients to see other practitioners in your clinic instead of you. The easiest clients to transition are those you haven't yet seen, so make a decision to no longer accept new clients. Besides, as your availability to your current clients becomes more scarce, your diary will become very full very quickly anyway.

4. **Close any waiting lists:** If you have a waiting list of clients to see you, don't add any more clients to it. It's now closed. Contact each client on the list already and either book them with a different practitioner, or manage a transition for them by offering to see them for one final appointment so you can introduce them to their new practitioner.

5. **Acknowledge blank appointments are your best friend – don't try to fill them:** This is one of the most confronting mindset challenges to overcome. As a small business owner, you've been used to doing everything you can to maintain a full appointment book. With gaps in your diary from late cancels or reschedules, you will feel tempted to book people into those times, but you must protect your diary. If you cannot commit to keeping gaps in your appointment book ruled out, then you need to go back and review your intended outcome for this process and make sure it is sufficiently motivating for you to see it through.

Step 4: Prepare your team

Complete the following to prepare your team:

1. **Meet with each team member individually:** A critical part of this entire process is ensuring your team is aligned with your outcome. Your team needs to understand why you're doing this, and you can help them understand by meeting with them individually to discuss your intentions

and vision for the clinic once you're no longer consulting. This is a great way to help nurture those who may be feeling insecure or confused about your reasons for no longer consulting.

2. **Bring your team together:** Hold an all-in team meeting to discuss your reasons for coming off the tools, and formalise your strategy for your appointment book. They will have lots of questions, and some may still have some concerns about the change. Make this a meeting that's different to other meetings – perhaps hold it off site, over dinner or drinks, or connect it with a quarterly strategy meeting. Tell your story and be honest. The whole process should invigorate and energise your team. Aside from the fact they will benefit from more of your attention, they will also find opportunity for more clients as you manage a transition to other practitioners, and more responsibility as you start systemising and delegating your usual tasks to others.

3. **Identify practitioners to whom you will transition your clients:** Meet regularly with two to three practitioners and use this time to discuss clients you are sending their way, and also to train them specifically on how you treat those clients.

4. **Introduce your clients to them:** Even if your clients don't know about your plan to come off the tools, it's important for clients to be familiar with other people in your clinic. Talk about the other team members during your appointments, and introduce your clients to other practitioners – even if only in passing.

5. **Encourage those team members to observe as many sessions as possible:** Having other team members observing makes it much easier to transition clients over to them. For difficult transitions, being open and honest in your handover process is very valuable. Have the new

practitioner sit in on a number of consults with you, and then you can check in on their progress once the new practitioner has taken over.

6. **Be thorough in your clinical notes:** Make sure you have all your clinical notes up to date and add useful handover information for the next practitioner. This will enable a smooth transition and support your team to continue the conversations you last had with those clients.

7. **Reinforce your outcome:** Talk about the process, your final date and where your focus will be after this date. Spend time with your team and reinforce your commitment to them on a weekly basis.

Step 5: Communicate to clients and referrers

Work through the following with clients and referrers:

1. **Tell your clients:** Take some time during your appointments to tell your clients that you won't be directly consulting one on one with them anymore. Here's an example of how the conversation may go:

   'I have come to a decision to step back from my consulting role within the business. The main reason for this is that the business has grown to a level where I feel I need time to invest in our team more to continue to deliver a high-quality service for all the clients who see us. I want everyone who visits our clinic to receive the same level of care that you expect when you see me, and I think I will be able to influence more clients positively by doing this.

   I am putting you in the capable hands of [practitioner] and will ensure they have a thorough handover of your treatment plan and progress. Thank you for your understanding. I'm not going anywhere – I'll be hard at work ensuring your expectations are not only met but also exceeded long into the future.'

2. **Train your reception team:** When clients call to book an appointment with you, your reception team need to know what to say. It's important to be direct, but also conversational. Ask your reception team to respond as they normally would to any enquiry (with something like, 'How can we help?' or 'What have you done?'). Then they can use a phone script similar the following, which we used at our clinic:

'I'm sorry, Daniel's books are closed until the end of the year, but he is working very closely with the other superstar podiatrists here to make sure everyone is well looked after ... Mary specialises in that concern so I would recommend you book an appointment with her and Daniel can monitor your progress with Mary.'

We also used the following script for when a new client was referred directly to me:

'I'm really sorry. Daniel is the director of our clinic, but isn't consulting with clients anymore. We've got other amazing podiatrists who Daniel mentors, however. Can I make an appointment for you with Mary? Everyone loves her.'

Once you've written a script that works for you, print it and place it near every reception phone or computer so it's easy to refer to.

3. **Meet with referrers and other people in your professional networks:** Arrange a time to talk with people who refer to your clinic about your decision and how you intend to use your time training and mentoring your team to deliver the same high level of service they have come to expect from you. Ask for their support during this transition by referring to your clinic rather than directly to you. You can also reassure them that you can remain involved in the progress of special clients by offering to be present during the consultation, or reporting back on their progress personally.

Step 6: Be present throughout the process

Be present in your clinic! Coming off the tools doesn't mean you are no longer there – at least for a period of time. Take responsibility for everything that happens in your clinic, and look for solutions in the form of new systems.

Remember – you will lose some clients. But that's okay, and a normal part of the process. As they regain trust in you, they can return – especially if you make it easy for them to do so.

Some clients may be upset because they've been transitioned to a different practitioner earlier than others. If they see you still consulting, they may wonder, 'Why can they see you and I can't?' Be ready to acknowledge and nurture those clients and continue to be present in their treatment journey, even if you're not directly providing the treatment. Consider the following:

- Check in with your long-term clients by phoning them after they've seen one of your other practitioners (perhaps after a couple of visits).
- Pop in for a quick hello whenever your clients are seeing a different practitioner – just to reinforce that you're still around.

Overall, with good communication, a solid commitment to the process and a team supporting the transition, you can be confident that the process will have the best chance of going smoothly.

Core element: Habits

The habits element is about installing the right support structure to help you transition from plateau to progress. And focusing on your health and longevity is very important for your clinic's sustainability.

Key focus: Health

Principle: Take care of yourself

> Habit is the intersection of knowledge
> (what to do), skill (how to do),
> and desire (want to do).

Stephen Covey (author of *The 7 Habits of Highly Effective People*)

Care for your health

Your health and wellbeing is central to being able to sustainably grow your clinic. If nothing else, your health is necessary to enjoy the fruits of your labour.

The long hours and constant stress that come with not growing your clinic effectively can have you looking for comforting food and habits. While perhaps comforting in the short term, these don't provide the long-term energy, vitality and mental acuity you need to make good decisions. To do the work required to grow your clinic, you need your health.

Lead by example

As health professionals, we should do what we can to represent health in the way that we show up for our clients, our team and our network. This means eating and sleeping well, exercising, getting rest when you need it, and working reasonable hours. If you don't do these things, you can't expect your team to. And if you don't have a team of happy and healthy people, your business won't last long.

We often flog ourselves in the effort to sustain and grow our clinic, at the expense of our own health and wellness. But there is no sustainability in leaving your health behind. All the effort and great plans in the world will not help you if your physical or mental health fails.

Key focus: Renewal

Principle: Regularly fill your cup

> My mission in life is not merely to survive,
> but to thrive; and to do so with some passion,
> some compassion, some humour, and some style.
>
> Maya Angelou

Boom, bust and burnout

The tyres are spinning fast but you're going nowhere; this is burnout.

As health professionals, a 'fire in the belly' inspires us to help people. Our can-do attitude drives us into the profession and allows us to make a meaningful difference for those we work with as teammates and for the clients we care for. This attitude is a reflection of our conscience – a conscience that guides us to say yes and figure out how later. A conscience that allows us to develop empathy for the clients we serve so that they experience the care in healthcare.

Your personal charter is likely to be the best version of yourself and help others do the same. You give everything you have, to your clients and team members, and to your spouse and/or kids. And guess who's left to last? That's right – you. It's why so many health professionals face burnout to some degree or another.

The challenge for every health professional is 'filling their own cup' in a way that allows them to take care of themselves. Health professionals commonly feel as if they have nothing more to give. All too often, the demands from clients, team members and partners build up and combine with the pressures of running a business. It can feel as if the internal fire to consistently and genuinely care for the people and work they do is burning itself out.

Avoid burnout with a strong connection with your personal mission

One key to avoiding burnout is maintaining a strong connection to your personal mission. Reminding yourself why you do what you do will keep you going when times get tough. And your 'why' has to be more than just wanting to be happier and less stressed. Your why has to be more specific and personal if it's going to inspire you to do the hard stuff. When you're still at the clinic late on a Friday night trying to solve a billing problem, you need alignment with your mission to keep going.

Your personal mission could include:

- creating something meaningful that is worth sharing with the people close to you and having the ability to reach further and deeper
- having more time for your own wellness
- doing more of what you love to do
- having more time for yourself
- having more time to give back to the community
- starting a family
- having more time to share meaningful experiences with your family without worrying where the money and time will come from
- having more time with your partner
- having more time to study
- having more time to travel.

Note: If your why is to start a family, nothing is more satisfying and relieving than knowing your clinic will allow you to take a break when your first child is born and that everything will keep going. You must systemise your business to start a family and be able to work from home. (See Degree 4: Systems.)

Update like your phone

Your phone gets a better deal than you do – it can easily be recharged so it can perform the multitude of functions you demand of it every day. Better still – every couple of months, it undergoes an operating system update.

The times when you involve yourself in high-value work for greater gains often demand substantially more time, effort and energy on your behalf. And no-one can sustain that level of workload.

You can get through these periods if you know an equal or greater rest peak is coming – usually in the form of a holiday or period of refreshment. The learning point is around playing at that transactional level in your mind. That same level of thinking may be filtering through to other areas of life as well. Ultimately, you want to work smarter not harder, doing higher-value work for greater gains in less time.

The legacy test

How long are you going to be in your business? The majority of clinic owners aim to be in their business for multiple years; others aim for decades. Imagine you're 93 years old, perhaps in your rocking chair, and you're looking back on your life and your career, and considering what you're most proud of and grateful for. You're probably not thinking, *I wish I had spent more time managing the low level operations at work, or fiddling with the practice management software.* You're likely going to reflect on the time and impact you had with your family and friends, with your patients, and the causes that matter to you.

The ultimate luxury is time – time for yourself, your health, your family and friends. Time to connect with your team, your clients, your network and the causes that matter to you. It's not unlimited, so you need to invest your time wisely. It's not always about more time, but it certainly is about quality time with all of those people who matter. Quality time doing the work that needs to be done. Investing your time in a way that 'spreads you thin' is not sustainable. It doesn't represent the best version of yourself and certainly will limit your capacity to make the impact you seek to make. And what you are doing will not pass the legacy test.

Too busy to take a break

Are you so busy launching the next clinic or onboarding the new team member or seeing the case load of clients that you forget or avoid taking a break? Perhaps you're in a really good state right now, and you don't want to break the momentum. But consider the sustainability of constantly and immediately going onto the next thing. How could you instead shift gears? We often go from one thing to another without thought or a pause in between.

In Degree 2: Purpose, we cover shifting from corporate 90-day work cycles to 120-day rhythms that allow you to pause, play, take a break and spend your time doing things that will pass the rocking chair test.

'It feels like an indulgence'

'I find it hard to give myself permission to take a break, because sometimes it feels like an indulgence. The team thinks I'm not working.' Does that sound like you? We hear this often from clinic owners. But, as already discussed, maintaining your health so that you can maintain your clinic is so important, as is modelling that behaviour to your team. Everybody in your clinic must understand that you all need to work at a sustainable pace, which includes taking breaks. And they are not simply going to guess this by themselves; you must share this with them. You must tell your team how you want them to work and how you are going to work, and why. Then they will understand that taking a break is not an indulgence – it's a vital part of a sustainable work routine.

Renewal boosters

You can use the following renewal boosters to keep yourself on track and maintain your focus and energy, especially when times get rough:

- **Go back to your personal desire statement:** Returning to your statement (refer to the Mindset element) provides fresh perspective on whether your actions are in alignment with where you want to go and, most importantly, why it matters to you. What are the meaningful reasons for bringing that world to life for you and your family? Realigning yourself may mean committing to something or someone else, or letting something go.

- **Assess your work–life integration:** Review your ideal week, and better accommodate the realities of what actually happens in the structure of your week. Set yourself up to succeed. Allow enough time and space for team meetings, your own health, time with family and whatever else is important to you. For example, Dave, who runs a musculoskeletal clinic, wanted to be more present as a father after the recent birth of his fourth child. His work had been a great focus and he wanted to better integrate the 'life' part of his week. So Dave decided to give himself a score of how 'present' he had been each day as a father. Instead of journaling in long form, this simple score – one number – was what he kept track of. He also decided to get all his work done in work hours to protect the evenings and weekends with family. Consider making a similar change to not only free up your time, but also free you up mentally so that you don't feel like your business is taking over your life.

- **Take a holiday:** Vacations are a great opportunity to celebrate a business that is less reliant on you. It's important to enjoy your holidays, take some time off and recharge. Often that recharge means you are twice as effective when you return, meaning over the long term your efforts will pay off significantly.

Planning for an extended break has some great benefits:

- Preparing for your time away involves implementing systems and structures to be able to run things from a distance.
- It can spur you into action prior to your vacation in a way that catalyses you to close the loops on open projects, rapidly develop systems, policies and procedures, or delegate those tasks you've been meaning to do for some time.
- Your team have the opportunity to step up into new roles.

Use holidays and extended leave as a chance to see how the business runs without you. Things typically rise to the surface when you're away.

Renewal is exactly what you need

When you're at your best, what are the things you're doing, focusing on or experiencing? This is an important question that we asked George after noticing a pattern of big ups and big downs in his own state and in the progress of his clinic. One key response from George stood out, and it has been characteristic of many clinic owners' responses over time.

For George, he was at his best when having a week's holiday or renewal. This allowed him the distance, distraction-free environment and perspective to get clear on what matters, and provided the opportunity to look at all parts of life and how he was integrating them, or not. Through allowing you to look holistically at family, health, self and clinic, and giving you the time to slow down and make important decisions with a clearer mind, renewal time is central to sustainability.

Another important tip is to always have your next renewal time booked in by the end of your current renewal, so that you've always got something to look forward to. Half of the fun of a vacation is planning it and looking forward to it. And then, when work starts to get on top of you, you can look at your calendar and see that your next renewal is not too far away.

Setting boundaries

It's important to tell your team what level of connection they can have with you and who might be the go-to person in your absence. Taking time away from the clinic is no help if your phone keeps pinging with messages and emails. Your team must learn to work effectively without you.

Some examples of the kinds of boundaries you might set include:

- You're available via phone only – but your team can call anytime if it's important.
- You're available on Slack only, between 9 am and midday each day.
- You're not available at all – and your team should contact specified team members for all decisions (only call you if it's an absolute emergency).

Key focus: Comfort zone

Principle: Growth happens in the above and beyond

> **So many of us choose our path out of fear disguised as practicality.**
>
> Jim Carrey

The perfect trap

It's very common to hear health professionals say, 'I'm a perfectionist'. This is the 'perfect trap' – and it's a trap that will hamper your ability to grow your clinic as a business owner.

Perfectionism is understandable, particularly in healthcare. Perhaps our industry attracts a certain type of person. More likely, it's a factor of our conditioning and training as health professionals. Through our studies, we're challenged to stay up to date with the latest evidence-based practice. That's a good thing. You want to deliver great patient outcomes.

However, while you're focused on growing your business, being a perfectionist can slow you down and severely hamper your progress. You may feel the need to get up to speed on all aspects related to running a business before you actually do it. You may want to read every book, sign up to every website and listen to every podcast before you take action. You may want to be involved with every single decision in your clinic when others are just as capable as you and can do certain tasks without you. With this perfectionist approach you'll be 93 and in that rocking chair before you make any progress.

Or you might take action, but do so reluctantly, or without conviction, because you want things to be perfect but nothing ever is. And you can sabotage yourself by not giving your all. That sabotage might take the form of avoiding the camera and not creating videos for your marketing, because you don't think you're good at them and they won't be perfect. Or it could be not working on your website because it's not coming together exactly as you'd hoped.

If you feel this way, you're not alone. Many clinic owners ended up running a clinic by default, after sort of 'falling' into it. Perhaps there was a spare room to rent, a 'good' opportunity with a colleague, or you were so good with your clients that things grew without you even trying. But now, years later, you're resenting parts of it, you're emotionally exhausted and, if you reflect, your perfectionism isn't working within this business you've created.

Many clinic owners are perfectionists. It's ingrained in health professionals that you need to have studied all the evidence and have the required experience before you can pull it all together in a clear, logical and progressive plan for your patient. That's as it should be; you need to provide the best solutions for your patients.

But being a perfectionist is a trap when starting, running or growing a business, and – paradoxically – pursuing perfection will result in worse outcomes over time. This book is all about using – and adapting – those perfectionist traits to be successful in business.

Doing what you know versus knowing what to do

As we mentioned in the introduction, you didn't learn how to run a business at university – and that's alright. (You completed a healthcare degree, not a business degree.) Focusing on the business side is what we're here for.

The perfectionist is waiting for that ideal time for knowing what to do – when you get that extra funding, when you're not so busy, when you have enough team members … the list of IFTTT statements goes on. Remember, as Trevor Hendy says, 'Conditions are always perfect'. You don't need to know all of the variables and all of the outcomes before you start. If you do try to know all the variables and possible outcomes, you'll be frozen by analysis paralysis. You'll become so obsessed with trying to solve every single problem and find every single solution that you won't know what to do and when, or where to even start.

You may be thinking, *I don't want to have my team do it*, or, *My team don't do it as well as I do*. But if you want to grow, you have to be good at delegating. While you shouldn't lower your standards, you must adjust your expectations – especially the expectation that it will be done to the standard you want right from the start. Rather, expect that with the right training, autonomy and structure, the standard will progressively get better. And your team will start to own it and take the reliance or burden off you. That's the ultimate goal for any business owner.

Set the vision

As a leader in your clinic, you must be the best version of yourself. Personal mastery is about your constant and always evolving improvement as a person – and especially as a leader – to become the best version of you.

Personal mastery is the first of the 7 Degrees because your capacity to grow and your ability to be effective are vital to making sustainable progress in all of the other Degrees to Grow Your Clinic.

Your business will not be able to outgrow you as the leader, so your personal mastery journey will be a real source of growth for your clinic.

'Imagine if …'

Using 'Imagine if …' can be a great catalyst for personal insight or team collaboration when setting the vision for your clinic, because it allows you to embrace abundance thinking. 'Imagine if …' is just a sentence starter – you get to fill in the blanks to explore the possibilities of your clinic vision. The key is to remove restraints that feel real to get to your big picture – restraints such as time, money, resources or people. The goal is to imagine having an abundance of each of those elements – what would/could you do? You can do this exercise across the different areas of your clinic, from team, to client experience, your brand, community, causes and so much more.

Here are some examples from clinic owners we've worked with:

- **Marion, speech pathologist:** Imagine if we could build a playground next to our clinic for the families who come to see us and the community at large.
- **Lauren, speech pathologist:** Imagine if we could own a forest and plant trees for every client who achieves a meaningful outcome through our therapy.
- **Michael, physiotherapist:** Imagine if we could host our next team retreat in Bali instead of Sydney.
- **Tess, podiatrist:** Imagine if we had an internship program that attracted the best therapist talent from around the country to work with us.

These are just some of the abundant and highly creative, out-of-the-box ideas you can create to paint a picture of the impact, experience and meaningful growth you want to embark on with your clinic. This exercise can also be an ongoing discussion and activity with yourself and your team.

Lead by example

The age-old saying of 'lead by example' is so valuable for you to enable and see growth in the people around you, your team, your partners, network and your client community.

You're often required to complete a certain number of hours in professional development each year to stay up to date. Most progressive health professionals will do more because they are committed to delivering the best for their patients. Take the same approach with getting out of your comfort zone, and growing yourself and your clinic.

Importance of your circle and community

As motivational speaker Jim Rohn famously noted, you are the average of the main five people you spend time with. This is key to also raising your standards and supporting your development. Most clinic owners say that they feel lonely; often their friends or family don't understand the realities of running a business and managing the dynamics of life outside of work. One of the keys to sustaining your growth and personal mastery evolution is to surround yourself with a peer community who do understand, who can relate and who can contribute to your growth, both now and ongoing.

You don't simply want to stay up to date – that's the minimum. You want transformational growth. Again you need to be as good at personal development as you are at professional development – with the distinction that personal mastery must be focused on every day.

High-impact action

Consider the following key insights and actions when embracing the personal mastery journey:

- Conditions are always perfect so embrace progress over perfection as you grow your clinic – because it doesn't get easier, we get better.
- Check in with yourself about what beliefs need to change to grow your clinic, because they are the precursor to results, especially the belief that you need to do it yourself (DIY).
- Meaningful growth matters so define your version of success and then ensure your action matches that ambition.
- Play to your genius by focusing yourself on the high-value and most impactful actions that come with relative ease for you to do.
- Pressure is a privilege so embrace your opportunity to make meaningful decisions to impact the lives of those you work with for the better.
- Strive to create more workflow, not workload, so that you can enjoy the journey of growing your clinic along the way.
- Take care of yourself and your own health – your clinic growth should never come at the expense of your own wellbeing.
- Avoid the boom, bust and burnout by regularly filling your cup with renewal boosters (time), setting firmer boundaries and giving yourself the upgrade, just like your phone.
- Growth happens in the above and beyond so get out of your comfort zone, set a bold vision, imagine and move beyond the perfect trap by doing what you know.

Personal mastery summary

Growing your clinic requires you to be the best version of yourself. With so many demands and pressures on you every day, it's important to take care of yourself so that you can sustainably play the game of business. Embracing the personal mastery journey will allow you to experience more flow, enjoy greater freedoms and experience the fulfilment of creating Clinics For Good.

DEGREE 2:

PURPOSE

Amplify your impact

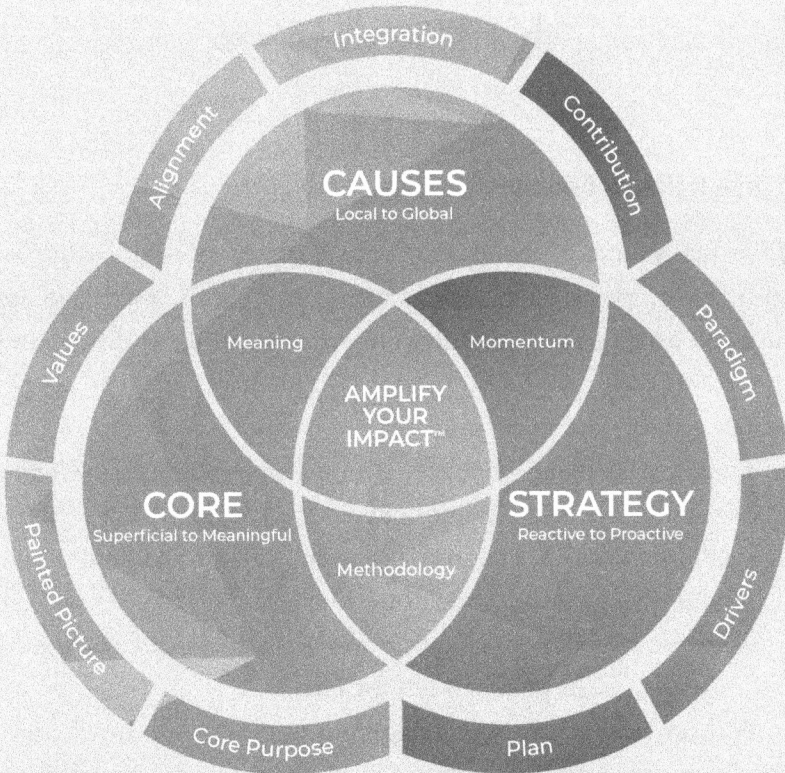

Core element: Your core

The first element to master in Degree 2 is your Core. This relates to you imagining where you're going and how you'll show up along the way so that you go from a superficial to a meaningful experience in growing your clinic.

Key focus: Core purpose

Principle: Be a force for good

> Never believe that a few caring people
> can't change the world. For, indeed,
> that's all who ever have.
>
> Margaret Mead

'I love helping people'

The first focus for establishing your Core is to clarify why your clinic exists by defining your *core purpose*. This allows you to capture the driving force behind your strategic goals so that you can inspire your team and engage your community. Your core purpose is about playing a bigger game!

However, this 'bigger game' is not always so easy to embrace or play. Greg, a Clinic Mastery client, was keeping it real when he opened up conversation at our 12-month progression session with, 'I thought this purpose and culture stuff was total B.S.' As we came to see as we talked more, that position was understandable; the past few years had been pretty rough for Greg.

Perhaps you're in a challenging position right now after a few team members have resigned; maybe your health or a family member's health has taken a turn for the worse; perhaps you've been sued, racked up a big debt or are experiencing burnout. Whatever the reason, you might feel the same way as Greg. *Don't you know what's going on in my business and life right now?* you might be think-ing. *I can't think about this pie in the sky, warm and fuzzy, purpose fluff.*

Well, perhaps when you're feeling like this, it's exactly the right time for you to focus on purpose. Perhaps the reason you're in the state you're in right now is because you're facing a lack of purpose and intelligent design around integrating why you do what you do into your clinic.

Remember why you do what you do. At your core as a health professional, no doubt, it's a version of 'I love helping people'. As you grow your clinic, the opportunity builds to find new and better ways to help more people, help them more often and add more value to their lives. By identifying the causes that matter to you and integrating these causes into your practice, you're able to find another gear and unlock a more resourceful version of yourself and those on your team.

Daniel Pink, best-selling author of *Drive*, wrote that people on your team can get a 'paycheque' anywhere. What they're really in need of is doing work and being of service to something larger than themselves.

The power of purpose and the impact of BlackRock

Larry Fink is the founder, chair and CEO of BlackRock – one of the world's largest investing institutions (with around US$9 trillion in assets under management). In 2018, Fink wrote a polarising letter to CEOs of companies around the world, which he titled 'A sense of purpose'. In the letter, Fink basically said, 'You need to do more than make profits'.

Fink's letter was a call to action for companies to become more socially conscious and for business owners and managers to design their business to be a force for good – locally and globally. Trust in government organisations might be waning in the community, but Fink argued businesses could be catalysts for change, socially and economically, through their employment decisions, service solu-tions, investment actions and more.

According to Fink:

> To prosper over time, every company must not only deliver financial performance, but also show how it makes a positive contribution to society. Companies must benefit all of their stakeholders, including shareholders, employees, customers, and the communities in which they operate.

For Fink, the connection between purpose and potential was clear: 'Without a sense of purpose, no company, either public or private, can achieve its full potential'.

In his 2019 letter to CEOs, Fink returned to the connection between purpose and long-term performance, and again emphasised sustainable and long-term growth. Fink argued, 'Purpose is not the sole pursuit of profits but the animating force for achieving them. Profits are in no way inconsistent with purpose'.

If you're like many health professionals, a sense of purpose no doubt inspired or called you to this industry in the first place – a purpose to help more people live a better quality of life. Though, as you grow your clinic, the realities of business are also a powerful force. At times, we can overlook and wrestle with ourselves over our sense of purpose versus our pursuit of profits as we navigate ambitious plans to grow. We can also be so committed to our purpose and want to be noble in our pursuit that profit becomes an afterthought – putting the sustainability of our mission in jeopardy. To grow your clinic sustainably you must be able to allow profits to be the animating force for your purpose. Clinics For Good are good businesses (profitable), that also do good (purposeful). This is the new paradigm of being a clinic owner, and will help you amplify your impact for the causes that matter to you and your team, clients, industry, profession and community.

Core purpose and strong leadership

As a clinic (and as a clinic owner), you must know why you exist. Who is it that you help? And what are you trying to achieve? The answers to these fundamental questions allow you to determine your guiding North Star. This is the stuff that gets you excited, gets you out of bed in the mornings, and allows you to commit to something bigger than yourself. When the going gets tough and you feel like the pressures and the challenges are all too much, your core purpose will keep you on track and pull you through the barriers to stay committed for the long term.

Defining your core purpose is no small or insignificant matter. It is easy enough to write down a basic core purpose – though the rubber really hits the road when your back is against the wall and you feel like throwing in the towel. Will you still stay committed to the very reason you dived into the deep end and decided that your purpose was worth facing all of the challenges?

A multitude of concepts and methodologies can help you discover your core purpose. Our method has evolved over time, and has been contributed to by so many of the greats who have gone before us. The remainder of this Degree outlines our method in more detail, but the answer ultimately lies with you.

The following table provides some examples from other brands and businesses to get you started.

Examples of core purposes

Nike	To unite the world through sport to create a healthy planet, active communities, and an equal playing field for all
Walt Disney	To make people happy
Patagonia	To save our home planet
Upwell Health Collective	To re-imagine the healthcare experience
Profeet Podiatry	To keep you happy, healthy and active
The Physio Co (TPC)	To help seniors stay mobile, safe and happy

Inspire CA	To be Australia's most impactful accounting firm
Clinic Mastery	To amplify the impact of Clinics For Good

Relatable experience

Bec Farthing is an experienced osteopath and the founder of Total Balance Healthcare. The core purpose of her and her team is to help people achieve their total balance. Bec shared how she and her team were able to put this core purpose into real action:

> *Huge personal win. I managed to get us in to the Country Fire Authority (CFA) Swan Reach fire base camp [set up to provide support during the 2019–20 Black Summer fires] to provide osteopathy and other practitioner treatments to the volunteers. Last night was the first night and it was absolutely amazing. We treated our butts off from 7 pm to 11 pm and we still couldn't get to everyone. We have over 30 practitioners rotating on a roster for the next three weeks. I have had amazing help from three osteo colleagues to organise, systemise and orchestrate. It is amazing! Aim is to keep the momentum going for the next eight weeks or until the camp closes. They were so appreciative last night – which I felt really a little embarrassed about because they are the ones we are so incredibly thankful for and that is why we are there.*

Key focus: Painted picture

Principle: Get clarity on your future reality

> The only thing worse than being blind
> is having sight but no vision.
>
> Helen Keller

Bold Brendon

The Richmond Football Club had many critics in 2010. Despite this, CEO Brendon Gale stood by his plan to rebuild the club. And his plan was bold: retire their debt, build their membership to 75,000 members and win three premierships over the next 10 years. An internal document that detailed these aspirations was released earlier than planned and quickly put the spotlight on the organisation.

In 2010, Brendon spoke in the media about the plan's details – including investing in new facilities, enrolling new team members and developing operational plans. But, he said, before all that, 'It starts with a vision'.

To create a vision at that time was challenging – the competition was expanding with the addition of two new teams in the coming seasons, and the Richmond Football Club were in what most would describe as dire straits, financially and operationally. Zooming out from the chaos of the moment to be more purposeful about where the club was headed took courage.

Brendon also stressed the one non-negotiable needed to bring this vision to life – making good decisions in alignment with their vision. In much the same way, Larry Fink (refer to the 'Core purpose' key focus) also emphasised that sustainable company growth required looking beyond the quarterly objectives.

Brendon focused on having the 'right people in the right places to work together and make the right decisions' – and ensuring the club had measurements and metrics around achieving that plan.

Bringing it to life

In October 2020, the Richmond Football Club, led by Brendon Gale as CEO and Peggy O'Neal as president (the first woman in AFL history to serve as a club president), had realised their vision, achieving all of their outlined objectives.

Here's what they put in their vision in that 2010 document and how their results compared:

- Five-year vision (by 2015):
  - Three years of finals appearances – achieved.
  - $0 debt (retired debt) – achieved.
  - 75,000 club members – achieved.
- 10-year plan (by 2020):
  - Winning three premierships – achieved.

If you choose to accept it

Running a successful clinic requires much more than just going through the motions each day. You must rally your team towards a colourful, meaningful picture of what sort of impact they could have if they achieve the vision you have laid out.

Social entrepreneur Dan Pallotta wrote a *Harvard Business Review* article in 2011 with a title and premise that asked a poignant question – 'Do you have a mission statement, or are you on a mission?' In the article, Pallotta expanded on this idea, arguing 'A person or organization on a mission is inspiring. A mission statement is an abstraction'.

While no standardised method is available to define – and act on – a mission or vision (much of the language is interchangeable), we're going to adopt the approach that having a meaningful and measurable mission and vision is pivotal if you are going to find and deliver on the purpose for your clinic.

Cameron Herold, author of *Vivid Vision*, says that a 'painted picture' is an ideal method of doing just that. Herold's painted picture is a detailed three- to four-page document that lays out a clear, logical vision of what your company will look like in three years (or even 10 years if you're Brendon Gale).

You must identify your painted picture (or three-year mission) for your clinic so that you have a guiding goal to help you amplify your impact. The elements of getting to a meaningful and measurable painted picture as a clinic owner are:

- **Owner-inspired outcome:** This is your personal desire statement. As the business owner, it's important that the clinic you build makes an impact in your life. Your desired outcome should inspire you to grow your clinic in a way that offers you meaning, fulfilment and success as you define it for yourself. What does your ideal week look like, what roles are you playing, how much are you earning?

- **Business-facilitated impact:** Here you consider what the clinic looks like – including number of site locations, the service experience, client feedback, financial status, brand reputation, marketing presence and results, and the contribution and impact you're making to the cause(s) that matter to you.

- **Team-focused missions:** Here you focus on culture, pathways, training, development and recruitment. You can look at the professionals who are on your team, and aspects such as length of stay and years of experience, employee satisfaction, the recruitment ecosystem status and types of roles fulfilled.

- **Client-centred goals:** Your focus here is the number of new people you're helping each month, how many meaningful goals clients are achieving each month, and their feedback on the service – captured by tools such as your net promoter score.

A blueprint for business decisions

Imagine if many of the symptoms or challenges in your clinic could be remedied sustainably by zooming out and aligning the team with a painted picture. What's it all for? If nothing else, it would help you make better quality and clearer decisions because you have a picture of where you want to go.

An important part of this is setting and celebrating milestones along the way. Setting yourself and your team a goal of doubling your number of patients, team members or locations in 12 months might seem like a daunting objective.

But what about if you break this goal down into more manageable milestones? Can you achieve a 10 per cent increase in two months? Suddenly that doesn't sound so daunting, does it? You can set regular milestones along your 12-month journey. This allows you to know where you are headed, and know whether you are on target as you progress (rather than getting to month 10 and realising you are falling way behind). It will also help with your motivation because you are not looking at a huge 12-month goal but rather a series of smaller, more manageable goals.

And make sure you celebrate each milestone as you achieve it. We're so often thinking about the next thing – the next team member, system or clinic location – that we can overlook the highly important act of putting our progress into perspective and celebrating our wins along the way. As soon as we reach one milestone, we put our heads back down and start striving for the next one. But celebrating as you go will help keep you and your team motivated and on task, and they will know that you value their work.

Key focus: Values

Principle: Core values are core actions

> **Values are not something you create; rather, they are core actions you identify and then purposefully amplify.**
>
> Ben Lynch

More than words

Core values are more than words; they are core actions. Core values are a set of principles that govern and guide who you are and who you are committed to being. Values are the cultural expectations of how you act as a team, how you engage with your clients and what you do in the community.

Core values are the things you do that define who you are and who you are committed to being as you grow. Your core values are represented in your actions and the way you do business. Values are verbs, and verbs are doing words. Therefore, values need to represent doing words (they are actions). You see, values already exist in your business. You may not have articulated or communicated your values and 'hung them on the walls of your clinic', but they exist in the form of how you show up each day.

Values are not something you create, but rather identify (they're what you're already doing 'naturally' when you're at your best) and amplify with a sense of purpose and intentionality. This also means that you can filter all of your decisions through your core values so that your actions align consistently.

You can then use and infuse your values into your decision-making and action taking. Identifying and amplifying your core values is one of the most powerful brand strategies you can undertake – because, after all, your brand is built on reputation. Do you do the things you say you're going to do? Your reputation develops based on the associations, stories, memories and experiences people have when working with you as clients, team members and partners. So start with what are you saying – in other words, what are you promising to others in how you will show up for them (core values)? Then you need to follow through with actions and deliver on that to build reputation and establish your brand.

Your VIP: Values in practice

Coming up with your core values can quickly become a word-smithing exercise.

If you're anything like us, that can be a really indulgent experience. However, after plenty of experience doing values sessions helping other clinic owners identify their core values, we know how important it is that these values actually get used.

One key way to ensure that your values get used is to avoid landing on nouns such as 'integrity', 'honesty', 'care' or 'humility'.

As already mentioned, core values are core actions, so they need to be verbs, and be clearer, more meaningful and more measurable. Some examples include:

· We make it happen
· Be outcomes focused
· Find new and better ways
· Bring the energy

So after running many values sessions, we've created a framework to articulate the values for your clinic:

· **Identify:** Identify the things you naturally do as a team and that are the best representation of you. These are what characterise who you are as a team. Again, core values are core actions. They are things you already do – and, depending on the state of your culture, should be the things you do well when nobody's looking.

· **Clarify:** Clarify the underlying core principles behind the actions you have identified and connect the dots between what you identified. Group the examples of actions you've highlighted into about three to five groups. Clarify what the common thread is between those groupings and summarise the key theme that connects the actions. Having a few summaries for each grouping is fine.

· **Simplify:** At this stage, it's useful to simplify your core values with words and language that resonate and reflect your culture. This is the wordsmithing stage, where you can distil your values into common phrases that are easy to remember, using a vernacular that is reflective of your team.

· **Amplify:** Finally, you need to put your core values into practice – use them when hiring, in marketing and with partnerships. You can also use them to help navigate tough conversations with team members, leaning on your shared commitment to how you are going to show up and behave. For example, say your clinic's core vale is 'make it happen'. If a team member didn't follow up a patient after their session, you could talk with them about how they didn't embody this core value.

Core values are the representation of how you and your team consistently 'go about your business' with integrity to who you said you would be when you articulated your core values. Core values are the principles that govern and guide how you act and how you behave. They are the cultural expectations of how you act as a team, how you engage with your clients and what you do in the community.

Be deliberate about using your core values. Most clinics will have 'unspoken' expectations of how each person should show up every day. The catch is that if you haven't defined your core values, you leave your culture up to chance. You become reactive to how people feel or show up on any given day without an anchor to come back to – core values.

If your values remain unspoken you don't have a reference point or standard for people to align with because you've never explicitly communicated the principles that you operate by. This can leave you vulnerable to inconsistencies in how you engage as a team or how you deliver your service. Outlining these expectations allows you to keep yourself and your team accountable to delivering your service with a standard and flavour that is unique to your clinic. It's about being more deliberate and consistent in the way you act or behave when you're at your best – because your team and clients deserve the best version of you every day.

Values can evolve as you grow

The essence and intention behind your core values will always exist as you grow your clinic. However, you'll likely get better at communicating exactly what you mean by your values so that they better reflect who you are, how you do business and how you want to do business. You just need to identify your values (through a reflection process) and then amplify them. You're no doubt well aware that your actions need to reflect your words, and you amplify core values by deliberately infusing them into everything you do.

Activity to amplify

It's important to get clear on your core values; however, they're also your core actions, so infusing them and amplifying them is key. The following provides some ideas.

Measurement and acknowledgement

At weekly team meetings, you can use your outlined values to measure your success in your service delivery for your clients/ members.

At the same meetings, you can also acknowledge weekly team and individual wins, using your values to identify these wins.

Performance review and mentoring

As part of your regular mentoring, training and reviews with your team, you can ask them to reflect on how they've lived out the core values in the clinic. You could use a rating system and open-ended questions to explore how they used a core value in their work. Using a 'focus sheet' (survey form) prior to mentoring sessions is helpful, because doing so provides opportunity for documentation and reflection to prepare for the face-to-face mentoring session.

Core element: Causes

The second element to master is your Causes. This relates to you identifying the movements, organisations and initiatives that matter to you so that you can amplify your impact from local to global.

Key focus: Alignment

Principle: Play a bigger game

> This Agenda is a plan of action for people,
> planet and prosperity.
>
> UN Global Goals

Aligning for impact

The first focus to have for Causes is to align your clinic, your purpose and your actions with the projects, initiatives, movements, churches or charitable organisations that allow you to make an impact. And why reinvent the wheel here? The best way to make an impact is to align on one or more of the Global Goals already outlined by the United Nations in 2015. (These Global Goals are officially known as the Sustainable Development Goals or SDGs.) Aligning with these goals allows you to channel your efforts towards supporting the most important needs of local and global communities.

The 17 important Global Goals outlined by the UN are:

1. No poverty
2. Zero hunger
3. Good health and well-being
4. Quality education
5. Gender equality
6. Clean water and sanitation
7. Affordable and clean energy
8. Decent work and economic growth
9. Industry, innovation and infrastructure
10. Reduced inequality
11. Sustainable cities and communities
12. Responsible consumption and production
13. Climate action
14. Life below water

15. Life on land
16. Peace, justice and strong institutions
17. Partnerships for the goals

These goals are designed to be a 'blueprint to achieve a better and more sustainable future for all'. Aligning your clinic with one or more of these causes is a way for you to amplify your impact and create the change you want to see in the world.

Key focus: Integration

Principle: Walk your talk

Well done is better than well said.

Benjamin Franklin

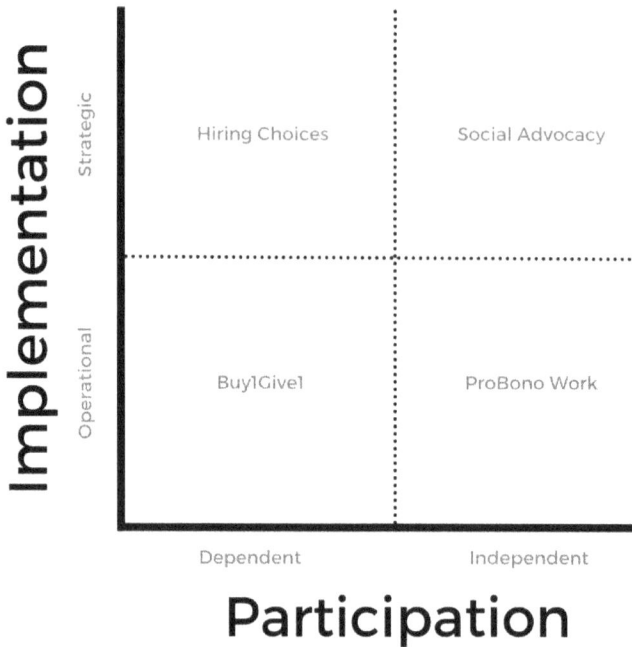

Implementation: Strategic versus operational

Integrate the causes that matter to you most into the very fabric of how you grow your clinic. This requires you to consider the type of participation and the level of implementation you are willing to commit to so that you can sustainably amplify your impact.

You can implement your impact in two ways – strategic or operational:

- **Strategic:** Using this option means you're choosing an impact that is based on future, more substantial and longer lasting approaches. This might include:
  - hiring a person with a disability to join your team who might otherwise have limited or no job prospects; this could align with SDG 8, Decent work and economic growth, or SDG 10, Reduced inequality.
  - partnering with schools, clubs, networks, groups, associations, professionals and businesses that align with your purpose and commitment to the SDGs.
  - becoming a B Corp and/or Clinics For Good certified business that has proven and promised its commitment across a number of standards to balance purpose and profit.

- **Operational:** This approach means your impact is related to the daily actions and activities of your clinic. For example, you could:
  - include some pro bono work in your schedule, such as providing outreach clinics to underserved communities; this could align with SDG 3, Good health and well-being, or SDG 10, Reduced inequality.
  - choose socially conscious suppliers (such as using Thankyou hand wash in your clinic, which helps support an end to global poverty); this could align with SDG 1, No poverty, or SDG 12, Responsible consumption and production.

Participation: Dependent versus independent

In a similar way to implementation, your participation can be based on two things – whether it is dependent or independent of something else happening:

- **Dependent:** This means your impact requires or relies on something else to happen first. The Buy1Give1 model is based on this concept, and Kula Health in Queensland provides a great example – for every consultation they provide, they give 30 days of clean drinking water to someone in need.
- **Independent:** This approach means your impact can happen without dependence on anything else. For example, you can use your social platforms to shine a light on the causes that matter to you and your team and to strategically create a profile and a presence within the community. Examples of this approach include joining committees and boards, and using your marketing voice and your advocacy in supporting a movement. Performance Medicine provides advocacy to the LGBTIQ+ community as well as SDG 10: Reduced inequality for women as part of their social media presence.

What opportunities do you see for better integration of your causes into your clinic? A great exercise is to introduce the idea of causes and their integration into the clinic with your team and ask for their collaboration and input. Consider having an evergreen way for ideas to be contributed or leading a team training day (or retreat) to catalyse some ideas.

Relatable experience

From episode 165 of the *Grow Your Clinic* podcast between Ben Lynch and Paul Hermann

Growing up as a tall, pale, skinny, freckly red–head kid had its challenges for Dr Paul Hermann, osteopath, speaker, lecturer and founder of Stay Tuned Sports Medicine. Kids can be very imaginative and cruel when coming up with nicknames for their classmates, especially those who stand out from the crowd. Red-haired kids are sometimes one of the 'only'. While not wanting to compare this to the pain children experience who suffer bullying through racism or other forms of discrimination, being a minority can make for a lonely and difficult school life for any child. But as the director of two successful allied health clinics, Paul is now a little older and a little wiser – and he has embraced his inner 'Ranga' to help the orangutans of Borneo who can't help themselves.

His belief is that we should all do what we can to help those in need, and this belief delivered the Stay Tuned organisational philosophy and mission: 'Everybody deserves to feel good'.

In 2017, Paul followed his passion to learn more and help these amazing animals, volunteering to work with the Borneo Orangutan Survival (BOS) Foundation in Samboja Lestari, Borneo. He also started the Stay Tuned for a Ranga Foundation, raising vital funds that are all donated to BOS for projects that help protect, rehabilitate and release orangutans back into the wild.

Key focus: Contribution

Principle: Pay it forward

> ### The secret to living is giving.
>
> Tony Robbins

Spreading Christmas joy

Gabby, a generous clinic owner, found out one of her virtual (off-shore) team members couldn't afford to buy a bike at Christmas for his son. He'd been working hard and had even helped her to identify she had more than $12,000 missing from unpaid invoices.

Spreading the Christmas joy and buying a bike for this team member seemed a no-brainer – and it made Gabby so happy that not only did she have a dedicated team, but she could also reward those efforts! Through months of work animating their core purpose to help more people, Gabby and her team has been able to amplify their impact with a commitment to contribution!

Implement your structure

Once you have identified your causes, your final step is to implement your structure for making your contributions so that you are an active partner in creating progress. This goes beyond the saying of giving a fish versus teaching how to fish, and encompasses your entrepreneurial spirit as a business owner to change the whole fishing industry. In other words, your investment and commitment needs to have substance that creates a measurable momentum and lasting force for good.

This means you must plan how much money, time, resources, assets, insights and/or services you are going to contribute, and how often it's needed to make the difference you seek to make. How can you use your resources, experience and insights to help others, and how can you make this a permanent part of the foundations of your business? Contribution is about following through on what you say you're going to do once you've identified the ways that you'll integrate causes into your approach to growing your clinic.

Core element: Strategy

The third element to master is Strategy. This relates to you being able to translate all the meaningful intentions you have identified and turn them into sustainable progress. Strategy is about shifting from being reactive to being proactive in your decisions and actions. Making this shift allows you to go from feeling a sense of chaos to a sense of control as you grow your clinic.

Key focus: Paradigm

Principle: Simple is sustainable

Run it through your filter.

Shane Davis, co-founder of Clinic Mastery

Simplicity at every stage of business

The Clinics For Good paradigm is a perspective and methodology to simplify how you implement your core purpose, values and causes, and approach growing your clinic as a clinic owner.

No matter what stage of development you're navigating right now in growing or starting your clinic, no doubt more is always being added to your to-do and ideas list. This might include landlord negotiations, clinic refurbishments, onboarding new team members, preparing systems for accreditation, opening a new clinic site, managing your waitlist – and anything else in between. You always have many important actions to focus on as you grow, and it can be overwhelming, stressful, exhausting, exhilarating, inspiring and joyous. The one thing it should never be is unsustainable.

Unsustainable growth has grave consequences for your health, finances, team, clients, community and the impact you seek to make. Our paradigm allows you to navigate any stage of business sustainably by using a simple model for operating as a clinic owner. This is a self-sustaining model that allows you to be a catalyst for progress, because you're able to know where your high-value focus needs to be for the greatest impact at any time.

Among your ever-growing list of things to do, you need to be able to prioritise and compartmentalise your focus so that you can sustainably amplify your impact. Very simply, the Clinics For Good paradigm has four steps:

1. **Lead inspired teams:** You take care of the team.
2. **Transform client experiences:** The team takes care of the clients.

3. **Grow your clinic:** The clients take care of the clinic.
4. **Amplify your impact:** The clinic takes care of you.

In this way, the steps are more of a cycle, as shown in the following figure.

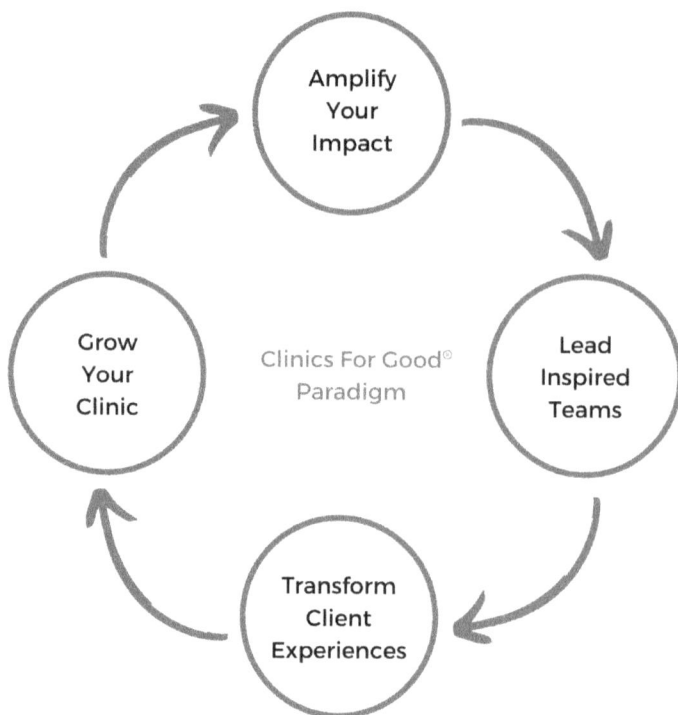

The cycle keeps repeating through the following:

- **Leaders support team:** As you grow your clinic, realising you can only do so much by yourself is important. You need a team of people to help amplify your impact. The first and foremost impact is to help more people (clients). Therefore, you need to focus on building the performance and capacity of your team.

- **Team supports clients:** As a health professional, your primary role is to help people live a better life. Your team of therapists directly and the support team indirectly help clients within your community to help more people and help them more often (through a comprehensive journey and across multiple episodes of care), plus add more value by finding new and better ways to improve the quality of life.

- **Clients support clinic:** Clients vote with their feet – by choosing to work with your team to improve their health. In turn, they support the growth of your clinic. With client-centred care being delivered by the team, your clients will show their support by enrolling into their recommended care journey and showing up for appointments. Those clients will also help grow the clinic through referrals to friends, family members, colleagues and others within their network. In turn, your clients contribute to a productive and positive atmosphere in your clinic as they achieve meaningful progress and allow your team to live their core purpose of helping more people.

- **Clinic supports leader/s:** By transforming client experiences, you'll help more people – allowing you to grow your clinic. That growth helps to boost cashflow so that you can invest in and reward your team – through improved facilities, equipment, training and experiences. This in turn accelerates your growth. Growing your clinic could then facilitate expansion opportunities as you open in new locations and add more team members. This type of growth also gives you the confidence and consistency to sustainably grow to the next stage of your development with a strong framework behind you.

At the core of your paradigm

At their core, Clinics For Good are two things: good clinics (businesses) that do good (change makers). This means, to be a Clinic For Good, you can't sustainably do good if you don't have a good clinic (business). So you need to create a sustainable clinic as your primary objective. The Clinics For Good paradigm is the model to support you in doing just that.

We expand on the ideas behind the Clinics For Good paradigm throughout this book. For now, the important point to note is that the paradigm provides a sustainable cycle for you to amplify your impact and make meaningful progress, personally, professionally and as a practice.

Key focus: Drivers

Principle: Stay the course

**You do not rise to the level of your goals.
You fall to the level of your systems.**

James Clear, author of the best-selling *Atomic Habits*

Chasing the shiny ball

A Clinic Mastery digital workshop for clinic owners featured guest speaker Lydia Lassila OAM – an aerial skier, five-time Winter Olympian, gold medallist and the first woman to perform the quad-twisting triple somersault. In the workshop, Lydia stressed that, 'You are the sum of your daily routines'. As a clinic owner, if your daily routines are structured around doing the deep thinking and immersive work required to grow your clinic, and live a meaningful and healthy life, you'll make sustainable progress.

Plenty of things can distract you from your bigger vision, and subsequently affect your ability to make the impact you seek as a Clinic For Good. Nir Eyal, a former Stanford lecturer and author of *Indistractable: How to Control Your Attention and Choose Your Life*, says that distraction (or chasing the shiny ball) is inevitable – the trick is being more aware about why. For Eyal, the opposite of distraction is *traction* – and traction is any action that you do with intent, is what you want to do and moves you towards your goals. Distraction, then, is any action that pulls you away from what you plan to do, or pulls you off track.

Common examples of distractions for clinic owners include:

- looking mindlessly at social media (such as scrolling through a Facebook group for clinic owners)
- checking on Slack or email to see the latest from the team
- starting a new project to avoid the new system that you promised to create for your clinic team.

And the triggers for allowing yourself to be distracted are often internal rather than external. Only once you know why you got distracted can you take steps to fix it so that it doesn't happen again in the future. Think about your internal triggers that drive you towards distraction, and start to understand the deeper discomfort of why you are using these tools as an escape from some kind of uncomfortable sensation.

Relatable experience

Adam, clinic owner of a multidisciplinary musculoskeletal clinic, had started to feel overwhelmed when trying to implement multiple projects in a variety of areas within the clinic. He felt he had a lot of 'open loops' and that his team were feeling uncertain. Using our typical 'radical candour', we advised Adam to stop being so 'busy' and start being productive.

His sense of overwhelm was reduced by focusing on important projects and not getting distracted:

> I just wanted to send a special thank you to Clinic Mastery for guiding me over the past three to four months – to billing appropriately, designing a career pathway for our team and transitioning our team from casuals to permanents. It was tough to not get distracted by other shiny ball projects, but we got there! Our team are really happy and it's boosted our team culture.

Same old boring strokes

When you play a shot in golf and hit your ball it's called a 'stroke'. There's a mantra that to be a good golfer and score well, you should keep the game simple by playing the same old boring strokes. If you score well consistently, you're then able to sustainably improve your performance over time. This is an important mantra for amateurs because they tend to make an already difficult game harder by trying to do things outside their skill level, beyond their capabilities or outside of their risk–reward control. In other words, they try to play in a 'flashy' way. And their performance often ends up very inconsistent.

To grow your clinic, you too can adopt this mantra of 'same old boring strokes'. New things to do in this year to grow your clinic are always going to pop up – including new technologies, updated strategies and improved methodologies. However, in many respects your focus needs to be on doing the same old boring strokes, day in and day out.

How well you grow your clinic versus a peer or your own goals often comes down to a lack of discipline – or lack of commitment to the same old boring strokes – not a lack of skill, or adequate strategy (or anything else).

Often you're on the right track, but for lack of patience, persistence or several other reasons, you don't continue with that approach: implementing and repeating the same old boring strokes that would sustainably allow you to grow.

A lot of sound fundamentals to growing your clinic don't change as the calendar year ticks over. Each and every day, you still need to do them well. Fundamentals such as:

- lead inspired, engaged, connected teams
- transform client experiences
- grow profitably and sustainability.

Again, these fundamentals are covered throughout this book. The key is that the same old boring strokes can be the difference, allowing you to make the progress you want personally and professionally.

Key focus: Plan

Principle: Plan to grow ASAP – as sustainably as possible

Rome wasn't built in a day.

Proverb

Your manifesto

Man·i·festo: A statement declaring intentions, motives or views.

Having 'one of those' seems like a good idea, right? Yes, you have goals and very objective, purposeful, strategic components for what's to come, but what if all the parts and pieces could be captured in a nutshell – your manifesto?

A manifesto is essentially a key thought – something that should always be top of mind in everything you do. It's a self-preservation thing (for all), because, inevitably the road ahead is going to have challenges.

When you have 57 things on your to-do list, 12 people wanting to connect, 96 emails in your inbox and only eight hours in a workday, how can you navigate the next steps?

Having your manifesto as an anchoring thought or intent will help. It's something your teammates can remind you of (always humbling), or you can remind yourself of. Your manifesto needs to be shared and kept front and centre.

The manifesto for 2021 inside Clinic Mastery (among many other intentions) was to 'Keep it simple'. This was chosen for a few reasons:

- **We've learnt from 2020:** Simplifying our focus and workflow enables sustainability, especially amid the chaos of the COVID-19 pandemic.

- **A condition of success:** As we grow, complexity can creep in. This impacts our ability to be consistent, efficient and effective. Simplicity allows scaling of results for clinic owners.

- **Have more fun at work:** We all want to have fun and enjoy the work we do. Keeping it simple allows us to give more attention to our relationships, focus on our projects and make more progress as people.
- **Amplify our impact:** Simplicity allows us to stick to the plan and replicate what works so that we can help more people (team, clients, partners, communities) and create more Clinics For Good.

What simple looks like

For us, keeping it simple can mean focusing on a specific critical driver, or a specific project, system, campaign or process. For example, a measurable objective for the next 120 days could be 180 new patients or three new therapists, or reducing cancellations from 25 to 15 per cent.

We keep things simple for our clients – we find what might be the underlying cause of their condition or presentation and then present possible remedies. You need to translate that skill across to the business side of things.

Plan with perspective

When we ask clinic owners how many years they plan on being in business, many of them answer with many multiple years! So growing sustainably is important – for your personal energy, financial rewards, team continuity, social impacts, systems, implementation, growth and motivation.

Detailed five- to ten-year plans are crazy for clinics. You must have a clear painted picture of the next three years, but even knowing what's going to happen in the next 12 months can be difficult. So getting some direction and making progress is what's important here.

We also deviate away from the 90-day (three-month) rhythm and planning of corporate projects – because this always feels more like a sprint. You need time to rest, reset and refine. The corporate

90-day model is designed and aligned for shareholder reporting. They have massive resources such as huge teams and bucket loads of money – which we, as small business owners, don't have. It makes sense to use a model more reflective of a sustainable lifestyle not a corporate entity.

We preference a 120-day (four-month) alternative that's much more sustainable for clinics. This approach creates sustainability for:

- your financial position
- the community and planet
- your team members
- your own energy and passion for business
- the systems in your business
- your continued growth
- your status as a Clinic For Good.

To make it memorable, we refer to this four-month planning program as the ASAP method, with each month represented by one of the letters in the acronym:

- **Month 1: <u>A</u>ctivate** – Do your big strategic thinking and planning before you then launch new initiatives, campaigns, projects, systems, policies and procedures.
- **Month 2: <u>S</u>ustain** – ensure you have the tracking mechanisms and dashboards in place for the initiatives you activated the month before. Refine any details, systems and/or components of what was activated as you prepare to go all in next month.
- **Month 3: <u>A</u>mplify** – now that you've activated and ensured sustainability of the new initiative, it's time to invest more time, resources and money to amplify the reach, results and impact of that initiative. Don't introduce anything new in this month – just keep your head down as you focus on disciplined action to amplify the initiative.
- **Month 4: <u>P</u>lay** – in this month, close any loops from the previous three months and enjoy the fruits of your labours.

Ideally, you're taking some time for you – enjoy longer weekends, early nights or later starts. While you're not starting anything new, you can review and reflect on your purpose and prepare the plans for the next cycle – beginning with Activate again and consolidating profit so that you don't grow out of money.

Each month has a different set of actions and intentions to make the ASAP method a sustainable cycle for implementing change and making progress. Moving to a four-month cycle has been a subtle shift with a massive impact on our workflow and that of the clinic owners we've helped implement this over the years.

Take action ASAP

The four-month ASAP method can then be repeated three times (or what we like to call three trimesters) over a 12-month period.

The following table outlines a possible rhythm.

Example ASAP rhythm over a 12-month period

	Activate	Sustain	Amplify	Play
Trimester 1	November	December	January	February
Trimester 2	March	April	May	June
Trimester 3	July	August	September	October

Put your consulting hat on

No doubt you've got a massive to-do list of all the things you want to do in your clinic (who doesn't?). But perhaps you're not sure where to start as a professional development buff, or concerned that perhaps you're not even any good at this strategic planning stuff. A few common challenges that clinic owners face when it comes to strategy include:

- not sure where to start and what to prioritise
- struggling to allocate enough time to do the deep critical thinking, or sacrificing this time for the 'urgent' needs of the team, clients and the clinic
- not sure 'what's possible' (having limited awareness or lacking vision).

If you're facing similar challenges, this is where you need to use the consulting skills you already have. Wear your consulting hat and proceed as you would with a patient – first diagnose the problem, and then plan what you are going to do about it and implement that plan. You then need to track the results and adjust your approach as needed.

You can use the core element of Strategy, and its key focus areas, to help create more meaningful, profitable and sustainable progress as you grow your clinic.

High-impact action

Consider the following key insights and actions when infusing purpose into your clinic:

- Continue to be a force for good by reinforcing your passion and core purpose for helping people live a better life – it's an animating force for progress.
- Get clarity on what your clinic looks like three years from now in a really clear painted picture so that your team can align with impact you seek to make.
- Core values are core actions, so be sure to identify, clarify, simplify and most importantly amplify through daily actions the values that make you unique.

- Play a bigger game by aligning your clinic for impact with the 17 UN Sustainable Development Goals and build a better future for the generations to come.
- Integrate the causes that matter to you through the means of strategic and operational implementation as well as dependent and independent participation.
- Pay it forward by taking consistent action in accordance with your integration so that you tangibly see the impact you're making.
- Adopt the Clinics For Good paradigm because simplicity is sustainable. Amplify your impact by leading inspired teams to transform client experiences so that you grow your clinic.
- Stay the course by focusing on the key drivers of growth and avoid the temptation to chase the shiny ball with disciplined action and quality systems, no matter how boring.
- Forgo the corporate 90-day rhythm that creates overwhelm and adopt the 120-day rhythm that helps you grow your clinic as sustainably as possible.

Purpose summary

Purpose is about amplifying your impact. To grow as sustainably as possible (ASAP) you'll need to prioritise infusing meaning, creating momentum and defining your methodology for how you will play the infinite game of business. Remember why you became a health professional and clinic owner so that you can integrate and experience a higher degree of purpose as you create Clinics For Good.

DEGREE 3:

TEAM

Lead inspired teams

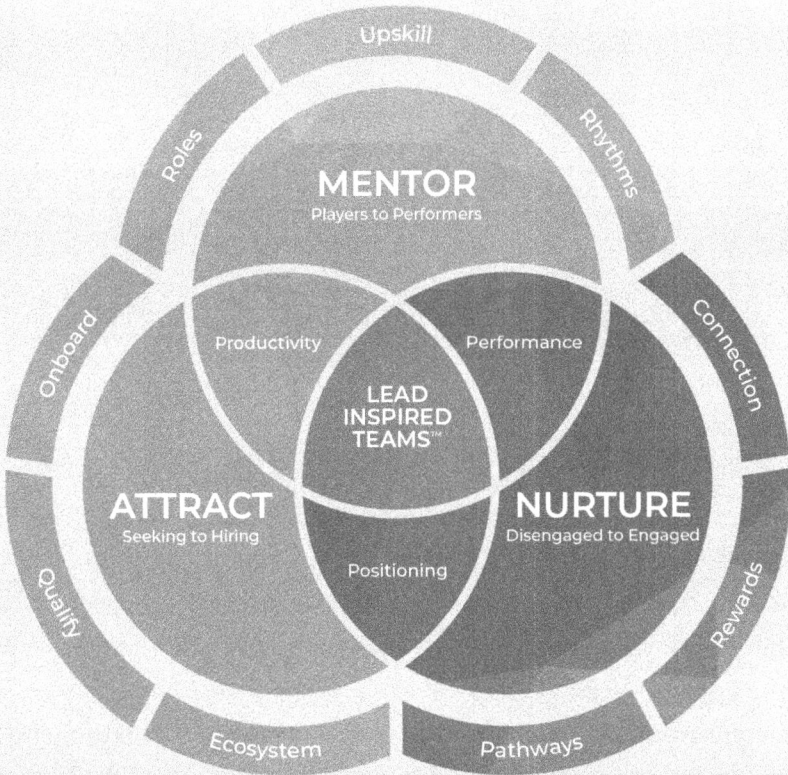

Core element: Attract

The first element to master in this Degree is Attract. This relates to you transitioning from seeking a new team member each time you have a vacancy to always hiring by positioning your clinic as a preferred place to work.

Key focus: Ecosystem

Principle: You're always hiring

> **Better to be looking at them than for them.**
>
> Shane Davis, Pro Feet Podiatry and co-founder of Clinic Mastery

Time in the market

Economist Benjamin Graham is famous for many things, including writing *The Intelligent Investor* (first published in 1949) and mentoring Warren Buffett, one of the richest humans alive today. Graham and Buffett share an investing principle that can also help in hiring quality team members, especially practitioners.

Their investing principle is 'time in the market, not timing the market'.

The opposite of the intelligent investor is to try to buy and sell assets at the 'right' time, when the market peaks and troughs are about to happen. This is an attempt to 'beat' the market, or 'outsmart' the market by buying and selling at what are believed to be optimal times to maximise gains. Instead, the concept of the intelligent investor focuses on time *in* the market, which involves a long-term approach, a methodical system, a comprehensive strategy and a more sustainable resource allocation. This leads to better returns on your investment of time, money and effort.

When we see clinics unsuccessfully hiring, we also often see an opportunity to adopt a similar principle to Graham's and Buffett's.

A clinic owner who is trying to 'time the market' sees they have a personnel need and puts a job ad out – typically at around the same time of year as most other clinics are doing it … that creates a fiercely competitive environment!

If you instead adopt the 'time in the market' approach, you're looking at 'always hiring' and investing in assets to develop your brand portfolio within the ecosystem of your industry so that you become a stand-out place to work.

At the end of the day, if you want to grow your clinic and amplify your impact, you're going to need to grow your team. It's valuable for you to invest in that growth, week on week, quarter on quarter, year on year by adopting the always-hiring principle and asset-creation practice.

To attract more ideal team members with ease, you're better to always be hiring, by establishing and owning your position in the industry as a preferred provider of healthcare, and as a preferred place to work. You need to adopt the approach of always hiring by perpetually adding value within an ecosystem – aka your industry – helping you attract more ideal team members with ease.

No wonder hiring is competitive

We commonly hear that recruitment is hard for clinics. Perhaps you're not getting enough applicants or not enough of the right applicants. Or, right at the crunch moment when you're giving someone a job offer, they go somewhere else and completely blow up your plans. It's so frustrating. However, some clinics (believe it or not) are getting an abundance of therapists applying to work with them; they're even being approached without the clinic having an active job advertised in the marketplace.

A few things separate these clinics from others and, while this is a journey about always improving, the principle that binds this together is *you are always hiring*.

No wonder hiring therapists is a competitive space for you if all of a sudden your hiring is reactive to your immediate need.

Suddenly, you need someone *right now* – you need someone to fill a position on the team and so you put up a job ad and hope that the wordsmithing you've done on your job ad completely blows away all the other wordsmiths out there. We've all done it. We write about strengths such as our culture, our team training and our support. The thing is everyone's basically saying the same thing, so how do you make your clinic stand out and attract the right people?

Build an attractive clinic brand

Making your clinic stand out comes back to your brand. If you've built enough brand equity, you can start to draw upon that. At the core of your brand is what you're saying to the marketplace and how you're backing that up with action. An important part of building your brand is adding value to your ecosystem through publishing assets that solve problems of your ideal team member avatars.

Next, once you've adopted this strategy of building your brand, you need to measure your progress. Just as you would in any other business domain – whether it's your financials or your client journey – you need to be looking at data and measuring how well you're doing.

Rather than jumping onto different strategies (trying to time the market), you can then find the incremental improvements or the marginal gains.

You can measure your success at each stage of your brand reach, essentially going from a broad spectrum of people within your industry and profession, narrowing it down to the ideal people and then enrolling them into your team.

Hiring journey framework

We have developed a stepped journey as a framework to give your recruitment ecosystem structure and outcomes. What you want to build is robustness in your ecosystem so that you're catching people at all of their career and contemplation stages.

The following framework helps you bring the best options to your clinic:

1. **Awareness:** Around Australia (and the world) are thousands of clinics, with more and more starting each month. You need to actually create a level of awareness that you even exist because without this, nobody will want to work at your clinic. But how? Some clinics already have a reputable brand, while others are absolutely still working on it. So this could be your first step – build a brand that people are aware of and respect. Building awareness is about knowing the needs, frustrations and desires of your ideal team member and then showing up in the place where they are in their greatest concentration, online and/or physically – in other words, go where the attention is. Measure this stage with data on reach – for example, number of podcast subscribers, Facebook group members or LinkedIn connections.

2. **Interest:** How do you actually measure that people not only know about you and your clinic but are also starting to be interested in you, and could possibly be on the pathway to joining your team now or in the future? You want to play the long game here. Yes, you might have a need now and you might have a few people ready to join your team, but how are you building robustness in your recruitment ecosystem so that 18, 36, 72 months from now when you need three extra therapists, you're able to do it with greater ease? The key is to build a database of potential team members and regularly communicate with them and add value to their careers. Measure this stage through looking at registrations – for example, number of downloads, registrations or database members.

3. **Evaluation:** This is where possible recruits are evaluating their career options, including whether you are a 'candidate' for their next move (not the other way round). Central to this stage of

attracting the best talent is being seen as a trusted advisor in the evaluation of career options in your profession. Focus on helping potential recruits through their evaluation process by thinking about their needs. When they start to think about any pains or challenges they have in their current role or if they're a new graduate progressing into the real world, how can you help them make the best career decision? In our industry we often build our brand for clients – we publish all sorts of content and form partnerships so that our clients receive value and also see us as a trusted voice and option in their healthcare. What about within your profession with your team? What if you were the preferred provider of employment? What assets could you produce that live and breathe in the ecosystem of your industry and your local and global community to help build this brand as the preferred employer? Whether you're in the country (rural or remote) and you're trying to convert people to move out of the city and join you, or whether you're in the city and the employment market is highly competitive and you're trying to get people to change where they're working, everyone has their unique challenges when it comes to recruitment. How are you building your reputation as the trusted advisor to help them make this jump? How can you help them consider the things to evaluate and then have an open, active dialogue with you? Measure this stage with data on prospects – for example, number of meetings, or attendees at a webinar or clinic tours.

Tell + Show + Involve: The concept here is to substantiate the things you communicate in your recruitment. Prove the things you claim through a process of tell, show and involve. For example:

– *Tell:* We offer 1:1 mentoring.
– *Show:* Provide video, infographics, downloads, presentations or webinars on how that mentoring works.

- *Involve:* Invite them to join you live or online to experience or witness what you offer (through shadowing, work experience or observations).

Every clinic will offer a benefit such as 1:1 mentoring, so prove you actually provide the things you claim to offer before someone joins your team – show them and involve them to stand out.

4. **Consideration:** At this stage, your potential recruits are actively pursuing – they're applying for a job you've advertised, they're requesting more information, they're actually knocking on the door asking if you have any roles and going through the traditional application–interview process. This is where you're also actively looking to hire someone. The problem is most clinics start here – that's coming back to the feeling of 'I have a need right now. Let's put up a job ad and maybe a little video'. It's just not going to cut it in this ever-expanding and competitive environment of employment options. Instead, you need to consider how you invest your time, money and resources in a way that helps build your clinic and its brand, and allows recruitment to become more free-flowing. You will then attract more people in abundance wanting to work with you. Measure this stage with data on applicants – for example, number of applicants and quality of applicants.

5. **Enrolment:** This is the sticky point of the ecosystem – where you want your ideal recruits to stick around and choose you. Personalise your recruitment proposal to remove competition from the conversation. During the interview process finding out the current problems, concerns, fears, challenges and wishes of your potential recruit is highly valuable. You can also capture their desires, aims, hopes and goals for a specified time period (for example, the next three years). By documenting these insights, you're able to then package them through offering a tailored role with a clearly articulated pathway right from the start. Most clinics will offer the role as it will be over the next 12 months, with loose lip service to what might happen

after that time. Why not remove competition about which clinic might pay slightly more in the first year of the contract? You can then move to discussing and documenting the pathway of a team member in your offer (proposal) as a documented reflection that you're committed to helping them progress personally and professionally. Measure this stage with overall data on successful hiring – for example, time to hire, cost to hire, positions filled, and applications to roles accepted ratio.

Again, some clinic owners get to this sticky point and offer the job, only for the person to accept an offer elsewhere. So what are some strategies that you can have that get your ideal candidate through the qualifying process and to the point where you can present a tailor-made solution?

Recruit with rigour

Are you measuring your 'always hiring approach'? If you are committed to hiring now and into the future to support your growth, you need to conduct your recruitment with rigour. That means having a recruitment dashboard to track your effectiveness and observe the opportunities to attract more ideal people to you. The following key focus outlines this in more detail.

Assets in action

Use the QR code provided here to download more information about the Clinic Mastery recruitment dashboard and how you can use this in your hiring processes.

Key focus: Qualify

Principle: Hire for culture add

As much as talent counts, effort counts twice.

Angela Duckworth, author of *Grit: The Power of Passion and Perseverance*

Don't settle

Polly and Tim, owners of a paediatric care clinic, made 'culture add' the central part of their hiring process when they were looking for a new admin team.

When advertising the positions, Polly emphasised they were looking for admin team members who could add to the experience of the families coming to their clinic by bringing a service-based approach. They wanted to break the mould of the typical receptionist who had worked in similar roles for years and was just going through the motions. They were looking for anyone with a strong service focus – perhaps a flight attendant, barista or retail assistant who could bring their experience, perspective and personality to the role in a way that added to their culture.

They advertised the position in a local Facebook group, with a three-day application time. From the applicants, eight people ticked the boxes on what they we're looking for, and they progressed to a group interview with Polly's team. They then interviewed four people and ended up creating two positions. Both are a great addition.

The 'Me Generation'

In an article titled 'The Whiny Generation', author David Martin described 'a handful of spoiled, self-indulgent, overgrown adolescents'. He argued,

> We have a generation (or at least part of a generation) whose every need has been catered to since birth. Now, when

they finally face adulthood, they expect the gift-giving to continue … the Whiners want everything now … What's their reaction when they don't get what they want? That's right – they throw a tantrum.

This could easily be viewed as a summary of the younger generation of therapists coming into our profession today. However, this was a *Newsweek* article from 1993 and Martin is a baby boomer. Martin was complaining about the younger generation at the time – Gen X, who were born between 1965 and 1979.

Endless examples of quotes, stories and articles spanning the globe and across centuries document and describe how the younger generation of the day is viewed as lazy, entitled and self-interested – and the list goes on. Be mindful of your beliefs and bias when it comes to hiring – they might be blinding you to who is right in front of you. Whether you have a bias towards age, experience, gender or life stage, it's time to ditch the bias for a system.

Substitute bias for systems

You need to thoroughly assess the people interested in working with you by using a multi-step, personalised and very purposeful structure so that the best candidates qualify for the role. Create a qualifying checklist in your hiring process. Some of the assets and steps to remove bias and add systems include:

- implementing qualifying milestones to progress through stages of hiring
- screening applications against established criteria
- using standardised interview questions
- implementing reference check criteria
- taking advantage of social hiring with group or team involvement
- considering objective and subjective history checks.

Aim for culture add

When looking to hire someone new, aim for a 'culture addition' rather than simply looking for 'culture fit'. Settling for culture fit might just be limiting your clinic growth or affecting your culture. If you simply hire people who are like you, you don't get the added value of diverse perspectives to see opportunities for growth. You might also perpetuate the cultural dynamic – including the performance and contribution culture – that keeps your clinic stagnant. You have an opportunity to think about finding people who align with your purpose, share your values and *add* to your culture.

Key focus: Onboard

Principle: Give your team the best start

> ### You're in the business of recruiting, inducting and training.
>
> Steve McKnight, investor and best-selling author

Zero to 100

The 'zero to 100' principle represents the first 100 days in a new team member's journey. It's a parallel with 'getting them up to speed' just like referenced when getting a car as quickly up to 100km/h as possible (and as is safe). It commonly aligns with the education (or probationary) period for new team members. The difference between it and most probationary periods, however, is that the zero to 100 approach is much more intentionally planned out and hands on from you as the clinic owner. It might include, for example, staggered training in clinic expectations and procedures, and weekly mentoring and training sessions. (See the 'Assets in action' breakout box, earlier, for more details.)

The results speak for themselves. Psychologist and clinic owner Jenna implemented the zero to 100 model for a new therapist, and received the following feedback:

> It feels so different to my other therapists where we've kind of just agreed to work together, then signed a contract at some point and then sent 1000 emails figuring stuff out as it comes up … The new standard has been set!

Relatable experience

Faye is a clinic owner and leader of a musculoskeletal clinic who had recently welcomed a new therapist. Within the first few weeks Faye received the following feedback from her new team member:

> *You're already going above and beyond my expectations, with the zero to 100 and the weekly tutes we do and the constant contact I have with Faye. It is amazing and just so reassuring knowing that I am cared about as a new grad and helped through the start of a new career and not expected to be the same as someone who has already been working for years. We are so lucky. This is so much better than what all of my peers are experiencing.*

As part of leading inspired teams, you have a duty to onboard new team members with a guided launch so that they can make the best possible start in their role and in their renewed career with you.

On repeat

For every new team member, you need to repeat the same induction process, including the basics such as helping them know where everything is and how to access the systems. Onboarding a new team member takes time. It's valuable time and it's a valuable process as well, ensuring you give your new team members the best start.

So what can you create in your onboarding so you have a system that's on repeat so that you leverage more of your time? The zero to 100 process also allows you to do that. The other side of Faye's new team member's onboarding is that Faye doesn't have to try to remember everything, and she doesn't miss anything! It's all documented and linked to all the assets – such as systems, policies, procedures, training and so on – that have been created before. This system means that her new team members can view the documents and assets one at a time as they learn them and try them out, without Faye needing to spend hours and hours going over and over the components! This also means their face-to-face mentoring time is far more effective.

You can empower an independent learner and do-er in your clinic. Don't put your time on repeat; put your systems on repeat.

Assets in action

To give you and your new team members the best possible start and to establish strong foundations for a thriving future, we've broken the zero to 100 onboarding process (see the 'Onboard' key focus, following) into three streams, with each stream spanning across three stages. This allows your new team member to graduate from the zero to 100 process with confidence and competence.

Here's how you can outline how the streams and stages work together for a new team member.

Streams

To help create meaningful growth, your role at [clinic name] will involve three streams of development: Personal, Professional and the Practice. Together, we are going to work on each of these areas so you feel confident in your role. Over your next 100 days, we're going to cover a variety of topics and key actions that make [clinic name] and this team unique. To simplify your focus, we've outlined the key objectives we have over the next 100 days for each of these three streams and growth areas.

Stages

To help create sustainable growth, your zero to 100 journey will be rolled out in three stages (three blocks of five weeks):

- Stage 1: Launch & Learn
- Stage 2: Rhythm & Role
- Stage 3: Engage & Execute.

Together we're going to gradually introduce and progressively train you in all things [clinic name] so you feel confident in your role. To amplify your success, we're going to use these staged time-blocks to allow you to embrace mastery in everything that you do across the three streams of Personal, Professional and the Practice.

The stages also help you refine and tailor your training as it's progressively rolled out.

Core element: Mentor

The second element to master in Degree 3 is Mentor. This relates to you transforming players into performers and expanding your team's capacity to help more people in your community.

Key focus: Roles

Principle: Conduct your orchestra

Accountability breeds responsibility.

Stephen Covey

Conducting = coaching + mentoring

As you grow your clinic, you need to undergo a transformation from being the talented do-er (playing all the instruments) to being the skilled conductor who is coordinating the talented team.

Conducting your team combines the two processes of coaching and mentoring while also connecting your team to the 'who, what, when, where and how'.

Coaching focuses on the 'why' and uses curious and open-ended questions to help your team members unpack their thinking and find answers themselves. It's a great way to boost autonomy and remove yourself as a bottleneck in decision-making. Coaching allows you to embrace the principle Stephen Covey (author of best-selling *The 7 Habits of Highly Effective People*) calls 'Seek first to understand, then be understood'. As a coach, some days you're going to be better than others at asking the right questions, so using a consistent framework to ask questions helps you get the best results. This framework could come in the form of 'clipboard' style prompts and questions while you work with a team member or it could be an online form (for example, through Google Forms) with questions they complete prior to the session to give you a heads up on what's to be covered. (See the upcoming 'Mentor session notes' breakout box for some example questions to include on such a form.)

Mentoring is about the 'how', tapping into your expertise or experience so that you can advise team members on what to do. Mentoring is about prescribing the 'here's how to do it'. It's highly effective when you're short on time, or the person you're working with doesn't have the context to uncover an answer themselves within a coaching framework.

Conducting is then about a combination of coaching and mentoring that leads to you connecting the team member with the resources and/or people they need to find the answers or help them implement the solutions. It's a step further than both coaching and mentoring because you are connecting them with what they need and so you act as a conductor – it emphasises the who, when and where.

Part of the conductor's role is also creating clarity for all team members about the components of their position, and defining their roles and responsibilities. This means you can then help them develop in the areas where they can make the greatest impact by playing their role and knowing how their role impacts others. Everyone needs to know their role and responsibilities. You then need accountability to that role through a mentoring, training and performance hub.

Mentor session notes

Coaching focus sheet

Provided here are some example questions to include on a coaching focus form your team members can complete before a training session with you. Before selecting and adding your questions, it's important to reflect on your objectives for this form and for the meeting to determine the best ones to choose.

Consider the following questions (and the area of focus or core value they relate to):

1. What has been your *biggest* win over the past month? (Bring the energy)
2. What is the most important outcome for today's session for you? (Be outcomes-focused)
3. What's happening in your world? (Keep it real)
4. To what degree are you feeling a *workflow* versus feeling a *workload* in your role? (Keep it real)
5. To what degree are you enjoying coming to work? (Keep it real)
6. How can we better support you in creating more flow and enjoyment in the coming month? (Be outcomes-focused)
7. To what degree are you clear about your role in the strategic direction of the clinic over the next one year? (Be outcomes-focused)
8. What are your strategic or high-impact priorities over the next month? (Be outcomes-focused)

9. If you had a magic wand, what would you change about your role or the clinic? (Keep it real)

10. What is the clinic's core purpose? (Be outcomes-focused)

11. What is central to your personal purpose and passion? (Be outcomes-focused)

12. How can we better align and infuse your passions and personal purpose with the clinic's core purpose? (Make it happen)

13. What parts of your role are you really enjoying and thriving with? (Keep it real)

14. What parts of your role do you loathe or find draining? (Keep it real)

15. How are you going to simplify your role in the next month? (Make it happen)

16. To what degree do you feel your ideas are welcomed in the clinic? (Keep it real)

17. To what degree do you feel like your feedback is taken on board? (Keep it real)

18. What behaviours do you need to change so that we can achieve our clinic objectives over the next year? (Keep it real)

19. What behaviours need to change in our team so that we can achieve our clinic objectives over the next year? (Keep it real)

20. To what degree have you contributed your candid feedback and voiced your opinion to the people who need to hear it? (Keep it real)

21. To what degree have you contributed your appreciation, gratitude and praise for the team members who need to hear it? (Bring the energy)

22. To what degree have you played above the line in the last month? (Keep it real)

23. Tell me what I don't want to hear but need to hear. (Keep it real)

24. What skill or concept have you learnt recently? (Make it happen)

25. How have you (or can you) apply this new skill or concept in your role? (Be outcomes-focused)

26. What was your #1 personal focus for the past month? (And what area was this from on your Wheel of Life/ desire statement?)

27. What did you achieve in this area of your life?

28. What is your #1 personal focus for the next month? (And what area is this from on your Wheel of Life/desire statement?)

29. What will you achieve in this area of your life?

30. How could we support you to achieve this?

31. What was your 'one thing' action point from the previous session, and how is your progress with it?

32. What is one thing you will achieve to make this next month AWESOME?

Mentoring, training and performance hub

A mentoring, training and performance hub allows you to align Personal, Professional and the Practice objectives from your zero to 100 process (refer to earlier 'Assets in action' box) in a central hub for accountability, mentoring support and high performance.

Assets in action

Key features of your mentoring hub could include are as follows:

- **Clinic excellence indicators tracking:** It's important that therapists take great care with their client case load by delivering quality outcomes. The clinic excellence indicators provide a way for health professionals to track and measure quantitative results of how they deliver their service. Factors to track include number of new clients, returning appointments, patient reported outcomes, cancellations and net promoter score (NPS). Tracking these numbers on a weekly basis allows you to keep your therapists accountable to delivering great healthcare.

- **Desire statement evolution:** As part of aligning your Personal, Professional and the Practice objectives in a sustainable way, a desire statement outlines the written goals of your team member. These are the goals your team member has identified as meaningful for them to pursue across the different elements of their life and work. Knowing these goals allows you to 'mentor' the human (person), not just the therapist (professional) or team member (the practice). Reviewing team member desire statements on a monthly or quarterly basis keeps you accountable to incorporating fulfilment along the journey.

- **Partnership nurturing:** As part of delivering holistic care for clients, therapists work and partner with a group of colleagues, including other therapists, businesses, groups, networks, associations, schools and clubs. It important to track and systemise how you nurture your and your team's network for the best most sustainable outcomes. This section keeps you accountable to follow up and follow through on your partnership promises.

- **Client journey delivery:** Every client deserves a high-quality and consistent experience. This requires having systems and checklists in place to ensure you deliver on your commitment every single time. The client journey delivery area is a way to track that important steps are covered every time for a client – for example, a management plan has been implemented, a client welcome pack offered and a new client follow-up phone call initiated. Monitoring these aspects helps put the accountability on therapists for their respective case loads and the client experience they deliver.

· **Mentoring notes and focus sheet responses:** Just as taking notes is an important habit and record for therapist–client interactions, it is also highly valuable for therapist–mentor interactions. This section is where you can integrate responses to focus sheets you provide to your team (question–answer survey sheets filled out by the therapist). In this section, you can also take notes about these focus sheet responses and document actions to make your mentoring outcomes focused. Mentoring sessions have tremendous value when we move away from informal 'top-of-mind' conversations to structured, purposeful and outcomes-focused support sessions. This section of the hub is the way to prepare for and record your interactions, much like you would do for a client with their healthcare.

Scan the QR code (or go to www.clinicmastery.com/grow-your-clinic/discovery-session) to arrange a time to get person-alised support from Clinic Mastery and discuss how to improve your mentoring for better team performance.

This mentoring hub is important for the following reasons:

· You can unlock practitioner reward structures when all expectations are met. (See the 'Nurture' core element for more on rewarding team members.)

- You ensure the best possible tracking of patient care, nurturing and outcomes.
- You enable more accountability on referral and partnership nurturing.
- You make stronger connections between work and life development.
- You have a framework for yourself and other leaders in your clinic to ensure you're mentoring consistently.
- You have a historical HR record for performance and mentoring.
- You can set meaningful goals that practitioners are engaged to achieve.
- Freelancer contractors can more easily make the transition to aligned employees for consistency.
- Teamwork and collaboration become actions that are measured, helping to create more holistic contributors.

Developing a mentoring hub has some clear benefits. But it needs to be simple and used often. Common mistakes or shortfalls with implementation include the following:

- lack of training on how to create it and/or how to use it
- lack of reference to it in subsequent mentoring of practitioners or admin team members
- unclear connection between what's in it for team members and the relevance to their role and pathways (or unclear communication of this connection)
- making it too complex to use and therefore too much time to update and fill in.

Your business owner position description

Do you have a position description as a clinic owner? If you're like most clinic owners, you probably answered no. Many owners operate with the thought that *I'm responsible for everything, so it's all in my position description.*

To a degree, you are responsible for a lot. It's your business. However, if you've got a team, you've likely delegated some of the responsibilities as part of their position descriptions. On paper at least, you've removed yourself as the bottleneck. To really focus on your areas of responsibility, writing your own position description is worthwhile.

Components of your role (that should be included in your position description) include:

- appointment, diary and therapist utilisation and management
- client experience
- culture and human resources
- financial compliance and performance
- brand strategy and marketing
- mentoring and training
- partnership nurturing
- recruitment
- strategic planning
- systems, policies and procedures.

Your position description is going to be unique to your stage of business. If yours is a more advanced and mature clinic with various portfolios established – such as clinical mentoring/training, marketing and practice management – you'll likely have less on your position description than someone who is just starting out with their clinic and looking to quickly grow and scale up. The important thing is that you are accountable to doing what's on your position description – and that starts with continued review of what you need to do. As you grow your clinic, your description will evolve with you. Holding yourself to account – just like you would for other team members, according to their position description – may be hard, but it's just as important.

Key focus: Upskill

Principle: Plan the work, work the plan

<blockquote>
Create the environment for
transformational development.

Ben Lynch
</blockquote>

Schools can help train your therapists

Learning from other industries helps you to break the conditioning, dogma and status quo of your profession – and break the mould of being a clinic owner. This could also mean breaking the mould of limiting beliefs and practices that restrict growth. To get you thinking about how you could break the mould, let's first consider schools and flipped learning.

In the traditional education model, students come to class and learn about a specific topic for the very first time in detail. They then explore the concepts further and aim to apply those concepts as part of their homework. For advanced learners, this might work well – you can learn new things in class, absorb these concepts and then be able to think about their application – perhaps even ask quality questions on the spot. You're then able to go home and work on the concepts independently. I (Ben) wasn't an advanced learner (and I'm still not).

If you're like me (and many other students), maybe it took you a little bit of time to digest things. If so, you may have felt 'lost' doing homework – aka when left to your own devices.

To combat this, 'flipped learning' is something that a lot of progressive schools are adopting. In this process, students learn new concepts as part of their homework, and then come to class to mastermind and work on how to apply the concepts and teachings.

Flipped learning is a supportive way to apply learning, and you have the opportunity during the induction and training of your team members to apply this concept more deliberately for better outcomes and also to leverage your time.

Consider getting team members to first learn about new concepts and the latest evidence independently – whether that's through a podcast, the latest journal article, a book or a workshop online – and then come to team sessions to discuss and apply these learnings further. These sessions could be one-to-one mentoring, or the group continuing professional development (CPD) sessions you run once a week, fortnight or month. In these sessions, team members apply their new knowledge through activities such as masterminding, applied case studies, role play or workshop solutions.

Embrace the power of the team's collective perspective. This kind of flipped learning is a really practical way to be very deliberate about transforming the growth and development of your team and yourself in the clinic. And remember – leaders are learners.

Grow and develop your team by providing upskilling in the form of courses, content, coaching, collaboration, case studies and observations. Help them to achieve a level of mastery so that your clinic can continue to grow and thrive.

Key focus: Rhythms

Principle: Rhythms build relationships

> **It's the little things that you do consistently**
> **that make the most impact as a leader.**
>
> Brigid Linden, founder of Boost Health Collective and
> Clinic Mastery mentor

Ships in the night

If you're like most clinic owners, it's likely you have a group of individuals at your clinic who work together, but don't regularly cross paths because their work hours, variations in locations of practice or busy consulting schedules don't allow it. The 'team', including you, can be like ships in the night.

A connected team is going to be far more effective at caring for patients, more likely to collaborate with their team mates, more engaged in conversation, more aligned with the direction of the practice and more fulfilled in their roles. Ensuring a good rhythm for communicating, collaborating and connecting allows your team to better perform in their roles.

You'll find that regular connections such as a team meeting help:

- Create focus:
  - You can set the theme and can create an outcome or result that you want to achieve by the end of the session ahead.
  - You can reinforce key messages or values of how the team will carry themselves or act throughout the day ahead.

- Connect the team:
  - Your team get to touch base with each other on a personal front.

- Celebrate wins:
  - You can share a story of a team member who did something great.
  - You can also share a story of a client who achieved a great result, outcome or win in their life.

- Align the team:
  - You can share cover notes on patients coming in that day.
  - You can update the team on other items to follow up – for example, return contact (phone calls, emails).

Relatable experience

During the recent COVID-19 lockdowns, clinic owner Polly hosted an online 'Home, sweet home' themed 'quarter cuddle' (all-team meeting) night for her team. In the weeks leading up to the event, each team member was sent a list of questions about their homes and lifestyle, which included the question, 'What is your favourite take-away to order in for dinner?' Then they had to take a photo of something in their home that was meaningful to them and send it to Polly. They were also split off into discipline-specific groups to share tips and seek assistance when needed while working from home. Next, they were placed into groups, and told the people in their group would now be their 'homies'.

The homies were told to check in on each other throughout each work day, making sure that nobody was becoming isolated and offering companionship and support. Each homie group decided how they would operate and the level of contact they would have.

On the night of the 'Home, sweet home' event, the team came online as a group. Polly screen-shared the photos people had sent her, and of the team built connectedness as everyone shared the story behind the item they chose. And during this session, a surprise delivery was made to everyone's house with their favourite food (based on their response to the earlier questions). The team were so incredibly grateful for the connection, food and activities.

Blue sky + strategic + operations

Meetings can be like time-blocking in that you're constantly finding new ways to do it better. This constant adjusting can be annoying. You might be thinking, *Why haven't we 'figured it out' yet?*

However, as you grow a bigger team, and evolve your thinking and the way your clinic functions, the supporting structures such as meetings need to evolve also. Whatever your evolution time-line – three months, three quarters or three years – your supporting structures will likely need to be revisited and evolved. And that's okay. It's not that you're doing a 'bad' job; you just need to take the next step in your evolution. This takes us back to the 'age for stage' concept from the introduction – you need to update your methods to reflect your maturity in business.

It's like a software upgrade – the changes may be subtle, yet they're significant in how things function moving forward. In fact, it's a moment to celebrate these slightest changes. They mean you're doing things better than yesterday. You're creating sustainability in your growth through margin gains.

As you evolve, your meetings can be broken into blue sky, strategic and operations. What to focus on for each meeting, and how often to hold them, is as follows:

- **Blue sky:** A blue sky meeting occurs once per year. It's a chance to think big picture about the next one to three years and then three to five years. Topics discussed include a measure of progress, painted picture, major projects, brand evolutions, exit or sale timelines and team expansions.
- **Strategic:** Strategic meetings occur once every 120 days (every four months). At these meetings, you can think about the next 'milestone measure' on the road to your one- to three-year goal, and then determine the one to three major projects to advance you towards that milestone.
- **Operations:** Operations meetings occur once per fortnight (every two weeks). They are a chance to update the team on how you're doing through providing reports on measures and the status of the project/s that are being implemented. You can also discuss course corrections and where help is needed. Nothing particularly new (in terms of projects or implementations) is discussed in operations meetings.

These three meetings are the backbone of your clinic's accountability towards meaningful and measurable progress. Most commonly you'll play in the operational space with your whole team, and if you have a leadership or exec team they will also be present in the blue sky and strategic meetings.

Examples of operational meetings include:

- professional development – for example, continuing professional development
- daily huddles
- marketing – for example, campaigns
- finance – for example, accounts
- all-team operations
- mentoring sessions.

Consider also the mix of who attends each of the three types of meeting. You may choose to keep a certain type of meeting one on one and another open to the whole team. Or you might choose to focus on a particular group, such as the practitioner team or the admin team. Finally, you may choose to meet based on function or portfolio, such as clinical leaders, or the marketing or client experience team.

Core element: Nurture

The third element to master in Degree 3 is Nurture. This relates to you being able to transition your team from a state of disengaged to an engaged state by nurturing the Personal, Professional and the Practice components of each member's role, especially beyond their onboarding.

An important part of this element is creating structures, schedules and spaces for your team to connect. It's important that your team connect as individuals and as a collective group to establish the trust and understanding of one another so that they can navigate the challenges and seize the opportunities that come with doing ambitious and meaningful work.

Key focus: Connection

Principle: Compound your interest

Compound interest is the eighth wonder of the world.

Proverb (commonly misattributed to Albert Einstein)

Can we chat ...

The three words 'Can we chat?' can change your state, real quick. If you've ever received this request from a team member in an email or SMS, you'll likely be familiar with that sinking feeling in your stomach – shortly followed by an episode of anxiety for what's about to come.

You might be thinking questions like, *What does this mean? Are they going to leave? What's happened? Did I miss something?* This can turn to, *Not now! How am I going to deal with this? Why is it all happening at once?*

So, when leading inspired teams and growing your clinic, responding to 'Can we chat?' can be one of the hardest things to do. We get it. It can also be one of the most rewarding!

It's rewarding because coming to work with people who really care about doing good work and making an impact naturally elevates everyone personally and professionally. However, this kind of enthusiasm and commitment isn't guaranteed to last. (To be fair, nothing is guaranteed to last except perhaps death and taxes – and not even taxes if you're set up in the Cayman Islands.) So we believe that one way to sustainably lead inspired teams is to compound your interest.

As noted in the opening quote in this section, many people believe compound interest to be the eighth wonder of the world. (Although there's no record of Albert Einstein ever thinking so.) Of course, most people consider compound interest in relation to a financial portfolio and not leading inspired teams; however, the principle is still just as profound in this context.

The principle here is that you can compound your interest in the individuals who are already on your team to expand your understanding, embrace your humanity and enhance your connection. This is just the investment you need to make to lead inspired teams.

Making investments into your team in a genuine, authentic way will pay dividends.

Just like the principal in your financial portfolio grows as you compound your interest, the same is true of your results with your team when you invest in this principle. Your investment truly compounds when you create leaders who create leaders who are interested to connect with their team mates just as much as you.

Build connection and they will stay

Clinic owners in our Clinic Mastery community have been able to share many stories on the benefits of building connections with and within their team. The following are just two of these stories.

As the tornado of COVID-19 caused a series of prolonged impacts on many clinics' ability to open and see patients, many clinic owners faced tough decisions – especially when it came to their team. From rostering to redundancies, everything needed to be reviewed to see how on earth to keep the clinic alive. In a humbling experience, Jane, a clinic owner of a musculoskeletal practice, had every single one of her team put up their hand to take cuts in hours and to offer hours to others. This was a moving experience that made Jane realise the powerful connection her team had created with one another, and she was brought to tears of gratitude for the selflessness that she witnessed.

Sam, a clinic owner of a musculoskeletal therapy practice, was similarly moved by a decision by one of his team members. One of his therapists, John, was approached by a new clinic opening up in a neighbouring suburb. They offered him a position but he declined. This was a massive win for Sam because one year earlier he'd had to say goodbye to another team member who'd taken up an offer from another practice – a month before Sam was planning to take leave for the arrival of his first child. John turning down this offer was a great reflection of the connection they shared, and they were able to navigate the conversation with an open dialogue and open relationship.

Your story is what connects

Matt reflected that one of the greatest lessons from a team development day was that a new team only really has one thing in common – they're all in the same place at the same time. The key to doing great things as a team then becomes learning how everyone got to this place, and the ups and downs they faced along the way.

Matt had his team draw their life timeline on a board and use the peaks and troughs of their journey to share what brought them to where they were now (together at Matt's clinic). The session was extremely powerful, and made the team connection even deeper while encouraging everyone to be mindful of others' life experiences and how they can adapt their behaviours to be the best, most inclusive team possible. We encourage everyone to do this exercise with their team mates at work, sport or even with friends.

Relatable experience

Michael Rizk, Clinic Mastery mentor and co-founder of iMove Physio & iMoveU, shared the following.

I've met a lot of cynical business owners – and, in turn, this produces cynical new grads.

I used to think I'd never be a cynical business owner … but then, something happens. You put your blood, sweat and tears into a clinic … you invest time and energy … people leave. And you get upset.

Then you think, *Maybe if I wasn't so emotionally invested.* So you try to protect yourself and become less emotionally invested – and then team members start saying 'My boss wasn't there … or when they were they micromanaged'. And then they leave because you seem distant or less emotionally invested.

So you flip and go the other way again – offering leadership chats, quarterly rhythms, retreats, professional development, offsites, desire statements, and on and on. And people still leave.

It's a tough cycle to break, right?

Richard Branson may have said, 'Train people well enough so they can leave; treat them well enough so that they don't want to', but that's easier said than done.

I feel the thing driving us apart more than ever are poor business owners and leaders who go on to create cynical new grads. This creates a cycle where, every three to four years, people just want to go and start their own thing – and this time 'do it better'.

I've been on both sides – wanting to hold on to team members so tight you crush them, and then flipping and feeling like, 'Well, screw this'.

But I try to remember this: professionals in their twenties and thirties will inevitably move, travel, have kids, fall in love, fall out of love and so on. So some people leaving your business is also inevitable.

I also try to see things from the perspective of the new grad. They've just put their blood, sweat and tears into a degree for three to four years. Then they get their first job and are basically told, 'Start again – you have another three to four years before you're really competent'.

So for owners I say, enjoy the journey, get comfortable with an infinite game and celebrate every year a team member stays – because it's so easy not to stay.

Key focus: Rewards

Principle: Praise you like I should

> Recognition is not a scarce resource.
> You can't use it up or run out of it.

Susan M Heathfield, management and organisation development

A win–win–win outcome

A great rewards system is a win for your clients, your team members and you as the clinic owner. The outcome is to provide a remuneration progression for team members that is sustainable and profitable, and reflects their desire statement or goals.

Many rewards models are available, but the model we provide here is one that's worked for us. This model uses 'rewards brackets' based on the revenue generated by the practitioner. When the practitioner achieves a certain level of revenue, they unlock a reward.

This model is not perfect and it's certainly not the 'only' way. However, we've seen it work across many different professions in clinics around the world because it balances the financial goals of your team members with the business objectives and best client care to create a win–win outcome. As Shane Davis, co-founder of Clinic Mastery says, 'Every time we see a client, they give us a note of appreciation at the end of their consultation to acknowledge the value we've provided to their health and life. That note comes in the form of a monetary note'. In other words, in the world of private practice and small business, people are recognising the value we bring to the community by supporting us with a universally agreed medium of exchange: money. Whether that's their own money or money that comes via their funding allocation, it's an acknowledgement of a value exchange. Therefore, using a financial tracker as one part of a therapist reward structure is an acknowledgment over the long term that value is being exchanged.

Having a rewards system such as the one provided here is important for the following reasons:

- rewarding the effort and hard work of team members who contribute in a variety of ways to the team culture, client care and business growth
- creating a progression that allows high performers to go above and beyond in their role, while also being rewarded appropriately (and so removing a 'ceiling' on their income)
- ensuring you have a remuneration model that allows the business to grow sustainably while you continue to invest in the team, clients and business (while being paid appropriately as well).

Profitability versus sustainability

We're always working to find the balance of profitability and sustainability for our team and our business. Therefore, we look at the remuneration of our team as being on a continuum – a model also recommended by our friend and colleague Tristan White, best-selling author of *Culture is Everything*. On this continuum, sustainability and profitability are on one end, and team and culture are on the other, as shown in the following figure.

Profitability and
sustainability

Team and
culture

The challenge for any clinic (and business) owner is finding a balance between the two.

For example, you could pay your team very well for their work – passing on, say, 70 per cent of their billing revenue – and it's likely that team and culture at your clinic would be great. However, this is going to come at the expense of profitability and sustainability for the business and for you, the business owner.

On the other end of the continuum, you could pay your team a low rate – perhaps only 20 per cent of billing revenue – and your business would likely be profitable in the short term. However, it's going to come at the expense of team and culture. You'd likely experience high team member turnover and poor retention because your team members didn't feel or see the value of their work, and would be lured by other clinics for more financial reward.

You need to find the point on the continuum that you're comfortable with, and that aligns with your values.

What you decide may also be influenced by your location, demographic and saturation of practitioners, and should be reviewed at least annually to consider if your balance is working for you, your team members and your business.

Next, you'll need to identify recognition and reward mechanisms for your business that resonate with your team and reflect their contribution to team mates, clients and the clinic. It's important to find personalised mechanisms that reinforce and sustainably encourage your team to contribute in those ways. The following 'Mentor session notes' box provides more information on the reward structure we recommend at Clinic Mastery.

Mentor session notes

Creating reward structures for high-performing team members

Shane Davis, Clinic Mastery co-founder, director of Pro-Feet Podiatry, and owner of Active Feet Ocean Grove and Geelong created the following sustainable reward structure through making many mistakes and investing in numerous advisors. This is the rewards structure we help clinic owners implement, and Shane outlines here how it works, through answering some frequently asked questions.

What would be a fair pay for my team member that I can sustain as a business? (Base only.)

Talk with a qualified employment specialist to help you identify the appropriate remuneration for your team member in accordance with relevant awards (and any relevant rules, regulations and laws in your jurisdiction).

Once you know the relevant awards, paying roughly 5 to 10 per cent above the award for your base salary is a reasonable place to start (depending on your profession). With this you can say you offer an above award base salary, which gives your team members certainty and stability as they progress through their induction period. (Here in Australia, we like to talk about base salaries including superannuation with team members.)

As a percentage of revenue, you may then aim to pay 35 to 45 per cent base plus reward for your team members (depending on your profession). Keeping your salary base at the lower end allows more room for incentives and a positive rewards structure.

You may like to review the award with an HR company annually to make sure you're paying the right award. Also note that some clinic owners choose not to talk about the specific award level with their team members (for example, level 2, year 4). It's important for owners to know what award they're basing pay rates on, but not as important for the team member to know.

Of course, 'fair pay' may be specific for your profession (for example, psychology typically has a higher base than physiotherapy). It may also depend on other factors, including:

- **Location:** If you're in a remote location, for example, you might need to pay more to attract people to your town or city.

- **Experience:** What you pay a team member should reflect the value they bring to the team, to clients and to the business, and this is often influenced by level of experience.

- **Ideal practitioner:** You might pay higher to attract a particular practitioner to your clinic (and instead of paying a recruiting fee of $5000 to $10,000).

An employment lawyer can help you with legal employment contracts.

What's the difference between a reward and a commission or bonus?

A commission or bonus payment traditionally has only financial objectives that team members need to achieve in order to receive additional remuneration.

A reward is a more positive word, and includes expectations of the team member as well as meeting financial objectives and practice objectives to receive additional remuneration.

We want to reward a team member for contributing value to the team, clients and business so that we have a holistic team player.

You get what you reward and recognise, so it makes sense to reward behaviours and actions that are sustainable and in the best interests of all involved.

Why shouldn't I talk about 'percentages' with a team member?

My preference is to not talk about percentages with team members because it can lead to confusion about their value and their anticipated income.

Rather, talk about your team member's desire statement. This helps you both understand what they want and what that outcome will mean for them.

Remember that someone being on a 60 per cent commission doesn't necessarily mean they will be earning more than someone on a 40 per cent commission, because it's relative to the amount they are billing. This comparison also doesn't convey the lifestyle considerations of their work.

Absolutely you should know what the percentages are as the business owner. However, aim to move away from framing remuneration with your team in this light.

What percentage of revenue is good for the practitioner to be taking?

Once you've done your calculations, you'll be able to see what your practitioners are getting paid as a percentage of the revenue they generate.

Knowing this will help you benchmark yourself against your profession and peers more accurately to know how sustainable your arrangement or the current performance of the practitioner is for your profitability and your team and culture.

If you can achieve a target range of 35 to 45 per cent for the practitioner (after the products and so on are accounted for) while maintaining a team/culture balance, you will be doing really well. We at Clinic Mastery know as business owners this range is definitely sustainable.

What if my team member wants me to increase their base salary? When would I do that and by how much?

We like to say to our team that you get out what you put in, and their remuneration reflects the value they bring to themselves, their clients and the business.

We want them to make it easy for us to say absolutely yes to a higher salary.

It's helpful to talk about the future in these conversations – looking, say, 12 to 18 months ahead, and the things that make it easy for us as business owners to say yes to pay increases. These factors might include completing practitioner dashboard expectations, providing partner nurturing visits or writing content for blog articles.

Ultimately, you can be guided by the award, with a yearly review with an HR company to help guide you towards best practice.

How often do I pay rewards?

Typically, we pay or 'unlock' a team member's reward at the end of each quarter of the year to reward consistency over time.

We like to use the calendar year as our timeline for unlocking rewards. So, for example, quarter 1 (Jan to March) ends on 31 March. On this date, we would calculate and identify the reward bracket reached by the team member and then 'unlock' or pay that reward within seven days.

Paying quarterly also helps to smooth out some of the ups and downs that a practitioner will have, including leave days where clients are typically seen in busier periods before and after leave.

How does a team member unlock their reward?

A team member's reward will be unlocked when the expectations are completed on their expectations dashboard.

The reason we require this is so that the team member is contributing on multiple fronts to the growth of the business, providing the best care for patients and developing their professional reputation.

We don't want to encourage a practitioner to focus purely on the financial aspect of healthcare by overservicing clients or being unethical. So it's important to have more requirements that contribute in other ways to the business that need to be completed to unlock their reward.

Do I 'unlock' (pay) a reward if a team member hasn't completed all of their expectations on the expectations dashboard?

The expectation is that team members complete *all* of the requirements on their expectations dashboard to unlock their reward.

Provided you have installed a regular rhythm of connection through your mentoring, the progress of a team member shouldn't cause any 'shock'. The mentoring is a framework to anticipate and improve performance in alignment with the team member's goals and the clinic's objectives.

If they don't complete all expectations, they're not eligible to unlock their reward.

This needs to be made clear to your team from the start.

However, if they have generated the desired total billing revenue for the quarter but only completed, say, 7 out of 10 expectations, we may still unlock that reward for the team member. The disclaimer here is that we need to discuss this with the team member first.

Our discussion would go something like this:

'Hey Johnny, just a quick one – I know you're not quite up to speed on your expectations dashboard so I'm just wondering if you can focus on completing those last three items in the next fortnight so that we can get your reward payment for you as well.'

Johnny will often say something like, 'Yeah, no sweat' – because, as if he's not going to hustle to get $1000 or $2000 by ticking off those last few items, even if that's on the weekend or after hours.

What if my team member doesn't have the time or capacity to complete the expectations on their dashboard because they are fully booked?

You might like to reassess your hiring strategies to ensure your busiest practitioners remain at around 85 per cent utilisation (effectively 'fully booked'), to then be able to have the capacity to complete these essential elements of their work.

At this level of utilisation, over a 38-hour week they will have close to six hours per week to complete these tasks.

Growing practices should aim to hire a new full-time practitioner when their current practitioner reaches approximately 75 per cent utilisation (depending on your profession and for what they are billing).

Some clinics may have no option but to have practitioners above 85 per cent utilisation due to circumstances outside their control, and in these situations there may be special consideration for admin support for those practitioners, or a reduction in the number of items to complete on their dashboards.

This needs to be organised in discussion with the practitioner, and with reference to their desire statement. Remember – you want to balance the rewards of their work and lifestyle to avoid burnout.

It's important to note that while this reward model has a great structure, we're always tailoring it to individual clinics, and you should do the same.

Key focus: Pathways

Principle: Provide pathways for purposeful progression

> Let us all be the leaders we wish we had.
>
> Simon Sinek

Like pruning the roses

The final focus for the Nurture element in Degree 3 is to ensure you offer pathways for purposeful progression within your clinic. Having a variety of opportunities for your team to choose from in how they expand and evolve their role is important for retaining quality people. Sometimes, however, this is easier said than done …

A 'sparse and pruned rose garden' was the analogy George used as he described his clinic after the fallout from the last 12 months. In the previous 12 months, three high-performing therapists had left his clinic to seek new opportunities. That, of course, had its repercussions. It led to a significant drop in patients and therefore revenue, meaning George needed to go from full-time business owner to picking up a full-time case load of clients. This adjustment to his working week meant that he wasn't able to support, connect with and mentor the rest of the team like he had previously done. The three team members had also left behind a toxicity among other team members and, without his usual availability in the week, George wasn't able to course correct their approach to work. This compounding effect meant that in the subsequent months a number of other team members also moved on. It was an 'on your knees' moment for George, when years of work seemed to be very quickly unravelling.

George had to take decisive action. Instead of trying to 'save' everyone, he changed tact to focus on the 'clinic champions' – the people who were still on board, engaged and contributing in a meaningful way. He focused on cultivating that small group to help support the larger group, and also help find new team members who would better represent and contribute to the clinic culture. The plan worked (over the next nine months), and George was able to come through to the other side of this loss and attract new team members.

This was when George was able to reflect on the previous year, coming up with his pruned rose garden analogy. He reflected that when you prune the roses (or team members leave the team), the garden can look baron. However, as long as you continue to water, feed and provide sunlight to the roses, your garden will soon be flowering, colourful and thriving again. In hindsight, George realised he could have removed some of the stress of all those team members leaving by seeing it like the pruning season and knowing that he was doing all the right things (focusing on clinic champions) to prepare for the flowering. He just needed time and consistency.

Not only was this a good reflection and perspective that could be useful in any future seasons of turbulence in the clinic, the experience also taught George the lesson that having the right people on the team is the best thing long term, even if it means temporary pain as you make changes. Having pathways for those emerging and senior team members was also important, so that you could retain them in the clinic.

Cultivate a subculture of champions

Not everyone on your team will come around to new ideas or change at the same time. When you respect that, you realise you don't have to waste your energy. When you're doing your best to create change, focus on the people who are receptive, give them the opportunities and champion the results of the change to help create a collective movement – rather than just being the 'boss' saying this is what we're going to do and you need to get on board. Have the right people on board and give them opportunities to inspire others on the team through leading by example and catalysing change using the power of social proof.

If you are serious about creating a fulfilling career progression for your team as health professionals and humans, break down their journey with them. At each of your mentoring sessions and quarterly reviews, reflect on the desire statement of your team member so they're progressing to their 'meaningful goals'. Ultimately your progression – and your team's – is a reflection of your passion, performance, dedication and vision! You will get out what you put in.

Planned progressions

Time-block now a regular quarterly alignment session (review) of each team member's progression in alignment with the clinic purpose, painted picture and their desire statement.

You may have industry benchmarks and pay progressions that form a template for the structure you can tailor; however, a typical career progression for your clinic champions could be as follows:

- **First year – establishing roots:** In this year, your team member is learning your systems, getting familiar with and engaging with your team and partner network, and getting into a great rhythm with provided professional development. Whether someone is a first-year or seventh-year practitioner, their first year at a new clinic is the same. It's all about rhythm, consistency and building a solid foundation with the team and community. Volunteering for events outside of the clinic is also important to increase cohesion with the team and get team members out there building their community.

- **Second year – refining rhythm:** The team member is now into a rhythm, confident with how things work and ready to focus. This second year at the clinic is about focusing on their ideal community and nailing their week with their required number of clients consistently. Your team member might be ready to jump into some of the other portfolios (such as in the area of clinical mentor, marketing or practice management) and start challenging themself. They may even start thinking about their ideal roster and look to target three-day weekends.

- **Third year – nailing niche:** In their third year, your team member is continuing to build their relationships with their ideal client and community. They are confident and are building a reputation in their niche. Their roster will reflect when their ideal clients would like to be seen and they may consider taking on one of the clinic portfolios.

- **Fourth year – building brand:** In your team member's fourth year, they have developed a solid community and ideal client and can now solidify this with working on their ideal roster – lining this up with their desired income bracket from their desire statement. They may transition to block days or a split roster. They will be responsible for at least one clinic portfolio and, depending on their experience, may become a senior or titled therapist.

· **Fifth to eighth year – amplifying impact:** As your team member moves into their fifth year and beyond, they will be responsible for at least one portfolio, and can start assisting and guiding another team member working on this portfolio. They can also start considering other work–life aspects, such as increasing income, working more, working less, building a side hustle, moving to profit share or ownership, specialising via exposure, giving back to the community and/or being a leader at the clinic.

Each of these pathways takes time and comes with a new set of learnings and opportunities. Your role as clinic owner is to guide your team members along the process and stay open minded. Remind team members we all need to learn before we earn. Encourage them to pick a path, but also let them know that this can change and will change and that's okay too.

Giving guidance on what's possible without being too prescriptive is important. Allow your team members to work in collaboration with you to create a mutually beneficial and feasible pathway as they move into their fifth year and beyond, taking into account their work and life goals. The following 'Mentor session notes' box provides more details on some options for your clinic champions.

Mentor session notes

Possible pathways for clinic champions in their fifth year and beyond

Michael Rizk, founder of iMove Physiotherapy, iMoveU training for therapists and Clinic Mastery mentor, and Annie Strauch, founder of Performance Medicine and Clinic Mastery mentor, provided the following further information for guiding the pathways for practitioners at your clinic.

Your team members and clinic champions can consider the following pathways as they move into their fifth year with your clinic and beyond:

- **High income:** Your team member may be working towards more financial security and, therefore, want to work more, see more clients and become the authority in their area. They may work a roster that is beneficial for their chosen community, and choose to earn more by helping more people, more often and adding more value to their life.

- **Expert clinician:** Becoming an expert therapist may mean that your team member is producing valuable content and education to your community via multimodal channels (including webinars, online education and course develop-ment). They may also take on further study or additional external courses to support developing their expertise.

- **Side hustle:** Your team member may decide to start their own page (such as a website or social media) about something they're passionate about. This could be something within their profession or completely different from it. Your team member could work with your clinic's existing network and exposure to businesses, people and social media to create something unique to them.

- **Leader at the clinic:** Your team member may feel they can take ownership and accountability of a key function of your clinic and demonstrate this through taking on a portfolio in professional development, mentoring, education, socials or expanding the clinic brand. They see an opportunity to improve things and feel they can really help out.

- **Contributor to the community:** Your team member may be super happy in their role and want to contribute to the community or causes that matter them as part of the clinic's outreach initiatives. They may wish to go on a trip, pilgrimage or tour of duty to meet other industry leaders, talk at conferences or give to less privileged/underserviced communities.

- **Clinic director or clinical lead:** Your team member may feel they can take ownership and accountability of a key function of your clinic – such as social media, running professional development, leading the space in partner work or expanding the clinic's brand. Again, they see an opportunity to improve things and feel they can really help out. Roles such as clinic director or clinical lead are pathways that require commitment and allow increased responsibility in the running of the business. These roles are bespoke to the person and this pathway is one that can take years to develop into, so patience and persistence is key here.

- **Profit share:** Your team member may want to take the next step in their career but can't afford to buy into a business. A profit share arrangement means they get a percentage of the profits – anywhere from 0.5 to 10 per cent of your clinic (make it win–win for you and them). This provides your team member with exciting opportunities to work with the team and help them achieve their personal goals, thus keeping the clinic healthy – which directly relates to their percentage.

- **Satellite clinic ownership:** Many therapists get to a point where they want to own and you can help your team with this and reduce the risk. The advantage of starting a satellite clinic is that your team member will have all your existing systems and structures in place. This helps mitigate their risk and keeps their team around them and together.

- **Work–life flexibility:** In line with your team member's desire statement, they may want to work more days for higher income or fewer days for more family time, trial split shifts, work at two clinics or have a three-day weekend. You can help them with developing this flexibility.

We do leaving well

For many team members, leaving your clinic will be one of the pathways they choose. 'We do leaving well' should become a key mantra within your team. You just don't know how things might play out in the future, and the health communities that we operate within are so 'close' that maintaining the connections you have is extremely important.

Lauren and her rapidly growing speech pathology team is an example of this. Lauren had a therapist move on. While this was upsetting, instead of blaming or distancing herself, she embraced the concept of 'we do leaving well' – in other words, treating team members just as well on the way out as on the way in. Fast-forward 18 months, and Lauren's team had grown significantly. She was now in a position to hire a leadership role – a pathway she didn't previously have available, but was building for. This therapist who had resigned (and left on friendly terms) was so excited to see the new role and applied straightaway.

High-impact action

Consider the following key insights and actions to inspire your team:

- You're always hiring, so invest your time in building out your ecosystem of assets to attract more ideal people.
- Be mindful of your bias in qualifying the right people for your team and look for the culture *addition* (not just *fit*) by substituting bias for systems.
- Give your team the best start with the 'zero to 100' experience that covers Personal, Professional and Practice development.
- Conduct your orchestra by getting the right people in the right roles with your ongoing mentoring sessions to support that evolution.

- Use flipped learning to accelerate development and leverage time in helping team members learn and upskill.
- Rhythms build relationships; focus on doing the little things consistently to forge strong connections with your team.
- Compound your interest in your team so that you build trust in your team for navigating the ups and downs ahead.
- Rewards should be win–win–win outcomes – for your clinic, your team members and your clients. Sustainability and profitability are the key considerations.
- Provide pathways for purposeful progression to your team and be the leader you wish we had.

Team summary

In order to grow your clinic sustainably, you need to lead inspired teams. It's important to focus on attracting good people, nurturing them to be the best versions of themselves personally and professionally, and as a representative of the practice. Finally, nurture them as humans to help them find success and fulfilment in their career path ahead. Create an amazing place to work that follows through on the things you say you're going to do for the people that you work with. See your clinic as the place to help attract, train and nurture good people.

DEGREE 4:

SYSTEMS

Reduce reliance on you

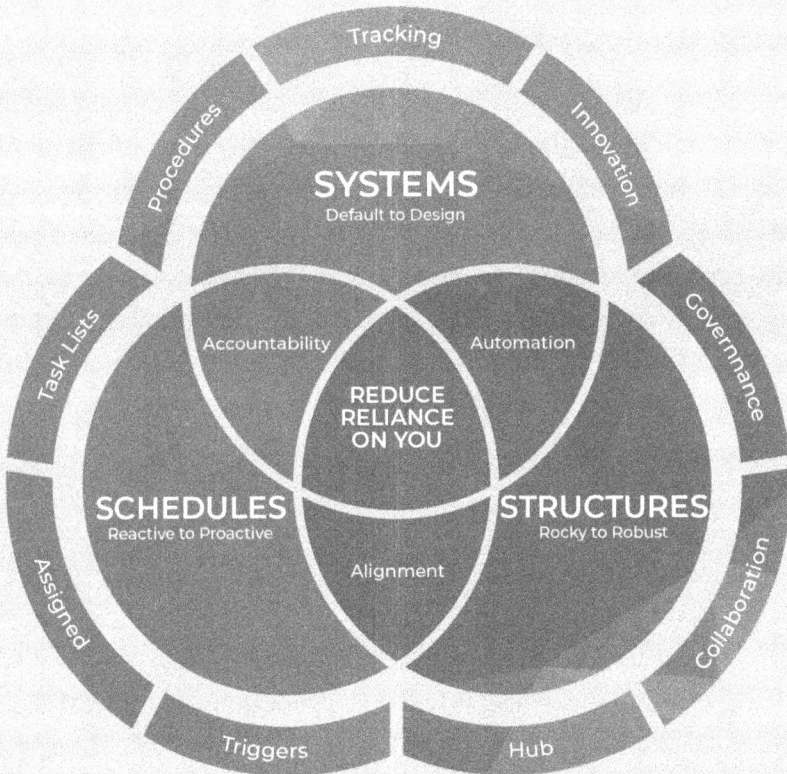

Tracking

Procedures

Innovation

SYSTEMS
Default to Design

Task Lists

Accountability

Automation

Governnance

**REDUCE
RELIANCE
ON YOU**

SCHEDULES
Reactive to Proactive

STRUCTURES
Rocky to Robust

Assigned

Alignment

Collaboration

Triggers

Hub

Core element: Schedules

The objective of Schedules is to transition from being reactive to being proactive in your operations so that you're more in control of growing your clinic.

Key focus: Triggers

Principle: Schedule your success

Timing is everything.

Buck Brannaman, horse trainer and leading clinician

An outstanding account

In a mentoring session, we asked Adam, owner of multidisciplinary musculoskeletal clinic, the dollar figure for his accounts receivable (money outstanding owed to the clinic) right now. His reply was shocking, uncomfortable and really positive all at the same time – his accounts receivable were sitting at $220,000. When we then asked how much revenue he was making per month, Adam told us it was $60,000. As a guide, maintaining the total amount of your outstanding accounts to less than 10 per cent of monthly revenue is the reference point we commonly use. (We combine this with the principle that you are your own benchmark and being better month on month compared to yourself should be your focus.)

Using our benchmark, with a monthly income of $60,000, Adam's ideal number for outstanding accounts would be $6,000. His clinic was 36 times over that amount. What had occurred was that a team member hadn't billed anything for about a year – and Adam didn't have a trigger to process payment or a trigger to review what was outstanding. As you can no doubt imagine, for his accounts to get this out of control, a few other things were also lacking from the leadership team and owners of the clinic. However, how much he was owed was positive because the situation could only get better – with the right triggers, systems and accountability in place.

Adam could now boost cashflow for his clinic, take more personal income and have confidence that their new lens of installing schedules around their systems would lead to more consistency and reduce reliance on a single person. Getting their accounts to the ideal reference point of 10 per cent of monthly revenue took a little over 12 months – and also involved moving on the admin team member and making way for another existing team member who showed a lot of promise to be promoted to a senior role.

You know what time it is …

A trigger is anything that prompts you to perform a certain activity, at a certain time. Triggers should prompt the right person to do the right thing at the right time in a way that's recurring. A system is a series of steps or a sequence of activities to be done at a certain time for desired results or outcomes, and to ensure accountability and consistency. Tracking is a way to then measure the results and keep accountable to the implementation of any activities so that you know if it was done, and by whom, when and how well.

Triggers can be:

- **Based on time:** This can include day, date or time triggers – for example, having a trigger of the last day of the month to reconcile accounts for the month in your accounting software.
- **Based on event:** The trigger here might be appointment type – for example a new client appointment.
- **Based on season:** A change of season could be a trigger for annual tasks, such as cleaning the air conditioner or launching marketing campaigns related to seasonal illnesses or injuries you serve in your clinic.
- **Based on requirement:** A trigger could be based on something an external body requires you to do, such as lodging your company tax at the end of financial year.

· **Based on behaviour:** Triggers can also be based on client or team member behaviours – for example, a patient cancelling could trigger a recall system.

How to trigger

Your triggers need to be scheduled to be recurring, globally accessible by the relevant team members, transferable to others on the team in the case of holidays or sick leave and accompanied by the relevant systems for how to do what's required. Some triggers will naturally require you to wait for someone to take some action or something to happen; however, where possible, being proactive and scheduling triggers (that is, reminders) to control your workflow is ideal.

Using a variety of frameworks to support the triggers for something to happen is also valuable. It's pretty frustrating to realise that something wasn't done for a client in their care or that a team member didn't realise they were meant to follow up a certain task – for example, ordering stock – to keep the operations of the clinic flowing. Triggers are a great reminder for your team to do the things they need to do in a timely manner. For example, triggers can be included in the following:

· **Task management system:** Systems such as Asana and Trello have the ability to be automated, with tasks scheduled, assigned and recurring.

· **Practice management system calendar or tasks:** Using the daily appointment calendar can be a way to also schedule and trigger team members to do certain tasks at certain times.

· **Operational meetings and agendas:** The structure of a meeting can trigger you to prepare something for the meeting or review and implement a task during the meeting itself.

· **Reminder prompts:** Using email or Slackbot reminders can also trigger you to follow through on actions.

Key focus: Assigned

Principle: Play your role with rigour

Everybody, Somebody, Anybody and Nobody

This is a little story about four people named Everybody,
Somebody, Anybody and Nobody.
There was an important job to be done and Everybody
was sure that Somebody would do it.
Anybody could have done it, but Nobody did.
Somebody got angry about that because it was
Everybody's job.
Everybody thought that Anybody could do it, but
Nobody realised that Everybody wouldn't do it.
It ended up that Everybody blamed Somebody when
Nobody did what Anybody could have done.

Condensed version of Charles Osgood's 'A poem about responsibility'

Avoid the octopus

An octopus has one head, arms all over the place and everything sucks. It can be a relatable parallel to your status as a business owner.

Acting like an octopus is understandable in business because we're often accountable for many and varied functions of the clinic – from marketing campaigns to attract more clients, to mentoring our therapists and delivering great client care. The bookkeeper is chasing you, your inbox is overflowing and it feels like everything and everyone is sucking your attention and energy away from the very important work you need to do to grow your clinic.

Simply assigning things to someone else and hoping they do it like you would (and hoping you can pick up the pieces later if not) isn't the answer – that's what's known as *abdication*. To avoid being an octopus and successfully reduce reliance on a single person – you – assigning roles through careful delegation backed by accountability is key.

Relatable experience

In a humbling and haunting experience, Kath revealed the following: 'I made a mistake. A tidal wave of annual leave is about to hit and I'm not sure how I'm going to be able to stay afloat'.

Six of Kath's therapists would be on overlapping leave over a six-week period. This was going to drain the reserves in the bank and require tapping into an overdraft account to keep the clinic alive.

Kath said, 'I've made a big mistake and it's going to be an expensive lesson'. The lesson was to delegate, not abdicate. Kath's leave approval process had been assigned to the practice manager – but, clearly, not effectively. Kath hadn't implemented any accountability or enough rigour in her training or the system behind the leave approval process.

Kath had the right intention: to reduce the reliance on herself and remove the bottleneck of decision-making. She'd also wanted to provide opportunities for her practice manager to take on greater responsibility. The problem was in the execution. Rather than handing over an important task in a careful and methodical way, the ball had just been thrown – and then dropped – and Kath and her clinic had a looming problem.

Falling into this trap is so easy as a busy clinic owner. When you don't feel like you have a spare minute in the week, the prospect of quickly offloading a task is very tempting. Whether it's leave approval, managing the banking, mentoring your therapists, the sterilisation of equipment or anything else, be sure to delegate, not abdicate. Investing the time when you assign will save you later. Just ask Kath.

Accrue your 'freedom hours'

Personal and professional sustainability for yourself means reducing the business's reliance on you. Think about your time spent effectively delegating as freedom hours accumulating for you.

Documenting a three-minute system that you do a number of times each day might take 30 minutes. This initial investment might mean you're tempted to just keep doing the minor task yourself. However, over time, the freedom hours you accrue by documenting this system pay back your initial time many times over. That 30 minutes is time very well invested.

You can use these freedom hours to learn a new skill, improve your health, spend time with your family, work on your business or travel. A healthy and happy owner is a great benefit to your clinic.

We don't advocate that you sit on a beach and have others work for you. The purpose-driven clinics we work with have great systems in place so that the owner can be very involved with the clinic but is not swallowed up by the day-to-day operations. They're also driven to amplify their impact, so they're inspired to do meaningful and substantial work.

Play to your genius

A key part of successful delegation is to assign the right roles to the right people for the best outcome. Delegation is more than just about getting tasks off your plate; it also provides the opportunity for your team members to extend themselves and to perform their role with vigour (because of your systems and training, and also because it's in their wheelhouse of competence, their genius). This will make a great contribution to your team's enjoyment at work and, therefore, your team retention.

Mentor session notes

Thank you to Daniel Gibbs, co-founder of Clinic Mastery for simplying how to ensure everyone knows the 'who, what and how' about tasks.

Team (the who):
- Everyone knows exactly what their role is.

- Everyone knows what everyone else does in their role.
- Everyone knows the impact their work has on everyone else.

Task list (the what):

- Every daily task (operation) of the business is recorded.
- Each task record covers what needs to happen, when it needs to be done and by whom.

Hub (the how):

- Written or video documentation of procedures is in place for every daily task or required operation and everyone knows where to find it. For example, you have documentation for:
  - team member induction (practitioner and admin)
  - team communication
  - training
  - monitoring (measuring clinic excellence indicators).

Key focus: Task lists

Principle: Prioritise progress (outcomes over outputs)

> **Don't confuse activity with productivity.**
> **Many people are simply busy being busy.**
>
> Robin Sharma, author of *The Greatness Guide*

A family retreat

Chris and Lauren had escaped for a well-deserved break from their speech pathology clinic. Like most clinic owners, before they left they'd been nervous and excited – nervous for what could go wrong, and excited that they'd be spending quality family time in the sunny north of Queensland, Australia. They'd already experienced some of what could go wrong the last time they'd had a holiday – therapists had left, causing massive disruption to the continuity of client care and financially squeezing the clinic.

But this time, things were different. 'We haven't heard anything,' they told us. 'And it's been three weeks.' What had changed since their last ill-fated break was the many new cultural elements and systems in their clinic. They now had triggers to activate certain tasks, work was properly assigned to the right people, and documented procedures and task lists were in place.

These allowed them to go away and have nothing go wrong. And better than that, the team demanded they stay offline and let them handle everything so Chris and Lauren could enjoy their time away with the kids.

They had achieved:

- **Alignment:** They had a good understanding of what their business was trying to achieve and their place in that.
- **Independence:** They enjoyed three weeks' leave without a phone call, email or message. Nothing went wrong!
- **Accountability:** While they still had some work to go on using their numbers as critical drivers, they had already seen good progress.
- **Empowerment:** A key team member had started taking things on without being asked, and achieving results. Previously, if she had any fear she could make a mistake, she would look for authority and support from Chris or Lauren before progressing with a task.

Going away is a valuable 'stress test' for your business structure and autonomy. How long could you leave your clinic for and still return to a smooth, up-to-date clinic? One day? One week? One month? One quarter? Your answer really shows how reliant the clinic is on you.

Activity to amplify

Thank you to Daniel Gibbs, co-founder of Clinic Mastery for outlining the following on how you can achieve more freedom through your task lists:

- Identify the tasks you do as the business owner that other people can do. Write a list.
- Support your team in being able to do the tasks you have identified the right way every time. Write a procedure for these tasks and create rigorous training to support your team.
- Create sound systems and tracking metrics to ensure quality and consistency. Create feedback channels and dashboards to report progress.

Understand the functional areas within the clinic with the following:

- Write a list of every task that needs to be done in the business, separated into the following three categories:
  1. Support (such as admin tasks)
  2. Operations (related to treating patients)
  3. Management (leadership, partnerships, marketing and vision tasks).
- Write down who currently does each task. (As the business owner, your name might be on a lot of things!)
- Work down your list of tasks and create systems for each, starting with the support (admin) and operations tasks. Establish these systems so that other people can do those tasks.
- Do everything you can as the business owner to get into and stay in the 'management zone'.
- Use your task list (the what) and systems (the how) to assign tasks to people in your team. You can use Asana, Trello or monday.com for this, or a 'to-do' app or even a spreadsheet.

Next, engage your team in the culture and vision for your clinic:

- Have regular team meetings, and speak to your clinic's vision and direction, and higher purpose.
- Train your team on understanding the functional areas you've broken tasks into – including what needs to be done and who's responsible.
- Review position descriptions, expectations, contracts, clinic excellence indicator benchmarks and salaries with a focus on reward for effort and alignment with your vision, mission and values.
- Ensure communication channels between your team are easy and used multiple times per day. Possible apps and online tools to help you include:
    1. Slack
    2. Voxer
    3. Bonusly
    4. Deputy

Finally, build out your systems around induction, training and procedures for key activities in your clinic:

- Work on your 'hub' (the centralised folders or intranet where all systems live), and refer to it often. (See the 'Hub' key focus at the end of this Degree for more.)
- Make sure all key activities and processes are being monitored and reported on frequently among the team.

Core element: Systems

The objective of Systems is to create consistency, repeatability and transferability of anyone's responsibilities to help grow your clinic with reduced reliance on any one person. This allows you to grow sustainability because of a focus on 'built by design' rather than by default.

Key focus: Procedures

Principle: Document, don't create

> ### Let the systems run the business and people run the systems.
>
> Michael Gerber, author and business skills trainer

Success requires systems

Systems are the backbone of automating your clinic and being able to have anyone – or almost any role within your business – jump into the driver's seat and know how to produce the same (or better) results that you do.

Systems are important for the following reasons:

- A good system beats a good person.
- Systems can be outworked regardless of who is there.
- While a team may change, systems stay the same.
- Systems allow you to work on your business, not be buried in it.
- Systems enable you to provide an increased level of service quality.
- Systems encourage the formation of new habits.
- Systems free you up to think about the next opportunity.

Remember that everyone has systems – it's just that some are better than others. Your payment process? That's a system. Your social media schedule? That's a system. The apps and cloud storage you use? That's a system. Pay attention to what you do all day and you may start to realise you already have quite a few systems in place.

Your systems must:

- be easy to access and simple to use
- allow you to build consistency and quality
- be repeatable to the same standard, every time

- reduce reliance on you or any one person
- create freedom and certainty.

Why aren't you building systems?

When it comes to consistently getting great results in your clinic, there's no doubt about the importance of systems and structure. However, perhaps you're resisting building conscious systems for the following reasons:

- It takes too long.
- You don't know where to start.
- You're not sure what to put in the system.

Clinics For Good are very deliberate about the process of designing their future – they don't leave it up to chance and they certainly don't just hope that it will evolve naturally.

The problem is that there's only so much you can do as a small business owner. Passion is not enough, and there are real barriers to your time, energy and resources. If everything that happens in the business needs to go through you, you are the bottleneck and you are slowing progress.

Too busy to create

George was flat out. He was managing a clinic renovation, hiring 12 new team members, managing a team of 30, consulting with patients for three days a week and juggling life as a husband and father. We started talking about creating systems to help reduce his clinic's reliance on him. 'Where should I start when creating systems?' he asked – shortly followed by, 'I just don't have the time to create systems'. The intention was to be able to delegate more tasks to the team. The best outcome would be that the team could follow provided steps for any task exactly. So they needed a system to follow. We know how precious your time is. In that moment, we could also see how precious it was for George.

Document, don't create

What if outlining your systems didn't mean any extra work for you? What if you made the work you're already doing more intentional when you're in the moment? That would mean you don't need to 'create' extra time in your schedule to sit down and write up a system. All you're doing is more intentionally performing any given task so that it's done properly and in that moment, also documenting yourself doing it. Essentially, you'd be killing two birds with one stone, as the saying goes. An example of doing this is simply turning on Zoom meetings (available for free if under the specified time limit) while you complete a task. Hitting 'share screen' allows you to capture what you're doing as you do it. Turning on 'record' and talking through the steps of a system allows you to explain each step in more detail. For example, you could record how to book new clients, or how to bill or invoice through your platform. All you've done is complete the task you needed to complete, but now you also have a documented walk-through of the task – with voice over commentary – so the next person can complete it just like you. And no extra time was used – that's leverage!

Let the team take over

Also showing your team how to document versus create means they will continue to make life easier for everyone. In George's case, his admin team now *love* documenting what they do. His team have increased their productivity and seen much more consistency between team members in how they complete systems and tasks.

Not only can your team run with this process, they can also find ways to improve upon it. That's the ultimate outcome: constant and never-ending improvement (mastery).

Here are some further upsides to documenting versus creating:

· You can reduce reliance on you performing systems by delegating to others.

- You can be confident in your team's consistency because you documented the standard.
- You're able to rapidly develop your content and systems library, which increases the dollar value of your business assets.
- You remove your clinic's reliance on key people so you're not so influenced if/when they leave you.

Systems are the key to consistency and they reduce the reliance on key people like you. When you're able to document as you grow, you leverage your time and remove yourself as the bottleneck.

Blame the system not the person

Ideally, you want to be able to trust that everything is being done right, every time. If you have good systems in place, you will know that when you have a problem, the system is to blame, not the person. This is a good thing because it allows you to get to the root of a problem and solve it, so it doesn't happen again.

For your business to grow consistently over the long term, your team need the structure, you need the confidence and, most importantly, your clients need the care and consistency that go with good systems.

Systems that don't work

A system may not work for four reasons:

1. You implement systems without the adequate training of your team.
2. You don't follow through on your words with action.
3. Your systems are too clunky and can't be replicated.
4. You don't have a way to track the system and keep your team accountable.

Remember – your systems are the essential life blood of your business, and you must value them as much as your business itself.

We know that this is one of the hardest things to implement because, as the business owner, you're so used to doing everything yourself. The good news is that it's easier than you think, and doesn't even take that long to do, especially when you embrace 'document, don't create'.

Let this be a moment when you decide to completely renovate your business from the ground up like you would with your house, not just patching over the cracks, but reinforcing the foundation, the frames and structure to create something you want to live in.

Remember also that your team won't be used to the changing pace of your clinic as you implement new systems, so you need to keep the conversation going, the communication flowing and your door open to help them feel engaged in the process. Follow through on what you say, and lead by example!

To empower your team, you need to support them by creating systems that allow them to layer on their own personality and flair. Again, if your business is reliant on you and you don't help your team to take care of the day-to-day operations, you don't own a business – you own a job.

By removing yourself as the bottleneck in the business and leveraging the strengths of each individual team member you can increase your capacity far beyond anything you dreamed.

Tools and techniques

'Document, don't create' approach to systems

When implementing a 'document, don't create' approach to systems, you need to document the steps in a task as you complete them. Here are some ideas for how to do so.

Step 1: Document

- Turn your phone camera on and video yourself completing the task.
- Turn your phone voice recording app on and record yourself speaking through a task.

- Use a screen recording app to capture your computer screen as you complete tasks. Options include Zoom and QTime (both free) or TechSmith Capture (paid).

Step 2: Record

- Turn your audio or visual files into text using a transcription service such as Rev or through uploading your file to YouTube as an unlisted video and then using the free transcription as a written system.
- Alternatively, ask a team member to act as scribe while you talk or act out the system in your training.

Step 3: Implement

- Send your team the recordings and transcriptions so they know what to do for each task.
- Get your team to send any questions they have via Slack or email.
- Track the performance and completion rate of the task in the following weeks.

Investing in structure

I recall a conversation with my business partner and co-founder of Clinic Mastery, Daniel Gibbs. Daniel said to me,

> You know I realised that the investment *needed* to succeed in business is structure, and I learnt that when I made the biggest shift in my professional and business career. I went from being six days a week working as a podiatrist to none in just 12 months. I was criticised, it took a lot of focus, but it was incredibly rewarding.
>
> In fact, my plan started as a five-year plan until a mentor challenged me to instead do it in six months. My mentor also challenged me to replace my income, and also increase the bottom line in my business by 20 per cent over the same time

period. That bit seemed unbelievable, but I have the results to prove it is possible.

I'm not saying everyone needs to do this, and if I did it again I'd probably do things a little differently, but that was my goal and by having a structure to achieve it I was able to do so.

I realised that to achieve my personal definition of success I needed to invest more of myself into my team, create a 'wow' experience for my clients, be more focused on working on my business, and be more present with my family. I couldn't do it all, and the answer for me was to take this journey of systemising the business – putting in place the structure for it to run successfully without me.

'But systems don't work for us'

We've heard people say this before, and we understand where that comes from, but digging deep into why they don't work reveals the same thing every time. The reality is that all of us already have systems in our clinic – it's just that most aren't particularly good. They lack the detail, accountability, implementation, training and tracking.

If you feel like you're constantly putting out spot fires, running from one problem to the next, banging your head against the wall because team members are making poor decisions or forgetting to do certain tasks, or even if you are just tired of repeating yourself over and over, it's time to invest in implementing some good systems.

Key focus: Tracking

Principle: Track your progress

> ### Accountability is the glue that ties commitment to the result.
>
> Bob Proctor, best-selling author of *You Were Born Rich*

Evidence of practices

From a clinical perspective, health professionals focus on using evidence-based practices in their therapy. These are the gold standard, evidenced-backed actions that you should take to help improve the health outcomes of a client. From a business perspective, clinic owners should focus on tracking the *evidence of practices* being used in their operations. This allows you to have confidence that the right systems are being followed, by the right people, in the right way, at the right time to deliver a consistent service experience as a clinic.

If you've ever implemented a system in your clinic only for months to go by before you realise it hasn't been performed consistently between people, completed regularly, or simply has been forgotten about, then you know how frustrating a lack of tracking can be. If an action hasn't been tracked and reported, then it didn't happen.

Tracking helps you sleep better

As clinic owners, it's normal to rest your head on the pillow at night and, right before you go to sleep, have a sudden thought about the business – such as, *Did that thing get done by the therapist before they went on holidays?* With centralised tracking and reporting, you're able to:

- see if it was completed and, if so, by whom and when
- know the overall progress status of a system
- identify what's next in a series of systems
- hold team members accountable to their role.

Tracking your systems helps you have more certainty about what's going on in your clinic, so you know how well you're doing and where you can be better.

Audit your opportunities

In business, your vision of the future painted picture can guide you as you grow your clinic, and help your team do work that is high impact and high ease. No-one wants to work harder than they need to, and we all want to make a bigger impact for ourselves, and our clients, team and community. Therefore, you need to track what you and your team are doing in your roles so that, over time, you can audit opportunities to get closer to this painted picture and do the work and make the decisions that are high impact and high ease.

You're able to track systems in your clinic using different methods. What's important is that people can record what they've done in the tracking method you've used, and people can see how the team is progressing. Centralising tracking helps reduce the reliance on you or any one key person in the team. This is important for being able to grow your clinic as sustainably as possible.

Over time, you're able to audit each system and consider key decisions and actions, including:

- what to automate – for example, using technology to make it easier
- what to eliminate – for example, removing systems that are not impactful
- what to delegate – for example, handing over tasks to others who can be more impactful
- what to dominate – for example, playing to your strengths for greater impact.

Reporting on what you've tracked

If 'accountability is the glue that ties commitment to the result' as Bob Procter says, then reporting is the mechanism for that accountability. Reporting is the communication about the results of the systems that have been tracked. Reporting on everything you tracked would be overwhelming and also unnecessary, because team members can go to your tracking source (for example, your clinic dashboard) for more information. Reporting allows you to capture the impact of the systems and it ties your commitment to the result.

In the case of your new client's experience, for example, you could report on the results or outcome of their experience by sharing their net promoter score (NPS). The NPS is a client satisfaction benchmark that measures how likely your clients are to recommend your products or services to others. The score a new client gives you is going to be a reflection of all the systems that are part of your new client checklist. If your new client had a bad experience, you could then look back at your tracking to see what was missed, or not done to the standard you'd promised, committed to or would normally deliver. The following 'Assets in action' box outlines what you could include in your new client checklist, and then track and report on.

Assets in action

You can use the new client checklist overleaf to track (and then report) their experiences.

As you can see, each of the steps in the 'What (steps and systems)' is clearly defined so that it can be delivered with high quality and consistency. In this tracking, you are then simply acknowledging that this system has been completed. In a digital document, you can link any of the steps in the new client checklist to a separate document (as required) that details all the specifics of that step, including the training in place and answers to frequently asked questions.

What (steps and systems)	Who	When	Status
Pre-appointment email sent	Team member name or initials	Date and time	Completed/ Not completed
Paperwork sent			
Reminder sent			
Paperwork prepared			
Client induction completed			
Client details entered			
Referral details entered			
Welcome pack given			
Next appointment made			
New client letter sent			
Referrer thank you sent			
Nurturing call complete			
Management plan provided			
Report sent			

Key focus: Innovation

Principle: Find new and better ways

> There is no innovation and creativity
> without failure.
>
> Brené Brown

Einstein story

We learned of a story about Albert Einstein and a conversation he had with his teaching assistant when he was teaching at Princeton University. He had just wrapped up a test to a group of second-year physics students when his teaching assistant approached him and asked, 'Dr Einstein, wasn't that the same exam you gave to this same class of students last year?'

Einstein paused for a moment then replied, 'Yes, it was the same exam.'

Perplexed by that answer, his teaching assistant then asked, 'Why would you give the same exam to the same class two years in a row?'

Without hesitation, Einstein replied, 'Because the answers have changed.'

The point Einstein was trying to make was that due to the number of insights and discoveries in the field of physics, the correct answers at that moment were very different from what they were even a year before.

We love this story because it's so reflective of how life operates across the board. What we think we know about the world and everything in it is constantly evolving and changing.

Your questions about your clinic will remain the same as you evolve and grow – for example:

- How do you attract, deliver and nurture more of your ideal clients to create more raving fans?
- How do you attract, mentor and nurture more of your ideal team members towards a pathway of career fulfilment and retention?
- How do you boost profit, accelerate cashflow and save tax to sustainably grow your clinic to support intergenerational wealth creation?
- How do you incorporate the causes that matter to you so that you can amplify your impact and be a Clinic For Good in the world?

The possible answers, however, will completely change – new and better ways, philosophies, methodologies and technologies will emerge.

Systems and processes that were once staples inside the most successful companies are no longer effective today because of the advancement of technology. How clients choose to engage with products and services today is completely different from even a year ago, because of the continuing evolution of many industries around the world. The best way to get your message in front of people and the form that message should take doesn't even resemble what it looked like a decade ago because of the rise of social media.

Although we claim to understand that the world of business is always changing, the problem is most of us are failing to change at the same rate with it. Perhaps we assume that just because the questions surrounding our business haven't changed, that must mean the answers to those questions haven't changed either. So, we stop 're-asking' the important questions. As a result, our assumptions, decisions and actions are typically just a continuation of what we've always done – which, unfortunately, keeps us right where we are instead of moving us forward.

So our advice is to take a page out of Einstein's playbook and continue to ask the same questions year after year. Not only will the answers continue to change, but you might also be pleasantly surprised where those answers lead you.

Treat your clinic like a lab

Creating an environment to encourage, foster and translate innovation into action is an important next step. Perhaps embracing your health sciences background, you could think of the clinic as a laboratory where you continually create hypotheses and run experiments to create innovative breakthroughs. From the way you train and mentor your team to how you nurture clients through their journey towards meaningful outcomes and how you scale new systems with simplicity, innovation can improve all areas of your clinic.

Be mindful of opening up an endless stream of ideas and make sure you actually close the loop by taking action or directing the course of ideas to achieve meaningful objectives for all involved. To do that, you need to connect the strategic needs of the clinic with the causative factors for the concern to identify the best next action and create a win–win outcome.

Questions and starting points you can use to come up with new ideas include:

- What's the real problem we're trying to solve?
- Imagine if …
- How can we make this simple, easy and fun?

Get on your bike

In 2002, British Cycling was barely a blip on the international cycling radar, having won only one gold medal in its 76-year history. And then they hired Sir Dave Brailsford as their head. Brailsford is both a former professional cyclist and a businessman, and he committed to applying the business world's concept of marginal gains to cycling. He and his team broke down riding a bike competitively to all of its individual elements, aiming to then improve each element by just 1 per cent. And they were thorough. As Brailsford outlined in the *Harvard Business Review* article 'How 1% performance improvements led to Olympic gold',

> We hired a surgeon to teach our athletes about proper hand-washing so as to avoid illnesses during competition (we also decided not to shake any hands during the Olympics). We were precise about food preparation. We brought our own mattresses and pillows so our athletes could sleep in the same posture every night. We searched for small improvements everywhere and found countless opportunities. Taken together, we felt they gave us a competitive advantage.

And Brailsford was correct. At the 2008 Olympics, British Cycling won seven of the available 10 gold medals for track cycling, and matched this achievement in 2012. As Brailsford highlighted, each marginal gain was important; however, 'Perhaps the most powerful benefit is that it creates a contagious enthusiasm within the team'.

The story of Brailsford and the marginal gains in the British cycling team is a valuable principle to apply as you grow your clinic as sustainably as possible. We commonly hear clinic owners compare themselves to others unfairly and feel 'so far behind' their peers. And we also hear clinic owners say that they feel over-whelmed and burnt out by the constant and growing to-do list. The British cycling team still had ambitious goals – to win gold medals. However, they coupled these goals with the patience to substantially and sustainably transform every aspect of their perfor-mance to succeed well into the future.

This approach worked for the following reasons:

- **Sustainability:** Instead of aiming to win a 'gold medal' next week, you can find small improvements every day, week, month, quarter and year. You don't need to overwhelm yourself with what needs to happen to create meaningful and tangible progress. As Simon Sinek champions in *The Infinite Game*, those leaders and businesses who achieve long-lasting success focus on building long-term value and healthy, enduring growth.

- **Simplicity:** You can make subtle and very simple shifts that over time lead to significant changes as progress compounds.

- **Substantial:** You're encouraged to look at all the factors that contribute to an outcome and ask whether what you're doing is necessary and, if so, how it can be better.

Core element: Structures

The objective of Structures is to weave robustness into the design of growing your clinic so that you have sustainability and longevity. Structures allow you to grow your Clinic For Good, meaning that it is built to last amid the changing health, economic and political landscape.

Key focus: Governance

Principle: Practise best practice

> ### There are no shortcuts to excellence.
>
> Angela Duckworth, author of *Grit: The Power of Passion and Perseverance*

Just like therapy

Governance is about practising the best practices in your business, just as you do in your clinical practice. As a therapist, you have to comply with various guidelines, regulations and laws that govern how you should conduct yourself. The same is true for you as a clinic owner. Governance is about holding you and the business accountable. It provides you and everyone you engage with – from clients to team members, accountants, the tax office, health insurers, regulators and law makers – the certainty and confidence that you're acting in a responsible way. From risk management to corporate compliance, tax regulation, employment standards, therapy conduct and more, governance is about following what is best practice when running your business.

But governance isn't just about doing the 'right' thing (or the bare minimum). Governance can also improve the performance of your business, as you improve productivity and unlock new opportunities sustainably. You're lowering your business risks while continuing to grow – and improving your reputation and fostering trust. Over time, these things build your brand. These are all aspects that mean your business is more likely to last for many years into the future.

That was good advice

Being across all of the rules, regulations and laws to be compliant as a business and a health professional can be challenge while trying to also grow your clinic. Engaging a team of specialists to advise you makes the whole process easier and safer. It's easier because you don't have to search for answers – you can go to the right people who can save you the time, effort and stress of figuring it out yourself. And it's safer because, in many cases, by engaging a professional to guide the governance of your clinic, you're accessing, early or proactive best practice advice to prevent saying or doing things that may results in a penalty later. For example, say you engage an employment advisor who helps you performance manage a team member out of your clinic, and the team member then makes a claim against you for unfair dismissal. While you can't prevent someone from making a claim, ideally, you followed best practice; therefore putting yourself in a strong position to defend against the claim. In most cases, of course, you receive sound guidance and avoid costly mistakes, so it's always good to take advice from a specialist.

As well as a board of advisors, your governance support team might include specialists in the following areas:

- accounting
- legal
- coaching
- human resources
- operations.

Key focus: Collaboration

Principle: Conduct an orchestra of minds

Alone we can do so little;
together we can do so much.

Helen Keller

Two pizza rule

Perhaps you've heard about the 'two pizza rule' Jeff Bezos instituted in the early days of Amazon: every internal team should be small enough that it can be fed with two pizzas. For Bezos, keeping each team small meant communication was easier and simpler, and members could instead focus on working on what needed to be done. They also fostered a decentralised, creative working environment.

Bezos's decision to keep meetings small in order to encourage productivity can be backed up by science. After devoting nearly 50 years to the study of team performance, the late Harvard researcher J Richard Hackman concluded that four to six is the optimal number of members in a project team, and no work team should have more than 10 members. According to Hackman, this is because 'communication problems increase exponentially as team size increases geometrically'. Ironically, the larger the team, the more time will be spent on communication instead of producing work.

In a clinic setting, perhaps you have 'the team', which encompasses everyone, and perhaps the next layer of the therapist team and admin team. As you grow your clinic, being intentional about the structure and function of your team(s) is important. Consider as you grow how you could embrace the 'two pizza rule' to facilitate better communication and productivity of your team(s), and perhaps move beyond the more traditional split into simply the admin team and the therapist team.

Adding more functional team units as you grow could include creating the following:

- **Clinical excellence team:** This team could be accountable for training, continuing professional development and therapist onboarding.
- **Education and marketing team:** Accountable for social media content, patient resources and client communications.
- **Clinics For Good team:** Accountable to the community impacts for causes, connection to partnerships, sustainability of clinic operations and pro bono work.
- **Client experience team:** Accountable to welcome room services, client nurturing and follow up and patient feedback.

Identifying what the clinic needs and aligning your team members' genius, passion and desires to contribute through the teams they're grouped in allows you to reduce reliance on your input. Using a range of functional teams that fit the 'two pizza rule' means you can delegate decision-making and outsource implementation. Importantly, also make sure you use centralised project boards such as Asana and communication structures such as Slack so that information can be freely shared and collaboration is encouraged.

Key focus: Hub

Principle: Centralise clinic intelligence

Create your own 'Dr Google' search engine to answer the questions and address the operations of your clinic.

Ben Lynch

Avoid the bottleneck

Facepalm moment. Not again. Your team member asks, 'How do I do that task again?' You know you've told them three times already. Yep, you've become the bottleneck. Again. As much as you're frustrated at the team member, you realise the system is the problem. It needs to be better.

You need a system where you and your team members can search and find useful documentation about how to do everything in your clinic – absolutely everything. Your system should leave nothing to chance or interpretation on how to do a task properly.

You already know your clients can search 'Dr Google' for answers to health questions – and how, sometimes, that can lead to interesting and funny conversations. (I once had a client tell me they had come to see me as a podiatrist to get orthodontics. They meant to say orthotics – the dentist is down the road.) In the case of your clinic, however, the analogy is useful. You want to create a 'Dr Google' for your practitioners and admin team. This is a centralised, global, mobile and live hub where all team members can search and find useful information about how to do everything in your clinic. It's like your online manager.

Relatable experience

Kate's blushing. Not only that, but she's also apologising for the 'mess' before we even see it. I (Ben) had asked Kate to share her screen during a Clinic Mastery mastermind session. As the screen was shared, we saw the hundreds of partially documented clinic systems scattered all over her desktop screen – in the form of documents, video recordings and more.

Kate said, 'I know it looks like a mess, but trust me – I know where everything is'. That might have been okay if it were just Kate in the clinic. However, it wasn't just Kate. None of the team had remote access to the systems. Even if they did have access, how would they know where to look for the answer to their question? And would the answer have been clear and complete?

We've all been in Kate's position. As you grow your clinic, the complexity can grow with it. Kate had started the right work – it just wasn't centralised or sorted in a way that would be of any use to her growing team. The key was to centralise her clinic intelligence by moving all of the systems (albeit works in progress) to an online hub.

Lauren, one of Kate's colleagues, had navigated the road ahead and was able to offer some sage advice – to keep her documentation simple, user friendly and fun for all. This started with Lauren sharing that she had created a persona for her hub, and it became known as 'TOM' (the officer manager). Now everyone on the team asks TOM as their first port of call. TOM has helped the team pass audits, impressed judges enough to win awards, onboarded new therapists and reduced the clinic's reliance on Lauren to create more freedom hours. This inspired Kate to do the same – and after months of inspired work, Kate had enough freedom to go on an extended honeymoon (for nine weeks).

In the lead-up to her time away, Kate was able to say the following:

> My team tell me they are feeling confident they will be absolutely fine while I am away for a two-month honeymoon over June–July because of the hands-on training and our HQ (internal hub) being so thorough.

On her return, she was even more ecstatic:

> Big win! Just arrived home from nine weeks away on our honeymoon to a jump in our NPS [net promoter score] from 91 to 95, and amazing heart-warming NPS comments for the team. Lots of these comments mentioned the great service they've received, from booking to payment. It has been so amazing to see

our patients acknowledging our whole team's effort to make their experience fantastic! Feeling pretty wrapped with our clinic's growth over the last 10 years and the team's commitment as they lifted the bar while I was off gallivanting.

High-impact action

Consider the following key insights and actions when getting your systems up and running:

- Schedule your success by using triggers to initiate the use of a system – for example, through Asana or Trello.
- Accrue your freedom hours by delegating not abdicating your tasks – implement training schedules when you launch new systems.
- Prioritise progress and the impact of your work through ensuring your tasks and systems have clear, objective outcomes.
- Leverage your time in the creation of systems by adopting the 'document, don't create' approach.
- Track your progress and ensure quality assurance through using dashboards and checklists.
- Create a momentum of change through playing the long game and aiming for constant marginal gains – be 1 per cent better every day.
- Seek out good advisors who enable you to practise best practice for quality governance and give you a safety protection buffer.
- Use the 'two pizza rule' to encourage communication and productivity – embrace more functional teams.
- Centralise clinic intelligence by creating your own 'Dr Google' operating and search engine to answer the questions and address the problems of your clinic.

Systems summary

Remember that Clinics For Good are two things: firstly, good businesses that, secondly, do good. It's important that the first part is established through the implementation of good systems that allow you to grow your clinic as sustainably as possible. This is the only way that you'll be able to do the second part of doing good, and making a meaningful contribution over a significant amount of time.

Systems provide you, your team and your clients with certainty, predictability and consistency – making it a more enjoyable interaction and experience every day.

DEGREE 5:

FINANCE

Grow profitably and sustainably

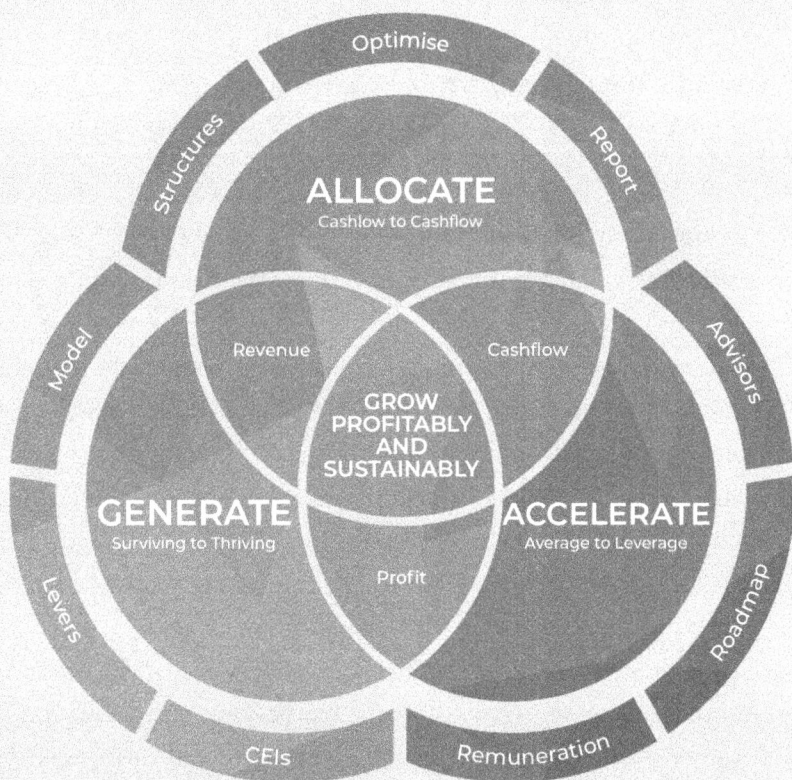

Core element: Generate

The first element to master in Degree 5 is Generate. This relates to you creating income streams so that you go from simply surviving (breaking even) to thriving.

Key focus: Clinic excellence indicators (CEIs)

Principle: Help more people, help more often and add more value

> ### If you don't know your numbers, you don't know your business.
>
> Marcus Lemonis, businessman, author and philanthropist

Knowing what to measure

The first focus for generating your income streams is to know and influence your clinic excellence indicators (CEIs). These are the numbers that reflect how well you are delivering value for your clients.

Knowing your numbers can be scary, overwhelming, boring or laborious. However, you *must* know exactly how your clinic is performing at any moment. If you don't, how can you expect to grow profitably, sustainably and with enough cashflow?!

This is not about being a 'million-dollar' health professional. Remember – as health professionals, our driving force is to help people and money allows us to do, be and have more, but it's the means, not the end.

The commercial reality to being in business demands you know your numbers so that you can reinvest in your team, reinvest in yourself and reinvest in your patients. Knowing your numbers helps you make better, more informed decisions on aspects such as when to hire, what to reinvest in, how much to spend on marketing and how many people you need on your team.

Given that your core role as a health professional is to see patients, knowing how to ethically influence these numbers is important for your clients' outcomes and essential for your business's success.

If you don't like numbers, or you're not good at maths, stay with us for a moment – we can simplify it for you!

What do the numbers mean?

Basically, every figure or metric is a measure of the effectiveness of the systems in place in your business. As highlighted in the previous Degrees, with good systems, when the business owner is on vacation, the money still comes in, the patients still get the best experience and the show goes on. When you're tracking and analysing your numbers, you're essentially checking that your systems are working.

Reviewing the numbers

In the 'corporate world' the numbers and results you'd be reviewing would be based on your (and your team's) key performance indicators (KPIs). However, we've jazzed these up, thanks to Brigid from Boost Health Collective and the Clinic Mastery mentoring team to call them clinic excellence indicators (CEIs)! Whatever you call them, the important thing is that they're tracked and reviewed. You can use a simple spreadsheet, simple Word document or detailed CEI dashboard, as long as it works for you.

The following table provides a list of possible CEIs that can be used in your clinic. This list is not exhaustive but does give you an idea of the types of CEIs that can be used.

One word of warning: don't fall into the trap of 'analysis paralysis' by trying to track all of the suggested CEIs. Just pick and choose what might work for you, and go from there.

Possible clinic excellence indicators for your clinic

CEI	Description	Variables	Calculation	Example target
Clients per day	A measure of the number of appointments per practitioner per day	Total appointments (a); number of days (d)	a/d	18
Rebooking %	The percentage of clients seen that have a future appointment booked	Total appointments (a); appts with no future appt booked (n)	$(a - n)/a$ ($\times$ 100 for %)	95%
Avg fee	The average fee received per appointment provided	$ total received (r); total appointments (a)	r/a	$100
Client visit avg	The average number of times a client visits over a particular time period	Total appointments (a); total clients (c)	a/c	14 (lifetime)
Missed appt %	The percentage of appointments booked where the client doesn't turn up	Total missed (m); total appointments (a)	m/a ($\times$ 100 for %)	2.5%
Cancellations with no reschedule (CNR)	The percentage of appointment cancellations where the client doesn't book another appointment	Number of CNRs (x); total reschedules (r)	$x/(r + x)$ ($\times$ 100 for %)	20%

CEI	Description	Variables	Calculation	Example target
Utilisation rate	The percentage of allocated consulting time spent actually consulting	Total cells available (t); vacant cells (v); extra cells (e)	$t - (v - e)/t$ ($\times$ 100 for %)	85%
$ per hour	The average amount a practitioner is billing per hour over a time period	Total $ billed ($); hours consulting (h)	$/h	$200
On time service	The percentage of appointments seen within five minutes of the scheduled appointment time	Total appointments (a); on time (b)	b/a ($\times$ 100 for %)	80%
Lifetime value	The average total $ received per client over their lifetime with you	Total $ turnover ($); total no. of clients (c)	$/c	$1200
Conversion rate (admin)	The percentage of phone call enquiries taken that result in an appointment booked	Total phone enquiries (e); appointments booked (b)	e/b ($\times$ 100 for %)	98%

Benchmarking

As well as tracking your CEIs, you also need to set targets or benchmarks to aim for in each measurement. You can build these benchmarks using the following steps:

1. Use the CEI to track what is currently happening in your clinic and get a baseline.
2. Compare figures from week to week or month to month at your clinic.
3. Compare figures between colleagues and other practitioners in your area. You can also ask your accountant for some industry benchmarks. Keep in mind these industry figures should not be your main benchmark, because so much context is missing when you compare to other clinics. Our belief at Clinic Mastery is that you are your best benchmark. Know your numbers and always improve on those. We understand a point of reference can be useful; however, you should run your own race.
4. Decide on your ideal targets, keeping in mind clinic expenses and wages.

The key to benchmarking is to keep it simple. Identify the three key statistics that you need to measure now to improve patient experiences and create consistency between practitioners. Start with what is most urgent – for example, if you get a lot of cancellations, start there. You'll notice great results when you can align your team with the business performance objectives.

Key focus: Levers

Principle: Money follows value

> **Money is fun to make, fun to spend and fun to give away.**
>
> Sara Blakely, businesswoman and philanthropist

Offering quality to clients

Once you've got tracking your CEIs under control, you next need to understand that certain indicators act as powerful levers in helping you generate more income. Simplifying your focus as you grow your clinic to prioritise these levers in your workflow will offer you a great opportunity to generate robust income streams.

One powerful lever is offering more value to clients, through offering quality services and products as part of your best client care recommendation.

Here's why offering this value is so important:

- **Clients deserve your best recommendation – you are the trusted advisor:** Your duty of care is to first provide your best recommendation (for both services and products) based on the client's health condition, problem or challenge. Your recommendation should not be based on what you believe they can afford. Affordability (time and money) can always be discussed and arranged after you have outlined your best care plan. Remember, any compromise in the plan is a compromise in the client's health and of your professional standards.

- **Clients deserve value – anticipate and meet their needs:** As an advisor, you should seek to provide more value to each client than anybody else. If you want to stand out in the crowded market, you should anticipate your clients' needs and look for new and better ways to serve them now and into the future. This is includes offering the best products, services and experiences.

- **Clients deserve your care – guide your clients in their health:** Clients already have likeability, trust and rapport with you because you are the health authority and guiding figure for them. That means they are willing to accept your advice and offers. In fact, that is what they really want – your best guidance for their health. It's not a 'sales pitch' if you realise that what you're offering is just an extension of your professional service and representation of your best care.

- **Clients deserve respect for their time – make it easy for them:** Time is precious, and by offering products and services together as a package you make the experience convenient. Clients shouldn't have to spend more time and effort going to another location, store or sales warehouse to get the services or products that they need and could otherwise be easily provided to them at the time of their appointment.

- **Clients experience better health outcomes – they can be more independent:** Offering products creates a great opportunity to improve client health between appointments. If clients can take control of their own health outcomes by doing home activities, exercises or rehabilitation processes using your products, they can maintain or even optimise their state of healing and wellbeing.

- **Clients need the right advice at the right time – nurture them through a journey:** Receiving guidance on using products and services is going to be more accurately tailored to the client if the caring practitioner is offering it, because you understand their health problem, injury or sickness. In fact, a client's health can commonly stall or go backwards if they are subjected to external services or products from providers who are not familiar with the client's condition and poorly advise the client on the use of products or services they need – for example, in the case of receiving products from retail assistants rather than health professionals.

Clients can experience better services and products

Boosting business income through offering additional products and services to clients in turn allows you to reinvest into client care.

For example, you can:

- invest in better client products (and so increase volume, create variety and/or boost quality)
- invest in better client services (through training your team, client resource development and/or better facilities or equipment)
- invest in the client experiences (through personalisation, better education, improved aesthetics and entertainment).

Your objective is to create a clinic that functions as a robust business, allowing you to grow profitably and sustainably. This means your clinic provides you with financial certainty, allowing you to:

- invest in yourself
- invest in your team through your remuneration structures, training and cultural experiences
- re-invest into your clients through the resources, equipment and facilities you make available.

This financial certainty also allows you to be abundantly rewarded for the risk and hard work of being a business owner.

Clinics can differentiate themselves to stand out in the market

A commodity is a product that is basically indistinguishable from its competitors. Don't commoditise your clinic. Provide more than price and convenience by packaging your products and services in a meaningful way that empathises with your client's experience and represents your brand. See yourself as more than a transactional 'therapist' and position yourself and your clinic as the place that helps your clients live better throughout their life.

Remember – generating more income is simply the result of providing more value to your clients and community. Making money is not the focus; it's just a measure of how much *value* you are providing (with value being better products, services and experiences leading to better outcomes).

Relatable experience

Jasmine, owner of a physiotherapy clinic, shared some feedback with us:

Had some fantastic conversations with team members this week about their desire statements, and also reviewed our profit and loss. We are shaping up to increase our overall turnover by 18.5 per cent on last year and our profit by 11 per cent on last year! All this hard work does pay off! I have also finally got to the point where every single person on our team is a weapon in their own way!

Last year was really tough and a long hard slog. This financial year, we continue to break revenue records! And by restructuring our admin hours we have just saved $22,000 a year! Stoked!

And she shared this recommendation:

Hustling really does pay off. Even though it may seem like it never ends, keep going, lean on this community, work hard with your coaches and keep that passion – it will pay off!

Key focus: Model

Principle: Build robustness

> There's a productive dichotomy between
> 'What if this all falls apart?' and 'I'm going
> to change the world'. You simply need to allow
> the dynamic dance between those two things
> to guide your pragmatism.
>
> Ben Lynch

Resting on laurels

People are always going to need healthcare, and that's good news for growing your clinic. Not only do they need it, in many parts of the developed world healthcare is heavily subsidised or incentivised for clients to receive. Whether through government initiatives (such as Veterans' Affairs, Medicare and disability schemes), third-party funding organisations (such as workers compensation payments and treatments and private health insurers) or anything in between, people often have access to resources that make accessing healthcare easier. What this means for many clinics is that they can establish themselves to serve a variety of clients or, in fact, specialise in servicing a specific stream of clients.

Accessing funding resources often provides clinics with a great commercial opportunity to serve clients. They have relative certainty about the type of clients they service, how to deal with them and what amount of money they can make to grow sustainability.

The challenge from aligning your clinic in this way can come in a couple of forms:

1. You need to adapt and deliver different healthcare to different people based on their funding source.
2. You can become reliant on one type of funding or delivery method.

You need to consider diversified income streams, including how you can help more people by adding value in different forms.

COVID has taught us many lessons but, in particular, it has taught businesses about the vulnerabilities of models that can only generate income from fac-to-face interaction with clients, or that rely too heavily on one industry. For example, if a clinic's main clients were from the arts and entertainment industry, when this industry stopped, so did the clinic's business.

Time versus outcome

Remember your first few consultations as a student? No doubt, an initial consultation would take 90 minutes, and you likely still didn't know what was going on. Fast-forward to the experienced clinician you are today, who can do the same consultation in 45 minutes with a high degree of empathy and acuity for diagnosing and providing quality solutions. The time isn't important; it's the outcome that matters. If the client can get the same result in less time, everyone benefits. The outcome doesn't just mean progress in their objective health; it also includes the outcome of client connection, empathy and establishing a client-therapist alliance.

Of course, being quick isn't the objective either. Sometimes even specialists and practitioners who are the best in the business can have the personality of a brick wall (and about an equal amount of care). They might be to the point, know what they're talking about and very efficient, but they don't create much trust. For you as a clinic owner, of course, building this trust is what ensures clients return and complete their treatment. So you want clients to feel comfortable while also doing this efficiently and providing a terrific outcome.

Clients are focused on the outcome – achieving meaningful outcomes for them. Your team also benefits from focusing more on outcomes than time-based billing.

Indeed, Brad Beer, owner of POGO Physio, has identified many risks from clinics focusing on time-based billing, including increased pressure on the practitioner, leading to burnout and attrition, and under-servicing of the client, leading to reduced commitment and trust from the client and client drop-outs. For Beer, time-based billing also creates a conflict of interest for practitioners (because more time with the client can potentially mean more money for the clinic). Beer expands on these ideas in a series of blog posts – you can find the first of these at www.pogophysio.com.au/blog/time-based-billing-problem-1-a-conflict-of-interest/.

The opportunity for clinic owners is to look at their business model from the perspective of emphasising, prioritising and delivering outcomes (not time) for their clients in a way that produces economic value for the business. This value is also produced in a sustainable and meaningful way for the niche you feel most compelled to serve. Instead of simply offering more services or products in a transactional manner based on the billing requirements, health insurance codes or 'standards' of a third-party system, you should focus on transformational support for those you seek to serve.

Core element: Allocate

The second element to master in Degree 5 is Allocate. This relates to you managing the income you generate so that you go from cash*low* to cash*flow*.

Key focus: Structures

Principle: Make it clinic specific

Embrace what you don't know.

Sara Blakely, businesswoman and philanthropist

Structure equals sanity

When you go into business you have big ideas and bold ambitions – and anything is possible. That passion is still all there, but perhaps you need to re-ignite that vision. Remember when you started and why! Capture that curiosity, that imagination and creativity. Put structures around you to help keep you on track. Here are three important financial structures to help you grow your clinic as sustainably as possible:

1. separate bank accounts for cashflow allocations – for example, for superannuation or pension payments, tax obligations, leave entitlements, operating expenses and profit
2. functional profit and loss for meaningful analysis
3. budget ratios for benchmarking improvements.

The bank account doesn't show a profit

Your profit and loss statement says your clinic made a profit but you don't see the cash in your bank. What's the issue? Importantly, your profit and loss may include sales that you have made but may not have received the cash payment for yet. This is the first key distinction to clarify with your accounts team: whether you're using cash or accrual accounting. Accrual accounting means you see the money included on your financial reporting based on when you billed for your service. Cash accounting means the money is reported when the money actually hits your bank account.

Most businesses use accrual-based accounting. If your clinic does, this means if you provided a service to a client and they have a third party that is paying for their care (perhaps WorkCover or the Department of Veterans' Affairs) and this third party hasn't yet processed the payment into your account, you are accruing the money as part of your accounts to be received.

Your profit and loss also includes non-cash items; for example, depreciation you're claiming. And it *doesn't* include items that make their way onto the balance sheet (and out of your bank account), such as loan repayments or owners taking out money from the business in the form of a loan.

Generally, if you want to 'balance' your profit and loss statement with what you actually have in the bank, you can complete the following exercise outlined by specialist allied health accountant Andy Wang from Clarico accounting:

1. Take your profit and loss figure.
2. Minus the stock you have on hand from your balance sheet. (This is inventory you have paid for but you don't get a tax deduction for until you sell.)
3. Minus your accounts receivable.
4. Add your accounts payable.
5. Add any payments you make that go to the balance sheet (such as asset purchases and loan repayments).

6. Add/minus your owner drawings (not any wages you receive, but drawings that get reconciled in the form of a loan).
7. Minus your prepayments of tax (PAYGI).

While it can give a slightly skewed view of cashflow, the profit and loss statement does help you determine the profitability and, therefore, sustainability of your clinic. It measures the performance of your clinic over a period of time (it's like a movie while your balance sheet is more like a photograph).

You have to meet three objectives to make your clinic sustainable:

1. be effective in converting assets into revenue
2. convert that revenue into profit
3. convert that profit into cashflow.

What to look at and look for?

When opening up your profit and loss statement, you likely navigate straight to the bottom line of the report and look at the total net profit number to see how you have performed. Of course you do – you're looking to see how much money you made this month!

However, you have a great opportunity to evolve:

- the structure of your profit and loss statement so that you make it more meaningful and useful for you as a clinic owner
- your financial understanding of your business so that you know where the opportunities are to improve that net profit number you're looking at
- the accuracy and structure of your budgeting moving forward so that you can see variances each month or quarter as you move forward.

Clinic-specific profit and loss structure

To get the best results for your clinic, you need to structure your profit and loss statement in a way that is relevant, meaningful and useful for you as a clinic owner. Your typical profit and loss will be set up as a template from your accountant or from the accounting system you're using. However, you can change this structure. You have the opportunity to become an expert in your own business performance by knowing your numbers really well.

Structuring your clinic profit and loss so it is functional for you and your clinic has the following benefits:

- You can accurately compare the following:
    - your past performance versus current performance
    - functional areas as a percentage of your total revenue
    - functional areas against themselves in different time periods
    - other similar businesses to benchmark and fairly compare.
- You can make quality decisions based on accurate and contextual data about aspects such as hiring, team performance and systems optimisations.
- You can separate practitioner salaries and wages from admin/ support team wages.

Looking at your profit and loss statement using a functional categorisation (rather than having all your accounts listed alphabetically) allows for more meaningful analysis. You can make better financial decisions through improving these categorisation structures.

When you use the default alphabetical profit and loss reporting structure of listing your line-item accounts, you'll have 'Accounting' next to 'Admin' expenses.

These expenses are very different, and so you need to categorise (group) your expenses with other similar expenses. The following outlines some of the categories you could use, and the individual accounts that could be attributed to each category:

- **Consulting Expenses (Group/Category/Heading):** Included here could be practitioner wages (employees), practitioner superannuation (employees) and costs from your practice management system.

- **Payroll Expenses (Group/Category/Heading):** This could include WorkCover fees and worker insurance.
- **Admin Expenses (Group/Category/Heading):** Admin wages and admin superannuation could be included here,
- **Occupancy Expenses (Group/Category/Heading):** Included here could be rent, electricity, cleaning, repairs and maintenance.
- **Marketing Expenses (Group/Category/Heading):** This could include marketing costs, Facebook Ads, Google Ads and website costs.
- **Support Service Expenses:** Fees for your bookkeeper, business coach, accountant, human resource consultant and lawyer could be included here.

Remember – if you are not paying yourself a wage or if you are paying yourself a wage below a commercial rate, your profit margin is going to look better than it might actually be.

Structuring your profit and loss statement in a way that suits your clinic allows you to do a functional analysis of the different areas of your business. For example, once you're able to group all marketing expenses together, you can see how much in total you're spending/investing in marketing, as both a dollar amount and then as a percentage of total revenue (aka sales or income).

For help with structuring your profit and loss statement in a way that works for you and your clinic, talk to your accountant or an expert in the cloud accounting software you subscribe to (such as Xero).

Be your own benchmark

Structuring your profit and loss statement in a way that works for your clinic means you have a much deeper understanding of your financial reporting, and how income and expenses are allocated. For example, what goes into your cost of goods and services or cost of sales accounts can be interpreted differently by different accountants. Indeed, many things in this process can be interpreted differently by different advisors, so it's important you understand these figures and pay attention to what's going on.

It's common to want to know how profitable other clinics are in your industry, city or stage of business. However, you'll rarely able to compare correctly when so many variables are possible, such as inclusions, exclusions and context for each clinic. So the best thing to do is play your own game, the infinite game, and benchmark against yourself with the aim to be better every week, month, quarter and year.

Relatable experience

Travis Kluckhenn, founder of Pathways Physiotherapy and Clinic Mastery mentor, reflected on the satisfaction of completing his review of the financial year. He said, 'There's something internally satisfying about going through the process of comparing our expense percentages and profit margin to targets/benchmarks using the profit and loss analysis tool and then setting our benchmarks for next year.'

High-impact action

Complete the following checklist when analysing your clinic's profit and loss statement:

- Is it current, and up to date?
- Is it accurate, and each transaction allocated correctly to its functional category and line item?
- Within the month:
  - What's the month view, with no comparisons?
  - What's budgeted versus actual?
  - How are the monthly comparisons and +/− percentages looking?
- Quarter on quarter: how are these comparisons and +/− percentages looking?

- Year to date (YTD):
  - How's budget versus actual looking?
  - What are your YTD percentages?
  - Are things falling within acceptable ranges?
  - Are there any outliers? (These may be expected.)
  - Do any outliers need investigation?
  - Are there any 'stories' and narratives that you can deduce?
  - Are there any opportunities for you to improve against yourself?
  - Can you spot any trends that may not be concerning now, but could be if left unaddressed?

Key focus: Optimise

Principle: Be a good steward

Money makes you more of who you already are.

Sarah Blakely, businesswoman and philanthropist

CREATE to solve cashflow

Once you have your head around your profit and loss and balance sheet, you need to optimise your cashflow by allocating resources for finding inefficiencies with how you're managing your money. You can then turn them into key focuses for sustainable growth.

You can solve a cashflow problem with CREATE:

- C: Use a **cash** allocation strategy
- R: Increase your **revenue**
- E: Decrease your **expenses**
- A: Reduce the **accounts** owed to you
- T: Increase payment **time** for accounts you need to pay
- E: Implement a rhythm to **evaluate** your performance and future plan.

Cash allocation

A cash allocation strategy allows you to manage the flow of money you generate by establishing best practice structures. This allows you to always have enough in the right areas of the business to invest or reinvest, to cover your employee liabilities and your tax obligations, and to ensure you're setting aside that rewarding profit that you need as a business owner to make it all worthwhile.

Your bank accounts can be structured so you don't only have one lump sum of money in a single account. Using a single account can muddy the waters, causing you to spend money or allocate money that is required to cover other areas – for example, liabilities and expenses. Speak with your bank and your accountant about how to effectively set up your accounts. Your accountant will be able to guide you on tax-effective set-up – for example, using offset accounts against loans – and your bank can help you minimise fees and set up your accounts in a user-friendly and cost-effective way.

Having a process for managing money once it hits your bank account is also valuable. This includes implementing a specific frequency and date/s for moving money across accounts during the month, using specific allocation percentages or dollar amounts and using specific accounts within your bank, appropriately labelled to move the money into. Examples of accounts established by clinic owners include:

- **Trading account:** Where the money is paid into for the services provided to clients.
- **Tax account:** Where you allocate money for tax liabilities such as those required in each Business Activity Statement (BAS) and Pay As You Go (PAYG) wage tax.
- **Entitlements account:** Where you allocate money to cover entitlements such as leave entitlements, and retirement and superannuation contributions (for yourself and your team).
- **Cash reserve:** Where you allocate money to be used later if or when necessary to cover periods of substantial income

shortfalls or 'Black Swan' events (more on these in the 'Accelerate' core element).

- **Profit distribution:** Where you allocate money to be taken as a profit distribution for all owners.
- **Investment reserve:** Where you allocate money to be built up for the purchase of new equipment, expansion of facilities, launch of new clinic sites and more.

Increase your revenue

Getting paid for your services is a reflection of a value exchange. You provide a valuable service and the client invests their money as a reflection of the value they received. In other terms, money is simply a certificate of appreciation given to us by our clients as a note of thanks and recognition of a 'valuable' exchange. Therefore, increasing revenue is a reflection of increasing the volume and rate of valuable exchanges. The simplest version of this equation in a clinic is to:

Help more people + help more often + add more value

This can come in the form of more new clients, more therapists to serve the waitlist of clients, and more clinic locations with more new clients and team members. This can also come through better 'retention' of clients according to their healthcare plan, and better products and complementary services that help increase the rate and volume of that value.

When you plan your next 120 days or next 12 months, it's valuable to include targets for increasing your revenue to meaningful and specifically measurable numbers that allow you to sustainably grow, as well as outlining what you'll do to achieve those targets.

Decrease your expenses

As your clinic grows, so do your expenses. The important distinction is to spend more strategically. Expenses can also been seen as investments – which is why we prefer to use the term 'strategic spending'. The alternative is to look at expenses as things you simply need to decrease. However, these are the investments you make in order to acquire the assets you need to deliver your products, services and experiences to generate revenue, and so run into cashflow.

Your expenses can be reviewed as raw dollar amounts as well as percentages to make meaningful decisions on what expenses could be cut and which are necessary investments. Let's say that you generate $10,000 per month in revenue and have a marketing expense of $500 per month. That expense is, therefore, 5 per cent of your revenue. Now let's say you're spending $5000 per month on marketing and thinking *Wow, we need to cut our marketing expense; it's 10 times what is used to be.* The question you need to consider first, however, is how much revenue are you now generating per month? If the answer is now $100,000 revenue per month, your marketing is still sitting at 5 per cent of revenue. This is a simple example to highlight that you need to consider your expenses in the context of dollars spent but also percentages against revenue as you grow so that you can moderate the 'strategic spending' – that is, decreasing expenses appropriately. It's valuable to look at your expenses monthly and identify at least one opportunity to strategically spend better.

Reduce the accounts owed to you

When you provide a service to a client, you will be paid for that service. However, for various reasons – such as third-party insurers or terms of services – you may not receive the money for the service you delivered until days, weeks or months after the day it was delivered. Shortening the time between service delivery and getting paid is the principle you should be working on, with the ideal outcome to be paid on the day and – for those in a very strong position – getting paid in advance.

We believe that you are the best benchmark for your business, and you should always be better than you were last week, month, quarter and financial year. However, we often get asked for a general rule when it comes to accounts receivable (accounts and money owed to you). So here it is: our general rule is to have less than 10 per cent of your monthly revenue outstanding at any given time. Some people like to look at their accounts on a time basis – say, 30 days old or 60 days old or 90 days old. We prefer simplicity – it's all 'old' and, more importantly, 'owed' to you. Therefore, if you are generating $100,000 per month, you should be looking to keep accounts receivable to $10,000 or less ongoing.

Often when clinic owners have blown out from this number, they'll say that they are at the mercy of a third party. While this might be the circumstance, you need to be firmer about your policy and terms for the service you offer. It's your business. Even if that means reducing your 30-day payment terms to 14 days (or even reducing your 14-day terms to seven days) – better is better. Julie, owner of an occupational therapy clinic, reduced her outstanding debtors from about $34,000 to $13,000 in a month, and has fine-tuned her invoicing and follow-up invoices systems so that the situation never gets that bad again. This means more in her bank account to offset the interest on her mortgage. The savings value is significant and ongoing.

Increase payment time

On the other side of getting your money sooner to improve cashflow, you should also look to increase the time that you need to pay those accounts that you owe. Extending your terms by an extra seven, 14 or 30 days can make a good difference in managing your cashflow. If you're unable to get a formal or fixed change to the terms of the bills you need to pay, you can still do two things:

1. ensure that you pay on the day they're due and not any time sooner
2. consider aligning the timing of your bills to be paid at two allocated times in the month to better manage the flow of cash out of the clinic.

For example, your accounts could be paid on the 5th of the month and the 20th. By aligning your billing rhythms to fall on those days, you have greater predictability, consistency and stability in the cashflow of your clinic.

Implement a rhythm to evaluate your performance and future plan

Your final focus in your cash allocation strategy is implementing a rhythm for reporting on your finances, so that at any given moment you know how well your business is going. You need a routine to help determine whether you are in a quality position for growth or consolidation, allowing you to make quality strategic decisions. See the following section for more on implementing reporting rhythms.

Key focus: Report

Principle: Your results rely on your rhythms

What gets measured gets managed.

Peter Drucker, management consultant, educator and author

Breakdown to breakthrough

There's sobbing on the other end of the phone line. It's Jenna, a speech pathologist clinic owner, as she describes her current mental breakdown and burnout. Jenna hadn't been into the clinic for a month, and she couldn't bring herself to even walk through the doors. 'I used to be happy, proud of my career, but now, this is all a burden.' Struggling with anxiety attacks and the constant comparison to other clinics, she felt defeated. 'I just don't care anymore. I give up.' Jenna had hoped opening a clinic would mean more time for herself and her dream to help people, creating change and making money but not working clinically as the owner.

Jenna didn't know how to login to her accounting software because she was scared of numbers; she had more than delegated the role, she had abdicated it. The software showed 12,000 unreconciled items. Her accounts were a mess – years behind – and she owed $40,000 to the tax office. (To put this into perspective, clinic owners should look to have all of last month's accounts reconciled by the fifth day of the new month or, at worst, by the tenth day of the month.) In particular, this debt was a huge weight on her and her family because it meant they had to continue with the instability of renting when they wanted their own home for their two young boys.

Two years later, Jenna was again on the phone, but this time she was clapping and laughing – and passionate about doing her new financial year budget. Jenna now had an up-to-date rolling breakeven spreadsheet, so she knew what she needed to make each week to breakeven. Not only that, but Jenna had also managed to pay off her tax debt. Jenna and her family could now use their savings to bid for homes on the market.

Numbers can be confronting. As health professionals, we love helping people – that's why we entered the profession and didn't become accountants. However, 'numbers aren't my strength' can't be the excuse if you're looking to sustainably grow your clinic. Ignoring your numbers will catch up with you. The reality is that, although you chose healthcare and not accounting, it was your decision to be a clinic owner and start a business.

From hoping to knowing

The world needs more clinic owners like you – someone purpose-driven to create a Clinic For Good. That requires you to transition from *hoping* your numbers will allow you to grow and be sustainable, to *knowing* what the financial health of your clinic is at any moment. Your results rely on your rhythms.

The following table outlines an example schedule for checking your financials, and how long each check should take. Schedule these checks into your calendar. They not only provide a moment to review and get up to speed, but can also lead to decision-making and action-taking. It's valuable to have a checklist and system (refer to Degree 4: Systems) to ensure you cover all of the right data points and decisions at the right time.

Your financial results rely on rhythms

Daily	• Accounts outstanding review (10 min)
Weekly	• Business dashboard review (10 min) • Reconciling accounts (30 min) • Cashflow forecasts (10 min)
Fortnightly	• Budget variation review (30 min)
Monthly	• Profit and loss analysis (30 min) • Cash allocation review (30 min)
Quarterly	• Budget review (30 min) • Tax planning with accountant (60 min) • Profit and loss quarter on quarter analysis (30 min) • Balance sheet review (30 min)
Yearly	• Budget for new financial year (60 min) • Reset allocation targets (60 min)

Depending on factors such as the size of your clinic and team, your number of sites and your company structures, your time allocations will differ, so the preceding table is an indication. As you complete your reviews more frequently, you'll develop systems to make the process more efficient. An easy and high-impact action is to time-block each of these sessions into your diary with the relevant frequency, time allocation, title of session and relevant checklist. Avoid simply putting 'finance', for example, as the name of your time-block – be specific.

Core element: Accelerate

The third element to master in Degree 5 is Accelerate. This relates to you being able to scale up your growth so that you can go from making the business average to accessing leverage.

Key focus: Advisors

Principle: Invest in your future

> Doing one thing better and better might be more satisfying than staying an amateur at many different things.

Angela Duckworth, author of *Grit: The Power of Passion and Perseverance*

Advice from a billionaire

In a famous government committee hearing involving Kerry Packer, one of Australia's media moguls, Packer highlighted the value of good advisors. Challenged by the inquiry on how he was managing his fortune in a tax-efficient way, Packer said,

> I am not evading tax in any way, shape or form. Of course, I am minimising my tax. If anybody in this country doesn't minimise their tax they want their head read. As a government I can tell you you're not spending it that well that we should be paying extra.

With the right advisors around you, you can have the guidance and support to downsize any unnecessary financial contributions, maximise your takings and protect your assets.

As part of one of his newly established financial rhythms, Harry, a clinic owner of a musculoskeletal clinic, experienced the benefits of Packer's approach in surrounding yourself with the right advisors.

Harry shared the following with the Clinic Mastery community:

If you think you're paying too much tax, you probably are. Getting a second pair of eyes to look at your accounting is definitely worthwhile. After speaking with a new accountant who amended my last two company tax returns, I received an $11,000 refund.

Change may be afoot

At a Clinic Mastery workshop, Harvee Pene, founder of Life Changing Accountants shared some signs that you need to change an advisor such as your accountant:

- They are reactive, not proactive.
- They charge by the hour, and for each email or phone call, rather than offering a fixed monthly fee for abundant support.
- They send you surprise bills for their service or from the tax office.
- They are slow to respond to your communications.
- They are technophobic and don't use cloud computer software (such as Xero).
- You have to prompt them to complete tasks and reviews.
- They charge you to ask questions.
- They are not entrepreneurial or business minded themselves.
- They are not strategic around tax planning to proactively save you tax and maximise your take home (thanks, Kerry).

Tiger Woods can't see his swing

One of the greatest golfers to ever live is Tiger Woods. He's so far ahead of the rest that his is the work of a legend. Despite being the best in the world, Woods is known (like all professionals) for investing time, money and resources in the advisors around him to be better.

The best in the world have a coach – someone to hold them accountable to rhythms, stay focused on outcomes and elevate them to the best version of themselves.

Coaches also help with what you can't see. Woods can't see his own swing, so his coaches and advisors help him aggregate marginal gains for better performance. His advisors are key to transformational growth.

Don't try to navigate growing your clinic alone. You can see across the 7 Degrees to Grow Your Clinic how many areas there are to learn and do. A key to sustainability is building your advisor team around you.

Penny wise and pound foolish

Breaking the mould of our own therapist mindset can be difficult as we transition to clinic ownership. We've been conditioned. The idea of 'penny wise and pound foolish' symbolises a bias towards the conditioning of a typical therapist mindset – where there is a focus on being overly cautious about lower-value things. The opportunity here is to transition to the abundance of the clinic owner or leader approach. If you've made this transition already, it's time to help elevate your team.

The following table outlines the difference between the therapist and the clinic owner mindset that we typically see.

Therapist versus clinic owner or leader mindset

Therapist	Clinic owner/leader
Paid by the hour	Paid for the value we bring to the hours
Therapy creates a big impact for others	Decisions create a big impact for others
Negotiates on present state	Negotiates on future state

Therapist	Clinic owner/leader
Spender	Investor
Wants to know it all	Gets advisors and support people who know it all
Do it yourself (DIY) approach	Hires to address weaknesses
$100 per hour work	$1000 per hour work
Focuses on personal security/ independence	Focuses on intergenerational wealth
Reactive to events	Strategic plans
Scarcity mindset	Abundant mindset
Focuses on *me*	Focuses on *we*
Focuses on profile, transactional	Focuses on legacy, impact, causes

The mindsets shown in the preceding table are not exclusive attributes; rather they provide a compare and contrast of the 'typical' approach of a therapist and clinic owner with respect to finance.

Engage progressive advisors and members of your support team, including an accountant, bookkeepers and financial planners who are able to create the appropriate business structures for compliance, best practice and maximisation of the money you generate.

Key focus: Roadmap

Principle: Build to sell

> Selling your clinic (part of or all) is an opportunity to realise the value you have created in the world.
>
> Ben Lynch

When, not if

Danielle told us, 'I would never sell my business — I'm going to be 75 and still running this clinic.' If these are your thoughts also, we have some news for you. You are going to sell your clinic — it's a matter of *when*, not *if*. And to sell your clinic successfully, you must start with the end in mind. This gives you options down the track. If you get to 75 and do want to sell but you haven't put in the structures to allow that to happen in a way that reflects what you've worked for and also want and need at that time, you'll be disappointed. But if you create your business in a way that allows you to sell it, that doesn't mean you have to sell it. Everything you do to make your business attractive to a buyer also makes it a stronger business for you to keep running. And everything we cover in this book will help to make your business more attractive to a buyer, including finding and keeping the right people, creating systems and good financial processes, and ensuring the business doesn't rely too much on one person.

Reasons for selling or exiting your clinic (all or parts of it) can include:

- You receive an offer that matches your desire statement.
- You're progressing to enjoy the fruits of retirement.
- You're burnt out or have had enough of being a clinic owner.
- You're keen to provide opportunities for others — including providing team pathways for progression.
- You're keen to pursue other aspirations or career options.
- You've made yourself redundant (and so not required for the maintenance and growth of the business).
- You want to liquidate some value to invest in other areas (such as property or shares).
- You want to spend more time with family.
- You need to focus on your own health.
- You are offered more money than your future time in the business is worth.

- You don't want to work as a business owner for the rest of your life.
- It's part of a plan in your goals.
- You want to give others the chance to run a business too (buying in).
- To go onto other ventures – business or personal.

No guarantee of tomorrow

Nassim Taleb, author of *The Black Swan*, explains the concept of his book with the following:

> A Black Swan is a highly improbable event with three principal characteristics: it is unpredictable; it carries a massive impact; and, after the fact, we concoct an explanation that makes it appear less random, and more predictable, than it was.

While 'highly improbable', you also have to be ready for the unexpected Black Swan event. For example, perhaps you have a plan to sell your clinic in five years and you are structuring the business around that plan. But then, sadly, something tragic happens for you, your family, your community or business. Because you were already building towards a sale, you'll be in a much stronger position to exit the business than if you had planned to stay in it until the day you die. Nobody wants to think about such circumstances, but they do happen.

Building business assets at every stage

You might have only just started in business and can't imagine selling. Or perhaps you're a little more experienced and are really hitting your stride … great! You should still think about building your clinic to be saleable – because, as mentioned, one day it will sell (even if it's a partial buy in of a team member)! So begin to make it valuable now.

As you grow, continue to build assets, and increase return on investment (ROI) and the value of your business. Do this by creating robust systems and structures, hiring and nurturing the best people, and developing your own intellectual property (IP) and your brand. You must start to think like a buyer. Whoever purchases your clinic wants to be able to step into your shoes and run the business without interruption – it's your job to create the structure for that to be possible.

Think like an investor! Because you are.

Mentor session notes

Milestones on the finance roadmap

The world of finance, especially personal finance, can be complex. However, with a few simple milestones on the finance roadmap, you can have some clarity and something to aim for as you grow your clinic. At times, you'll move almost naturally to the next milestone as you progress. But you'll also likely face times when you move backwards as you regress with the challenges of being a clinic owner. Nonetheless, it's important to simplify finance to make it sustainable – personally and for your clinic.

The list of milestones provided here is a guide. You could break it down into many more detailed milestones; for now let's keep it simple. We suggest you determine a specific monthly or yearly dollar amount that reflects each one of these stages for you – it's different for everyone. So many people have just one amount they're 'aiming for', but the reality is that your standards, expectations and needs change with the circumstances. To give yourself added clarity and certainty about your financial status and milestones ahead, use this simple exercise as a quick guide.

Certainty

At this financial milestone, you're breaking even. You're covering your personal and clinic expenses, perhaps with a small margin for safety and surplus. Financial certainty gives you the confidence that you can keep 'playing the game' of business. You're getting paid a market rate for your role (though perhaps the lower end of a range), but you're not quite profiting like a clinic owner should for all that goes into running a business. A good achievement at this stage is to build up enough positive cashflow to build a reserve for your clinic and your family. Doing so requires you to first pay off your overdraft and any outstanding liabilities (such as tax obligations or credit cards) to build a buffer. It's important to break free of any reliance on government grants or loan facilities. Stability in income gives you certainty to make better decisions.

Surplus

At this milestone, you're well ahead of the breakeven point and running a profitable business. You're seeing the fruits of your labour and have an income of a business owner. You're able to build up the reserves you need personally and for your business to have a number of months up your sleeve. You're now in a position to look at expansion and investment into areas such as team, businesses, equipment and facilities. This can further fuel growth when done with precision, but can also bring about financial strain if you're not a good financial steward.

Freedom

At this milestone, you have been a good steward and now your investments have multiplied your financial flow both personally and to the business in a way that releases you from any time-for-money transactions. You have used multiplication to provide you with various streams of income and a growing asset base to afford you many options about the direction of your business and life. The valuation of your business is substantial and you're able to contribute to the causes, clinics and community in many ways.

Abundance

At this milestone, you have amassed enough wealth for inter-generational impact and income. You have a legacy business and vehicle to support the people who matter most to you for decades to come. At this stage, you're able to substantially amplify your impact by partnering, directing and contributing in meaningful and material ways to advance the causes that matter to you.

Key focus: Remuneration

Principle: Pay yourself as you grow

Fit your own oxygen mask first.

Every airline's passenger safety instructions

Certainty leads to abundance

After having his first profitable financial year in over six years, clinic owner Greg reflected on how much more certainty he felt. He mentioned that the financial strains weren't apparent until hindsight brought some clarity. Greg had been making many decisions from a place of scarcity without realising what the underlying cause was – his own financial uncertainty. He was not earning a commercial amount of money to comfortably cover personal expenses let alone justify the demands of being a business owner. Greg's personal financial position was a self-sustaining cycle – because he couldn't make quality business decisions to break out of that cycle.

Only on reflection, however, did this become apparent. Greg reflected on how, when under the weight of financial uncertainty, he was closed to rewards and pathways for team members, not investing into marketing, and overlooking investments into the culture of the team and many other things. This is a narrative that is all too common for clinic owners, as they get stuck in a cycle of financial uncertainty that perpetuates the cycle of business stagnation.

You need to meet a primary need for certainty, especially when it comes to finances. For each one of us, that financial amount is different and so it is important to understand and calculate what that number is for you. Find the financial certainty and sustainability personally to unlock the abundance required to grow your clinic.

How much should clinic owners be earning?

How much you earn as a clinic owner is a reflection of the value you bring to yourself and your team, clients and community. As you grow your clinic, your ability to help more people can be recognised financially through a 'certificate of appreciation' – that is, money notes.

Setting meaningful and measurable earning targets as a clinic owner has two parts.

Part 1: What would be your ideal?

As part of your desire statement, what would you like to be earning from your clinic each year? Your answer will be dependent on a range of factors, but essentially you're looking at what value you want to receive for the work you put in. You're then able to choose a target amount for over the next 12 to 24 months.

You should then consider the tax implications in a discussion with your accountant. You accountant will be able to advise you on the most tax-effective way to earn that amount – because it's not what you make but what you get to keep that matters. You will likely have a salaried amount paid to you on a regular basis as an employee of your business (as part of your fortnightly payroll) as well as profit distributions paid on a semi-regular basis (perhaps quarterly) to you as an owner of or shareholder in the business. Knowing this overall number gives you an idea of an upper amount or target for how much you should take home each year.

Part 2: What would it take to replace you?

Understanding the market salary for your role is a useful reference for how much you should be paying yourself. For example, what would a therapist with your years of experience and case load be paid? Or if you were a CEO with your workload, experience and size of company, what would you be paid? Knowing this amount gives you an idea of the lower limit to what you should take home each year.

Factoring in how many hours a week you're doing the role/s is also important. For example, if you determine that the CEO part of your role should be paid $150,000 annually for a full-time position and you do the role for 20 hours each week, pro-rata the payment. In the end, it's your clinic (company) and you can pay yourself however you like (in a manner that's legal, of course) but if you're wanting it to reflect market rate and 'correct to effort' then the information here can guide you.

Remember that you have taken all the risk – you experience the stress and turbulence of being a clinic owner. You should be remunerated well for that. The reality is that you could earn a fairly 'reasonable' amount of money in a much 'easier' role at another high-performing clinic, so you need to receive a 'premium' on that amount to justify the things you go through as a clinic owner.

Good stewardship

More and more money is flowing around the world every day. Your role is to participate in the economy by providing value through your services as a health professional and improving the lives of those in your community. You don't make the money; you simply offer healthcare as an exchange to receive the flow of money. In other words, you simply need to direct the money through you.

The simple formula is:

$$\text{Help more people} + \text{Help more often}$$
$$+ \text{Add more value} + \text{Maximise your margin}$$

The distinction is that money flows *through* you, not *to* you. To multiply the money flow, you need to embrace this distinction. Those who hoard and save stop the money flow. To multiply money, you need to be a steward. The steward manages and organises the money in a way that produces more flow to themselves and others to support the causes and clinics that matter to them.

What you can leverage is the rate of money flow, which is the 'Help more people + Help them more often' part of the equation.

Money always flows towards and rewards value. Value determines the volume of money flow (the more value, the faster the flow), which is the 'Add more value + Maximise your margin' part of the equation.

Remember – the money is not yours. The money simply flows to you before you manage it to flow elsewhere. Don't stop the money flow. Direct the money flow to investments that allow you to multiply the flow into the future so that you can do more and help more people. Be a good steward.

Mentor session notes

Working out remuneration with multiple directors and time split between clients and admin

Shane Bennett, co-founder of Beyond osteopathy and Clinic Mastery mentor, provided the following as a guide when paying multiple directors of a clinic.

Question: We are two therapists running under the same business name but as two sole traders. We are looking to form a company with both of us being directors of the company. We both see different numbers of clients and complete a different number of admin hours. What is the best to pay ourselves?

Response: It will ultimately come down to what you as directors want to do. It can be valuable to separate out the emotion and go down the pathway of 'pay per job role as per market rate' for each role.

As an example, your wage comes from the following roles:

- **Therapist:** You're paid a market rate. You can work as much or as little as you want, as can the other directors who are also therapists.

- **General manager:** You're paid a market rate of what a general manager would cost you if you were to bring them in externally. No more, no less. *Note:* You could be pro-rated because you don't do the role full-time and the market salary is based on turnover and years of experience. *Note:* Operations manager and marketing manager can be on market salaries, which would be quite different in dollar amounts for each role.

- **Shareholder:** You're paid a dividend, like all directors, once all wages have been accounted for.

This set up means you're not all thinking that you're doing more than the other person – there's no bickering or infighting. It creates the freedom to have very different work weeks. So you can have people pulling bigger weights. It's not without its issues and it's not perfect; however, it's a practical solution. Accountability and remuneration should be to a job role not a person.

Question: How would you approach a situation where people start saying, 'Well, I can earn a lot more billing patients than being a marketer or manager' and then everyone just wants to see patients? Do you have a set number of hours they need to do other roles for to work on the business?

Response: We hope that anyone who becomes an owner/shareholder isn't doing it just for the money. I guess the same could be said for our clinical mentoring team (who aren't owners) – they'd earn more if they just saw more patients in the time they spent mentoring but the increased job satisfaction, diversification, progression, altruism and lack of hubris seems to trump the money motivation.

So we don't have set hours for other roles. Anyone who wants to do that definitely won't be chosen for our marketing role or management role. You could argue that the person who is smashing through patients is helping the clinic by providing more revenue than the other shareholders and showing the team how to be busy (big issue if they're not!). However, we think more is at stake here.

A good comparison for this model is to compare it to a company listed on the stock exchange – for example, BHP. If you are a shareholder of BHP, you are an owner, but those shares don't come with a caveat dictating you must put in hours for BHP to get your dividend. You get your dividend because you paid for your shares. So if people are becoming owners of a practice but aren't putting their hand in their pocket and paying a fair price, they need to pay in other ways – sweat equity.

It's an interesting argument because you can use the very same perspectives on both sides. For example, why not have the same wage for all owners if they are equal shareholders and we don't care about the dollar amount? Why is one role – whether it's manager, seeing clients or marketing – worth more commercially if everyone is pulling equal weight? You're all owners; just keep driving the business further and know the roles and demands will differ at different times. When it comes down to it, I hope no-one who joins the business would be like that, and I tend to think the same way, then why wouldn't they agree for everyone to just take equal wages?

Question: There are so many variables and it's interesting why many don't look at the other side and just say we're in this together, let's split it. Is it because we are therapists first so want to be paid for seeing clients differently from business roles?

Response: I think the reality is that it's probably pretty rare to find someone or a group of people who all think they're pulling equal weight. Paying separately also enables very different work weeks among owners, and that may suit different lifestyles and phases of life. Do we want to set up a scenario where everyone feels obliged to pull the same or do we want to create a scenario where it's completely okay to have very different working weeks – whether that be based on time, responsibility or risk?

You can pay everyone equally and then if you feel someone isn't pulling their weight, you could always kick them into gear, but we both should want to succeed. It's important to note that two people will never do exactly equal work and you have to be okay with that. They should both bring value and the reality is that they can do that differently. It's important to have clear expectations (position descriptions) and key performance indicators.

I think each option has pros and cons. It's important to run the decision through your filter and have the robust discussions upfront so everyone has clarity moving forward.

Note: Always discuss your pay options in collaboration with your accountant so you set up the most beneficial structures and processes to facilitate the best outcome for everyone.

High-impact action

Keep in mind the following key insights and actions for your clinic's finances:

- Measure your clinic excellence indicators to know what value you are generating and then set about doing four things to improve that value – help more people, help more often, add more value and maximise your margin.
- Ensure your clients receive the healthcare recommendations and most valuable care they deserve and remember – money simply follows value.
- Emphasise delivering meaningful outcomes for clients rather than time as part of your business model. Consider how you can deliver outcomes without reliance on any one income or delivery stream.
- Remember you are the benchmark – be better than you were yesterday and make your numbers clinic-specific. An example could be a functional structuring of your profit and loss report that works for your clinic.
- Use the CREATE acronym for improve cashflow – a pragmatic strategy to fuel your economic engine.
- Measure the rhythms of your results regularly and find the opportunities for financial optimisation by time-blocking your diary.
- Invest in quality, progressive advisors to help you comply with regulations and optimise the cashflow you generate in business.
- Start structuring and preparing today for the roadmap to selling (however far off that is).
- Fit your own oxygen mask and pay yourself a commercial wage so that you have financial certainty to make quality decisions.

Finance summary

Saving tax, boosting cashflow and accelerating profitability are key to the financial sustainability of growing your clinic. Remember the goal is not money – money is simply the reflection of scalable value you bring to your community and what allows you to invest in yourself, your team and client experiences to be able to do it over again in new and better ways.

DEGREE 6:

BRAND

Attract ideal people

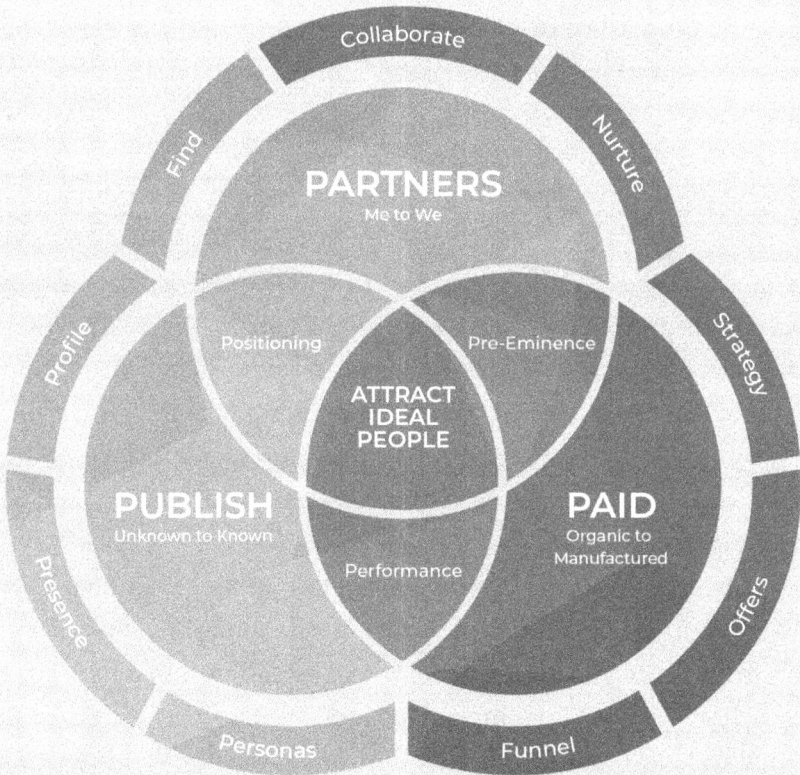

Core element: Publish

The Publish core element is about publishing the kind of content that helps you go from unknown to known in your industry and community. Your objective is to become and be seen as the go-to place for healthcare information – and healthcare. This includes establishing yourself as a preferred place to work, a preferred provider of healthcare and preferred partner to collaborate with.

Key focus: Personas

Principle: Help someone specifically

> You may not be able to change the world,
> but you can change someone's world.
>
> Anonymous

Yes, but who specifically ...

'I love helping people.' We've mentioned this a few times through this book, and it's worth returning to. When we get asked why we do what we do as health professionals, at the core of our response is that we love helping people. Helping a client achieve their meaningful goals and enjoy a better quality of life brings us great fulfilment, and reminds us of why we got into healthcare in the first place. It then inspires us to help more people.

However, wanting to help people can be a double-edged sword at times, because in an attempt to help more people, we can become a martyr trying to help everyone. The trouble with trying to help everyone is making a meaningful and sustainable difference for someone requires empathy – *practical empathy*. Your ability to understand the needs of a specific patient (persona), team member or partner in front of you is key to being able to publish work and create experiences that benefit everybody involved: you, your team and your patients. Reconciling that we're not able to help everyone can be hard, because as health professionals we care. We have a high degree of empathy.

Specificity creates sustainability

Having the diversity and depth of training or practical empathy in all areas of our profession to be able to help all of our clients in the same meaningful way is not sustainable. Even if it were possible to help everyone at some point in our career, it would likely take decades to become an expert in all the possible presentations, differential diagnosis, treatment interventions and best practice methodologies – and that's if you could also manage the demands of growing your clinic as a business owner at the same time.

A better way to sustainably help more people that doesn't involve trying to help everyone is available – you can help someone specifically. Think about that specific client and know them inside and out. Knowing the personas of your community allows you to help someone specifically, meaningfully, thoroughly and consistently. You're able to publish compelling offers that resonate, and deliver experiences that turn clients into raving fans. In the process, you're able to create a great deal of fulfilment as you deliver comprehensive transformations for those specific people.

Your brand is your reputation

Do you think that only big companies such as Coca-Cola or Toyota have to worry about their brand? Well, this is not true. Your clinic, no matter how big or small, has a brand just like any other company – whether you realise it or not. If you always run on time and give clients a great experience, that is part of your brand. If your clinic is clean, fresh and inviting, that is part of your brand. If your online booking system often crashes and your reception team are rude, that's also part of your brand.

If you are going to create raving fans for your clinic, you must always keep your brand in mind. Examples of doing so include:

- focusing on and regularly achieving meaningful client health outcomes
- keeping your clinic clean, welcoming and inviting
- consciously choosing who you are partnering with – such as complementary schools, clubs, networks, associations, groups, businesses and other professionals
- making sure appointments run on time
- offering personalised, engaging and memorable healthcare experiences
- having an educational and consistent social media presence
- always following up with a client when you say you will
- putting the wellbeing of your team and your clients above all else
- remembering small details such as how you answer the phone, the music in the clinic, your signage and your business cards.

Subtle shift, significant success

The best way to create raving fans is to consider their needs, and a great way to understand and empathise with their needs is to use your insights about them to create what's known as a *client persona*. Your objective is to know and publish the specific details and characteristics of a persona so that you can help them more specifically. Whether that be a team member, client or partner you're looking to attract or nurture, you can be significantly more successful with your approach with the subtle shift of knowing their needs better than anybody else.

Publishing your personas allows you to design personalised, engaging and memorable experiences. You also lower the cost and time of acquiring new team members and clients to your clinic because you're more specific with who you want to work with and who you can help.

Relatable experience

In over a decade of leading a multidiscipline musculoskeletal clinic in Melbourne, Australia, Nicole hadn't ever detailed the specific personas of her clinic. We said, 'That's alright, it will all happen in good time. Remember that Clinics For Good aren't built overnight and we're here to help you grow your clinic as sustainably as possible.' As we embarked on our 120-day plan with Nicole, helping more people was the focus, and our objective was to attract more new clients to the clinic. So we started with identifying Nicole's client personas and focusing on helping someone specifically.

As Nicole became clearer on the client persona she believed she could help the most – someone she was passionate about helping and who was ready, willing and able to be helped – she started to think more creatively about how to attract that person to the clinic.

She started boosting her profile as a trusted advisor by creating content, and through partnerships and engaging in public relations (for example, radio). Her strategy worked. By the end of her 120-day cycle she told us, 'All of our eight therapists are fully booked, a waiting list has formed – and we're now shifting to attracting the right team member persona'.

Not for everyone

Personas guide your marketing message, education-based content and patient journey so that you can boost your profile and be seen as the go-to place for healthcare because you help someone specifically.

Seth Godin in his best-selling book *This is Marketing* wrote about doing work that matters for a few people who care. The reality is that what you do is not for everyone. The therapy you provide, the content you produce, the offers you create, the products you sell, the training you deliver will help *someone specifically* – just not everyone. So focus on a few people who care and deliver remarkable experiences for them.

Assets in action

If you're going to position yourself in the community as the go-to clinic for career opportunities, health and wellness, as well as the preferred partner, you need to help someone specifically, meaningfully and consistently. For that you need to publish your personas and design practical empathy in your marketing, offers and experiences so that you resonate and attract more ideal people to grow your clinic.

Use the QR code provided here to download quality resources on creating your ideal client personas.

Key focus: Presence

Principle: Go where the attention is

> The sniper is far more effective than the scattergun approach because it is targeted.
>
> Ben Lynch

If only they knew …

As health professionals, we're lifelong learners. We're just as much in the education industry as we are part of the healthcare industry.

From reading journal articles about the latest research in treatment interventions, to attending professional conferences and the weekend workshop to hone our technical skills, we love learning. Not only do we love learning but, aligned with our highest shared value – our passion for helping people – we also enjoy teaching others what we've learnt. Finding out another therapist has left the profession or a client has taken unnecessary healthcare measures for reasons we believe we could have foreshadowed, and more importantly supported them through, makes us sad. We think to ourselves, *If only they knew …* Perhaps we ought to think, *If only we had a better presence in their world, perhaps we could have made a meaningful impact sooner. Perhaps we could have shared some of that knowledge we've developed and helped them make a better decision.*

Don't let critical colleagues decrease your impact

Do you sometimes feel as if everyone is looking? Judging? It can feel uncomfortable, even in the shadows. As health professionals, we are critical. And this characteristic serves us well when we're discerning the latest evidence-based practices to help our clients get the best outcomes.

The challenge is that when it comes to having a voice and creating a presence in the community by publishing our content, key ideas and offers, we're scared off by thoughts of our 'peer-reviewed' critics – our judging colleagues.

You have to start ignoring these images and thoughts. You have a lot of experience to contribute and ideas to share, and they're all backed by a passion for helping people live a better quality life. Everyone you come into contact with as a practitioner – from your clients, to team members and your community – needs the guidance and support you have to offer. Allowing the peer-reviewed critics to prevent you from showing up and having a presence means you're allowing them to decrease your impact. Your impact could keep therapists progressing in your profession and clients progressing in their health.

When we look into the mirror we realise the biggest critic we need to overcome is ourselves. That critic stops us from even showing up and having a go. Thoughts like, *It's not perfect, I don't have anything different or better to share, I need more experience* are all stories that prevent you from having that presence. Just as easily as you can find all the reasons why you can't, the reasons why you can must be as readily available. Play a bigger game and connect with your purpose – your reason why you do what you do – and help more people in subtle, yet significant ways with your trusted voice. Start to show up, and have a presence.

Show up (in all the right places)

It's all well and good to adopt the latest strategies to grow your clinic, but if you're showing up and implementing those strategies in the wrong postcode, wrong social media or wrong groups, clubs, networks, schools or associations, you're going to fall short of your ideal outcome – whether that be increased new patient numbers or new therapists, or a broader network of quality partners.

You can do better than simply showing up at every event you can get yourself invited to, and that's to be more purposeful with your presence. So, the question you need to answer is this: where (presence) are your ideal people (personas) in their greatest concentration, when they are in a state that is ready, willing and able to enrol in your services?

Go where the attention is

Your life is much more enjoyable by showing up and having a presence in an environment where your ideal people (personas) gather. You're able to create messages that resonate with them because of the practical empathy you've developed in understanding their needs. You'll have more meaningful exchanges.

Finding those places where your ideal people (personas) meet in their greatest concentration allows you to make your efforts more impactful. An abundance of your targeted audience is in a community that is going to be more receptive to working with you – meaning you'll have more measurable success in attracting those people (team members, clients and partners).

Finding people in a state ready, willing and able to enrol in your services is a way to make your life easier. If those ideal people are the right fit but you find them at the wrong time in their respective journey (for example, due to their career or illness), you're going to add more work for yourself. Find the right fit by considering factors such as access to the right funding models, health insurance, plan management, stage of life, proximity to care, therapy or injury timeline, family or health support, and money and resources. And then go where the attention is – online or in person. You'll get a better return on your invested time, money and resources.

Zero moment of truth (ZMOT)

In 2011, Jim Lecinski from Google published a report called *Winning the Zero Moment of Truth*. This was a call to action for you to show up and have a greater publishing presence. The report outlined the research process that prospective consumers will go through prior to purchasing goods and services, which includes researching, comparing, reading reviews and talking to friends and family for recommendations. This process occurs for any larger or important purchases, including choosing a health clinic. Lecinski also high-lighted the success of those businesses that have a regular presence in the community. Your presence helps boost your status and positions you as the logical choice for those clients, team members and partners you're hoping to attract, allowing you to grow your clinic sizably and sustainably. Your presence needs to focus on adding value to your community through the three Es: education, engagement and enrolment towards better health outcomes and experiences.

Future-proofing your presence

As more clinics open up in the surrounding suburbs and as the quality of that competition improves, those clinics that have a meaningful presence will be positioned to attract more ideal people. The best time to start is now. The best approach is to go where the attention of your ideal personas is and have a meaningful presence that adds value to your community. You should consider the people, processes and publishing schedule to hold you to account and enable a workflow that supports your proliferating presence. It's time to show up!

Assets in action

Content duplication and distribution system

Once you've started producing content, your objective is to leverage the work that you publish by duplicating it in different forms – from macro into micro, for example – and then distributing it out in a variety of different mediums.

For example, say you've already created a video education series for clients on a specific health topic. You can publish this video in other mediums, such as social media, but also leverage this content through the following:

- The video content can be transcribed and turned into blogs.
- Text from the blogs can be turned into multiple text posts for social media.
- Text from the social media posts can be used to create infographics and other images for social media.

You can then distribute the original video and its duplicated forms through a number of mediums, such as your partners, your own social media and your email database.

One last Clinic Mastery tip: outsource the duplication and distribution process using a virtual team. This allows you to focus on the $100 per hour work and outsource the $10 per hour work.

Key focus: Profile

Principle: Deliver on your promise

> ## Your identity is your most valuable possession. Protect it.
>
> Elastigirl/Helen Parr in *The Incredibles* (2004, Pixar Animation)

Inspired to be better

When you open up your clinic doors for the first time as a start-up, there's a breeze of optimism and creative inspiration. You're inspired to be better, and to deliver your version of healthcare experiences in new and better ways – from the treatment journeys for your clients, to the pathways for your team and the overall impact on your community with a modern-day clinic brand.

As your reputation develops for being a good practitioner who's able to help 'someone specifically', more and more people want to see you. When you reach that point of 'my books are full', you'll need to hire team members progressively to allow you to help more people.

The challenge can be that people still want to see you, especially if your name is in the clinic name. Your promise to 'be better' for your clients, team and community is stress-tested as your clinic brand expands beyond you. So as you grow your clinic, you need to think purposefully about the three profiles of your brand so that you can methodically deliver on your promises.

These three profiles are your:

1. practice profile
2. personal profile
3. professional profile.

Actions speak louder than words

Building a clinic profile that reflects the vision and inspiration you have to be better is possible. You need to clearly establish your identity within the community so that you build a profile that is *remarkable* – in other words, your brand is worth making a remark about. If your brand is your reputation and your reputation is based on doing the things you say you're going to do, your profile is about crafting and committing to the delivery of those promises across all three areas of your personal, professional and practice profiles.

To build your brand, you first need to understand that brand is simply your reputation. It's what other people say about you based on the experiences they've had or have heard about.

When you're establishing your brand, you need to clarify your identity – what do you want to be known for? However, most importantly, your brand will be sustainably built on following through on what you say you're going to do.

Brand is about making and keeping your promises to the people you work with and work for. Those promises relate to what they can expect in their experiences in working with you as a team member, client and partner.

Marks of distinction

Marketing is simply communicating your promises in powerful messages that connect with your audience, create value for their health or career, and lead them to choose you over another clinic.

To get that message across and ultimately influence your audience to take action, you must first capture their attention. This means you need to stand out, to define the status quo and transcend it to become truly remarkable.

What do you stand for and therefore what do you want to be known for? Think about the best health clinics you know of. No doubt their reputation is consistent with their values, and they are absolutely clear about what makes their clinic unique. They then demonstrate that through every element of a client's, team member's and partner's interaction with them. That's what ultimately leads people to achieve better health and life outcomes, and rave about their experience to others, making that clinic remarkable.

Breaking down your three profiles

Your practice profile includes the following:

- your core purpose and painted picture (refer to Degree 2: Purpose)
- your ideal client/team avatars – for example, who is and who is not a good fit for your clinic
- how you communicate your promises to those avatars through your positioning in the market
- your network of partners – such as schools, clubs, groups, associations and businesses
- your philosophy – for example, your clinic's approach to healthcare and client journeys.

Your personal profile includes:

- your niche/special interest
- your personal life story and experiences
- the causes, communities and movements that matter to you.

Your professional profile covers your products and services. It is what you offer your community to help them get better. This very much crosses over into the realm of client experiences and includes your:

- methodology – the application of your philosophy
- profession
- products and services
- online services (if any).

You need to earn your stripes – building your brand profile

Typically we see people think about the next marketing thing they can do to get a new client in the diary, or perhaps the best ad to run to attract the new hire they need quickly … While tactics that are short term and typically transactional can work, often they are unreliable – especially if you haven't also played the longer game of building brand equity.

Compare this to carefully developing your brand, which is playing a bigger game. This is about purposeful thinking about who you are, how you're going to show up in the world, and what you're going to promise and, therefore, deliver for your clients, partners and team. For example, your goal might be to become the most educational, engaging, experiential, results-orientated, progressive or friendly clinic in town.

Brand equity is your exit equity

Developing and focusing on the brand equity in your business is also part of a good exit strategy. When we talk about goodwill, that's the reputation of your brand, and it has financial value when it's time to sell your clinic. If all of the goodwill in your clinic rests entirely with your personal brand, then no-one will want to buy at an over-inflated price for your reputation, only to have clients leave when you do.

The goodwill in your business must instead be based on well-established teams, systems, assets and branding, so that the value remains in the business when you leave. Value must also be in the practice and professional brands to boost the equity value.

Even if you are not fully exiting, you may have team members come on board who want to buy into the whole thing or into locations that you have. Again, they will want to see value in what they buy into beyond the presence of the successful and well-known business owner.

Not just for Disney

Robert Iger is the former CEO of Disney, and he has shared some case studies on how Disney+ came to exist, and how Marvel and 21st Century Fox were acquired.

In the building of these brands and mergers, Iger kept on coming back to brand principles and alignment as key factors in the deals. Iger reflected on how the Disney brand had built equity in the community and stood for certain values that needed to be upheld in the deals moving forward, no matter the commercial incentives to deviate from them.

Iger's approach made us reflect on our brand principles – and we went to the butcher's paper and made a scribbling mess of ideas and iterations for our Behind the Brand asset (see the following 'Assets in action' box for more).

Brand is such an important thing to build as you grow your clinic because it helps you attract more of the right people, team members, clients and partners within your network. So often, though, the brand components are an afterthought or are managed at the superficial level of aesthetics, such as colours, taglines, images and logos.

Those clinics that stand out over the long term as the place to work, the place to heal and the place to connect with are going to have a strong brand presence and profile.

It's time to build your brand equity and assets. It's not just reserved for Disney.

Assets in action

What we call the 'Behind the Brand' asset is a centralised resource that documents and communicates all elements of your clinic brand. Given that brand is your reputation and your reputation is simply following through on the things you say you're going to do, you need to start with looking at what you are saying or communicating.

The Behind the Brand asset is the place to capture everything relating to this communication and all those brand elements, from styles to taglines, x–factors, clients, team promises, colours and communication guidelines, demographic insights of team members and clients, origin stories, brand strategy and much more. It's a resource that is used during training and onboarding of new team members, when guiding agencies who take over your marketing and when aligning your team on the delivery of your reputation to build your brand.

Your Behind the Brand asset is a strategic document that details your:

- x–factors
- differentiating value proposition
- promises to clients, community, partners, team
- strategic direction
- market positioning
- brand language, vocabulary and communications guide
- logos, visuals, colour palette and clinic aesthetics
- methodologies, approaches and philosophies
- purpose, values, 'painted picture' and causes
- team units and dynamics.

Use the QR code provided here to download a condensed version of our Behind the Brand asset, including a resource to help you compare the old way (or the status quo) with possible new ways.

Core element: Partners

The second element to master in Degree 8 is Partners. This relates to you transitioning from *me* to *we* by expanding your network to partner with other progressive schools, clubs, networks, associations, businesses, communities and professionals.

Key focus: Find

Principle: Seek purposeful partners

> Talent wins games, but teamwork and intelligence win championships.
>
> Michael Jordan

Seeing the bigger picture

Right from the start of our university education, we're encouraged to see our clients at the centre of a broader healthcare team. We're given the perspective that our role is just one role — although an important role — in the bigger picture of their health.

As clients present to your clinic for treatment, you have an opportunity to find, connect and collaborate with other healthcare professionals in their care. When it comes to growing your clinic, finding more of these health partners to collaborate with is important in not only adding more value to your existing clients, but also helping you find ways to help more people by receiving referrals.

When it comes to finding more partners to collaborate with beyond primary healthcare providers, we're often limited by only looking to traditional medical models or whoever might be closest or most convenient, instead of using that same lens we were taught to use at university: the lens of the client.

Breaking the mould

The opportunity to break the mould of the health professional comes when we look beyond partnering with other health professionals and find people who play other roles in our clients' lives.

More specifically, you need to find the ideal persona for partners for your business. This is important for the following reasons:

- A larger network for your clinic means more lead-generation opportunities.
- Having more services and products to offer your clients means you can help them get better quicker.
- You can build your brand positioning in the community through your associations and connections, creating trust and likability.
- You have more referral sources of new clients for your clinic.
- You can offer complementary services or products your clients can access and benefit from.
- Most importantly, you can build sustainable relationships based on connection, trust, rapport and value adding.

Trust over transaction

The first focus to have when expanding your network with partnerships is to find groups, clubs, schools, associations, businesses and other health professionals that can allow you to help more people, help them more often and add more value.

We all do business with people we know, like and trust. Therefore, you need to establish this rapport with a prospective new network before you can create a relationship that supports the growth of your clients and clinic.

How do you do that? You add value to that person or their business!

You need to position yourself as someone who can contribute greatly to those in your prospective network by offering them as much upfront value as you can.

Remember – you're not being manipulative or 'bribing' another person here. You'll never develop a relationship based on transactional thinking like this. Instead, you need to approach the people and businesses you believe have the greatest synergies with you and your client base so that you can work together. Your partnership needs to be a win for your clients, your team, business and, of course, your partners – otherwise, it's unlikely to survive and you won't be doing good in the world.

Key focus: Collaborate

Principle: Add more value

> Not adding value is the same as taking it away.
>
> Seth Godin

Building stronger relationships

If you think of relationships as a place to *receive*, they immediately become transactional and are very easily replaced or displaced. To instead create lasting connections, you must approach your relationships with the absolute best interests at heart for the other person, group or business. If you want anything to flourish, you have to put in the time, effort and energy.

Unfortunately, many people try to reap benefits for themselves at the same time – or, worse, before they have even sown any great deal of value into a relationship. This does not build a long-term relationship. You must first prepare by understanding the needs, wants and desires of the other party to the best of your ability. Then you can explore a multitude of ways to add value to their life. You can even identify ways in which you could provide value before meeting them.

Stronger partnership relationships can result in:

- more stable and regular new client growth (through generating more referrals)

- better nurturing and care for existing clients with better communication between the whole healthcare team
- increased access of one another's networks to amplify clinic growth through shared connections
- reduced expenses by combining business doings – for example, accessing buyers group discounts with suppliers or shared marketing costs
- greater knowledge of health and business with shared resources and training
- strengthened position in the community because of the collaboration – for example, through co-branding and joint ventures.

What's it going to take?

Next, you need to find complementary and constructive ways to collaborate so that your community, your partners and your clinic are better off. You need to find new and better ways to add more value to your partners and your community so that you continue to become the top of mind or pre-eminent choice for healthcare.

When you connect with a potential new partner, find out the following:

- their ideal client and special interests
- their specialty
- the best way to refer and care for mutual clients (both ways)
- the best way to communicate about existing clients
- whether they refer to your profession – including what for, what works, and what doesn't
- their biggest frustration with current referrers, especially within your own speciality.

If you really want to make a great impression, find out about as much of these insights as you can before you even meet with them. And then when you do meet with them make sure you take a bunch of notes! This shows you are keen to listen and act.

Dr Ivan Misner, founder of Business Networking International and the 'father of modern marketing' (at least according to CNN), distilled one of the core challenges of including partnerships as part of your brand into a single sentence. 'When you give a referral', he wrote, 'you give a little of your reputation away. If the business you've referred someone to does a good job, it helps your reputation. But if it does a poor job, your reputation may be hurt'.

Strengthen the relationship with existing partners and establish new connections so that you can build your reputation and grow your clinic.

Key focus: Nurture

Principle: Foster relationships

> You can make more friends in two months by becoming interested in other people than you can in two years by trying to get other people interested in you.

Dale Carnegie, author of *How to Win Friends and Influence People*

Developing your rhythm

The final focus you need to have with the core element of Partners is to develop all new and existing relationships. You need to implement a rhythm for developing your relationships so that you become a meaningful and powerful force for good within your industry and community. Your partnerships need to go beyond transactional and enter the realm of transformational – for your partners, your clinic and, most importantly, your community.

Developing a rhythm, and so a system, for your relationships is important for the following reasons:

- **Consistency breeds results:** To create momentum and see a return on your investment (of time mainly), you need to be consistently connecting.

- **Connect with more people quicker:** If building relationships is top of mind, you will see more of the opportunities in front of you that you could otherwise miss.

- **Provide better quality value to existing relationships:** If nurturing referral relationships is a regular activity, you also develop a sensory acuity to identifying the best ways to care for your referrers, rather than always trying to catch up because you've left it too long. With the right focus, you can deliver ongoing quality interactions and value.

- **Growth is continual:** Developing rhythms and systems primes you, meaning nothing is left to chance. It also means others can jump in the hot seat and take over by following the existing recipe.

I was recently given another great example of the importance of nurturing partnerships. We had just landed in Melbourne, Victoria, for one of our Clinic Mastery workshops and I shared the Skybus ride from Melbourne airport into the CBD with Andrew Zacharia, co-founder of PhysioFit and Clinic Mastery mentor. Andrew was talking about their most recent hire and I was amazed to hear that they'd recruited yet another person. I asked Andrew how many team members he now had – and he told me he was up to 22. I was amazed because Andrew and his business partner, Peter Flynn (also a Clinic Mastery mentor), had grown their team from just the two of them to 22 people in about the same number of months!

I asked Andrew if he were to attribute one thing to his massive growth, what it would be. Andrew said, 'When most clinics are nurturing or creating one partnership a month, we have been doing one a day'. The PhysioFit team were more focused and systematically committed to working alongside, collaborating with and supporting their connections to build great relationships with their partners. They focused on contributing value to their partners rather than trying to simply get a referral out of them. Some of the ways that they were able to add value are listed in the following 'Tools and techniques'.

Tools and techniques

Use the following tips to strengthen partnerships:

1. **Offer outbound referrals:** Show your support and belief in a partner's products or services by referring clients to their business.
2. **Train their team:** Provide continuing professional development (CPD) to their practitioners or admin.
3. **Send topical articles:** Send topical, trending or relevant articles and publications to your partners to keep them informed.
4. **Offer professional development:** Pay for a subscription to a journal or online provider of CPD and assign or gift to your partner.
5. **Connect with experts:** Connect your partner with other education experts in your network to provide education to them.
6. **Share team training:** Do shared team CPD training sessions for practitioners and/or admin training.
7. **Observe their team:** Ask to spend time observing partners in their own environment so that you can better understand their work.
8. **Connect with health professionals:** Connect partners with like-minded health professionals who could complement their practice and increase referrals.
9. **Connect with businesses:** Connect partners with complementary businesses (for example, a podiatrist with a shoe store) so that they can work together.
10. **Connect with clubs:** Connect partners with clubs, associations, teams or workplaces that are a good fit to partner with.
11. **Connect with suppliers:** Share your contacts list of people you trust to help your business operate – it's likely your partners need someone in some aspect of their business.

12. **Create a mastermind:** Meet regularly with a select handful of partners and actively promote one another's business.

13. **Offer a website feature:** Promote your partners by having them create content to host on your website that you then distribute.

14. **Be social on media:** Like, comment, share and tag people in your partners' content to support its reach and message.

15. **Include them in your welcome pack:** Include a promotional offer from your partners' businesses inside your new client welcome pack.

16. **Consider presentation opportunities:** Create opportunities or introduce partners to public stages and audiences to present (for example, for workshops).

17. **Acknowledge referrals:** Acknowledge client referrals in a timely, personal and genuine manner.

18. **Include in welcome room services:** Offer waiting room services and refreshments from your partners.

19. **Make a follow-up call:** Provide a follow-up phone call to new clients referred to you by partners to check on their experience and response.

20. **Collaborate on health outcomes:** Write reports to other health professionals in the client's care to facilitate a team approach.

21. **Share partner offers:** Share, repost and distribute special offers that your partners are promoting.

22. **Entertain partners:** Host a workshop, party or networking event to celebrate and connect your network further.

23. **Endorse publicly:** Review your partners' practice or personal profile (for example, on Facebook or LinkedIn) and recommend their skills.

24. **Send a personal note:** Acknowledge and regularly appreciate your partners in written and verbal form, publicly and privately.

25. **Offer your services:** Invite your partners to receive your services at a special rate or in a unique way.

26. **Purchase their services:** Become a success story and fan of your partners' products and service to deliver authentic recommendations.

27. **Source resources:** Help partners access new, limited or specialised resources and equipment where you get good deals.

28. **Increase community impact:** Work with partners to host or contribute to community and charity events with your time, money or expertise (for example, through offering free screenings or making donations).

29. **Consider co-brand positioning:** Jointly host online communities (for example, a Facebook group) and market products and services as a package.

Core element: Paid

The third element to master in Degree 6 is Paid. This relates to you being able to transition from organic expansion to manufactured results by leveraging your brand building through paid sources.

Key focus: Strategy

Principle: Get on brand

The essence of strategy is choosing what not to do.

Michael Porter, academic specialising in economics,
business strategy and social causes

Targeted and timelined marketing

Your brand is about educating, engaging and enrolling clients in their healthcare journey towards meaningful outcomes. That includes self-care and client–therapist alliances. The purpose of building your brand is to attract the ideal clients, partners and team members (in both quality and quantity) you need to grow your clinic as sustainably as possible.

In *Purple Cow: Transform Your Business by Being Remarkable*, author Seth Godin says, 'A brand is the set of expectations, memories, stories and relationships that, taken together, account for a consumer's decision to choose one product or service over another'.

Your brand is 'happening' every minute and every moment, and it includes marketing. Marketing is a targeted and timelined activity. If you have a waitlist of clients, you still need to focus on brand and marketing. If you don't have enough team members or clients, or you're seeing a decline, you need to adjust your brand and marketing. Your brand is based on what you deliver and marketing is the communicating of that to the community.

Marketing elevates your brand. You may already be achieving organic reach with your clinic. This is the reach achieved just by operating a good business, as people slowly find out about you and your business grows. You can now look at paid reach for your business – that is, manufactured exposure and results. This is where you get to control and craft the message that people receive about your business.

'I'm not sure where to start'

'I'm overwhelmed. I'm not sure where to start. I have so many great ideas to implement.' Does this sound like you when it comes to paid marketing? Well, what's your desired outcome of the marketing? If you are not sure of your desired outcome, you can't possibly work on your strategy because you'll have no basis on which to make decisions.

A lack of clarity about results means you will be unable to prioritise the highest impact action/s. A lack of clarity in your clinic causes problems for team engagement, hiring and retaining people, targeting your marketing, and much more.

Marketing strategy is about building your brand profile, presence and position – by educating, engaging and enrolling clients, team members and partners – each day, week, month, quarter and year in a way that achieves your objectives.

Your marketing strategy needs to be outcome-focused and results-driven so that the strategy is a sustainable investment of your resources, including money and time. To ensure your strategy achieves its specified outcomes, it's important to build systems for consistency, automations for leveraged results and pillars for robustness and repeatability.

Marketing systems allow you to feel confident that when a team member or marketing agency takes over your marketing efforts – from organic social media to paid advertisements – they're going to do so in a consistent manner. And that means consistent in frequency, quality, tone of voice, brand and audience representation, reach and results – and so much more. Documenting the 'how-to' in your marketing to the 'why' you do it and for 'whom' are some of the most fundamental aspects to effective marketing. Simplify your marketing by identifying how many clients or team members you want to reach, have join your database and then enquire about working with you to ultimately then join your clinic.

Automations allow you to save time by using technology and systems to replace the human effort – from editing production quality to scheduling and posting, some great software is available for free or a low fee to help take some of the effort out of your marketing.

Pillars are like the structures that support your marketing efforts over the long term and represent the mediums through which you distribute and execute your marketing. From podcasts through to blogs, your email database and much more, these are the areas of your marketing that need to be continually reinforced and used to build brand awareness and reach more of your ideal people.

Relatable experience

Dr Jin Ong, owner of MetaMed and host of *The Art of Listening to Your Body* podcast, shared the following with us on the direct results that came from her focused marketing:

> We had a huge week this week! We had 41 new patients through our two clinics. Average for this time last year was around 20 per week. I set the goal to push digital advertising and search engine optimisation and it's working!

Key focus: Offers

Principle: Make it compelling

Always deliver more than expected.

Larry Page, co-founder of Google

Importance of tracking new clients

Your new client acquisition marketing cost should be between 5 and 10 per cent of the lifetime value (LTV) of that new client. When considering what offers to use to enrol these new clients, first look at your current acquisition cost and determine if it's in that 5 to 10 per cent range. If it's higher, you'll need to look at ways to lower costs (make it more sustainable) or increase the LTV. However, if you have a buffer in that range, you could allocate this to new offers, such as improving your welcome experience through a new client welcome pack. So if LTV of the client is $1000, you have $50 to $70 (or $100 at 10 per cent as the maximum amount) to acquire and deliver the welcome pack or experience as part of their journey.

It's important to note that when launching a clinic for the first time or expanding into a new market, you're likely going to have to invest more to acquire new clients. For example, you may need to invest 20 per cent of lifetime value in the early days to get the saturation in the market to then be able to scale it back.

Know thy regulations

It's common to hear of concern, trepidation and at times conjecture around crafting offers to attract more ideal people (clients, team members and partners) to your clinics. In particular, when it comes to navigating the client-attraction strategies available to a more general business audience, health professionals need to assert a high degree of sensitivity. This is because most health professionals are rightfully governed by various regulating bodies (none higher than the law), about how they can advertise and market their services. You need to consider and comply with the codes of conduct or regulations stipulated by these governing bodies. That is the punch line.

However, many health professionals who act out of fear (or comment on offers out of concern) are not familiar with the current and explicit nature of those guidelines and so leave great opportunity on the table. You often have much greater scope and liberties to promote your clinic and offer your services than what's expected or hearsay among the often conservative healthcare community. You need to find a way to reconcile helping more people as core to your purpose and the need for the community to know what you have to offer them in a way that is run through your filter for maximum reassurance and impact. Delve into the details of any relevant guidelines and regulations and find out what you can and can't do, and what you're comfortable with. Seek advice from an expert in this area if in any doubt.

Compelling means it resonates

As health professionals, we solve problems and provide solutions to improve our clients' quality of life. What we offer is not 'one size fits all'. We offer a variety of solutions to a variety of problems. Often our community only knows a fraction of what problems we can help with and what solutions we have to offer. To be able to help more people, we have to better communicate how we can help in a way that compels someone to take action and commit to improving their health.

The art of crafting compelling offers is simply getting better at communicating and connecting the problems and solutions in a way that helps someone take action in their healthcare. A compelling offer evokes interest and captures the attention of a targeted audience within your community. It resonates with some but not all, because it's not one size fits all. The intention is to craft compelling offers that resonate with your targeted personas and offer them ideal solutions that solve their problems, meet their needs and move them towards their goals.

The following sections outline the nine steps of crafting compelling offers.

Step 1: Identify your target audience (persona)

Who is this offer for? Consider the following:

- You need to put your offer in front of the right people for it to convert at its optimum (team or clients).
- You need to understand the challenges and desires of your specific target group or persona to craft a solution that is right for them.
- You need to speak the language that resonates with your target audience so that they feel like you are an authority on helping them.
- You need an audience who is warm to you – it's much harder to put an offer in front of a group who don't know you or

haven't received value in advance from you (for example, through your content or existing solutions).

- You must be aware of each of the following aspects about your target audience:
  - demographics
  - interests
  - hobbies
  - careers
  - family status
  - life status
  - financial status
  - time status
  - location/geography.

Step 2: Define the problem

What is your target group's pain, frustration or opportunity? Keep in mind the following:

- You need to articulate and communicate the problem better than the target audience can.
- You need to understand what the problem is and what impacts it is having on the lives of your target audience so that they feel they can trust you to help them. The problem may relate to:
  - lack of time to …
  - lack of money to …
  - lack of freedom to …
  - pain that is causing them to …
  - pain that is stopping them from …
  - frustration that they can't …
  - frustration they have to …
  - anxiety about …
  - wish or hope to be able to …
  - wish they could just …
  - wish to work towards …

Step 3: What's on offer?

Package your massive value and ensure this is clearly articulated:

- You need to clearly identify your solution to their problem.
- You need to specify what's included in the transaction.
- You need to highlight all the inclusions in your offer, including:
  - products
  - services
  - experiences
  - resources
  - partners who are also offering inclusions.
- Also highlight the recommended retail value of each inclusion, including:
  - cost of products
  - cost of services
  - cost of experiences
  - cost of resources.

Step 4: Identify the universal truths

Use common connective language when communicating your offer to clients. This can include using 'universal truths' to build connection. Consider using one or more of the following:

- 'Treat the cause, don't just manage the symptoms.'
- 'Prevention is better than a cure.'
- 'Your body is meant to move comfortably without pain.'
- 'Your body can heal itself.'

Step 5: Highlight the benefits

How will your improve your client's life? Make sure your highlight the following:

- What are going to be the benefits of taking up this offer?
- How will those benefits improve your client's life on a day-to-day basis?

- What will those benefits then truly mean for that person? What emotions will they invoke and what feelings will they create?

Step 6: Run through the reasons to enrol in the offer

Once your clients are getting closer to making a purchasing decision, you need to really hone in on why they should buy the offer. Make them aware of the following:

- Any additional reasons why they should enrol in the offer.
- Any other advantages of this transaction for the buyer – for example:
  - more time to …
  - more money to …
  - less stress and anxiety
  - fewer distractions and interruptions
  - feel more comfortable to be able to …
  - feel more confident to be able to …
  - achieve their next/best version of …

Step 7: Make it compelling

Why should clients purchase now? To convert on your offer, you need to make it irresistible by stacking the reasons why now is a good time. You can make the offer more compelling with the following:

- Reducing the buying window through limiting:
  - time: for example, offer expires on 1 March
  - spaces: for example, only 12 available
  - money: for example, only a set dollar amount of funding allocated
  - offerings: for example, only three classes/workshops available
  - bonuses: for example, bonuses expire on set date.
- Highlighting again your position as authority in this area to confirm why they should buy from you and your clinic.

Again, position yourself as the expert through your training and published content.

- Clarifying why timing is short – for example, because of:
  - industry changes
  - political changes
  - health fund changes.
- Highlighting the advantages of them being an early adopter.

Step 8: Reverse the risk

Your intention at this step is to help your client feel comfortable and certain in their decision, so you need to allay any fear or feelings of risk they may have – for example, that their money is just going to disappear into thin air or they're about to be tricked.

To allay these kinds of fears, consider including:

- a free trial offer
- a money back guarantee.

You can also communicate what you already do – for example, perhaps you already offer:

- a fixed fee (which is all-inclusive, with no hidden additions)
- a tailored four-week plan (offering a personalised road to recovery).

Step 9: Offer bonuses

Finally, you can add additional bonuses. Keep in mind the following:

- The aim here is to include additional value that is practical and complementary to what you are offering – that is, it will be of use to the buyer when they buy the main offer.
- Include things that will help them get results more quickly, help those results sustain for longer, help the delivery of the results or help make your method be more ideal, pleasurable

and/or economical on time or money. For example, you could offer additional:

- products
- services
- savings or discounts
- resources.

Please remember to understand and abide by the rules, laws and regulations that govern the marketing of your profession. Don't assume what you can and cannot do. Always stay true to your brand, and be authentic.

Relatable experience

Matt, a podiatrist, told us about a successful compelling offer he used:

> We set up a campaign on Facebook and via email with a compelling offer to those clients who had not been into the clinic within the last three months. The offer took 30 minutes to create and a couple of hours to follow up on responses and reach outs. At the end of the campaign, we generated 86 appointments for around $8000 in additional revenue. The offer has truly given us $1000 for each hour worked! This was a great way to fill the books for the growing team and was helpful in contributing to the purchase of some new equipment and technology to add to the clinic.

Key focus: Funnel

Principle: Educate, engage, enrol

We need to stop interrupting what people are interested in and be what people are interested in.

Craig Davis, chief creative officer at marketing and advertising agency
J Walter Thompson Worldwide

Attracting your ideal people

The final focus for the Paid core element is to ensure you have a journey that offers your clients pathways for progression, also known as a funnel. This allows you to take a broad spectrum of people within the community and, across time, add value to them so that they continue to want to know you more and work (or continue to work) with you as a client, team member or partner.

The process is called a *funnel* because your focus starts off wide as you educate and engage your audience before it then narrows as you enrol them into your clinic. So you want to capture attention and attract a large number of people to your business to begin with. This is often done through education-based marketing or engagement-based advertising on social media, or through crafting compelling offers to enrol in working with your clinic.

As people come to your business, you can offer them more products, services or information. The idea is that the more they learn about your services and solutions and the more contact they have with you, the more your ideal clients will want to work with you while your non-preferred clients will find other solutions. Your clinic will be much stronger and more sustainable if you know who your ideal clients are, and you then only work with them as much as possible. Remember the personas from earlier in this Degree. You must have a persona of your ideal client, and know what their needs are – and how you can meet these needs.

We mentioned Jim Lecinski's 'zero moment of truth' theory earlier in this Degree, which refers to the process people go through before they are ready to buy. Your marketing needs to ensure you and your clinic get in front of people at this earlier stage in their journey to get them into your marketing funnel. Remember – you are not trying to get them to enrol into your services immediately. You are trying to get them into your funnel so that you can teach them more about you and what you do, so that they become comfortable and ready to engage your services.

Use systems, automations and technology to help you reach and capture registrations on a database through your social media platforms, partnerships and website. You can then 'guide' those people to the relevant products, services and experiences you offer. Using a 'funnel' allows you to identify the stage of consideration and deliberation a person (prospective client or team member) is navigating to personalise or customise your engagement with them so that you can enrol them into the appropriate pathway for progression that solves their problem and delivers meaningful outcomes in their life.

High-impact action

Keep the following key insights and actions in mind as you build and strengthen your brand:

- A better way to sustainably help more people that doesn't involve trying to help everyone is available – you can help someone specifically.
- A meaningful and sustainable difference for someone requires empathy – *practical empathy*.
- Show up in all the right places: where (presence) are your ideal people (personas) in their greatest concentration, and when are they in a state that is ready, willing and able to enrol in your services?
- Your brand is your reputation and your reputation is based on doing the things you say you're going to do.
- Your profile is about crafting and committing to the delivery of those promises across all three areas of your personal, professional and practice profiles.
- Seek purposeful partnerships where building connection and establishing trust is emphasised over creating transactions – because it's what good people do.

- Add more value to your partners because it's the right thing to do, and the law of reciprocity will help you identify how to curate your list of partners.
- Schedule your rhythm for nurturing partnerships – remembering that any relationship that's going to thrive does so off the back of regular connection and communication.
- Marketing is about communicating. Brand is about substantiating. Marketing elevates what your brand is known for. Do both parts well.
- Craft compelling offers to solve meaningful outcomes for your ideal clients and grow your clinic sustainably.
- Attract your ideal people with a pathway for progression, from education to engagement and enrolment.

Brand summary

In order to grow your clinic, you need to build a remarkable brand by meaningfully and consistently providing value to your community. You can then partner with other complementary service providers to add more value and use paid resources to amplify the impact of your results to grow sustainably.

DEGREE 7:

EXPERIENCES

Create raving fans

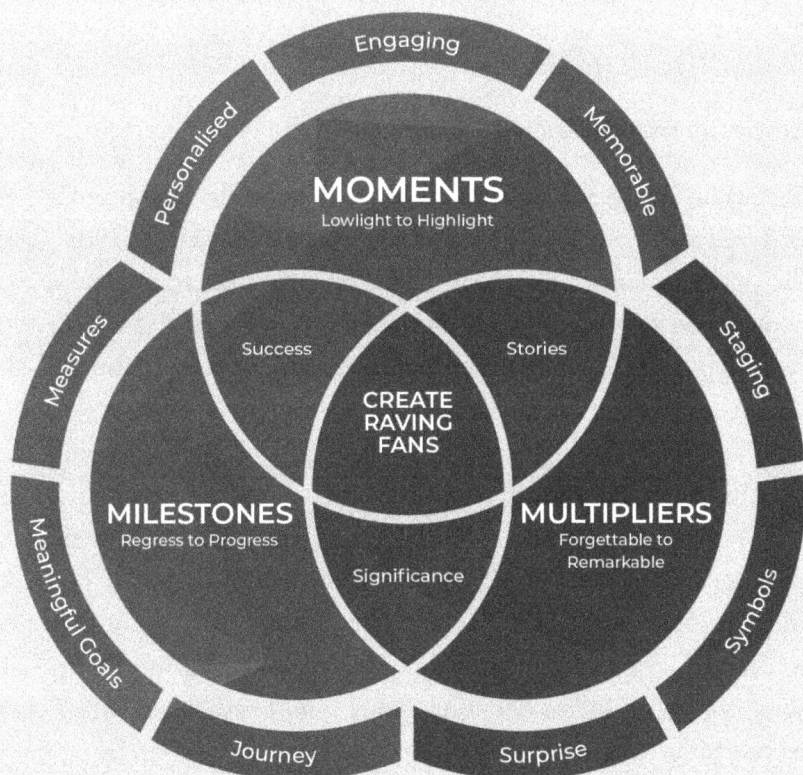

MOMENTS
Lowlight to Highlight

MILESTONES
Regress to Progress

MULTIPLIERS
Forgettable to
Remarkable

CREATE
RAVING
FANS

Success

Stories

Significance

Engaging

Personalised

Memorable

Measures

Staging

Meaningful Goals

Symbols

Journey

Surprise

Core element: Milestones

In their health journey, clients seek care at your clinic to help them experience measurable progress and achieve meaningful goals for a better quality of life. The Milestones element is all about crafting a client experience based on these measures of meaningful progress and goals so that you create more raving fans.

Key focus: Journey

Principle: Transform client experiences

The highest form of knowledge is empathy.

George Eliot, novelist

Empathy mapping client journeys

Experience fosters empathy. Empathy comes from experience. As you and your therapy team develop clinical experience, you foster the development of empathy – the ability to understand the *human* experience of your clients. The human experience is where biological, psychological and sociological influences contribute to the health and wellbeing of your clients.

Over time, this allows you to deliver a client experience that is empathetic because it maps the milestones in their journey in a way that matches and reflects their experience at each stage of their healthcare. Empathy mapping involves reflecting on the needs of your clients and understanding them in a way that allows you to deliver a journey of meaningful progress in their health and life. You can then document what your client says, does, thinks and feels. Using each of these aspects as headings and then documenting these empathetic insights under each heading is a great exercise to lead inspired teams to transform client experiences.

The healthcare landscape has shifted. Previously, the emphasis may have been on the years of experience of the *therapist*. Now, shifting client demands mean the emphasis is on the experience of the *clients* during the years of their care.

Your focus needs to be on the combination of health and care. You now need to consider the experience for the client in both domains, with an emphasis on the human experience of connection at the heart, because from that place we can have a great client alliance.

Clients deserve better

In the competitive private practice world, focusing solely on delivering a solution for your client's acute or presenting needs is just one aspect of growing your clinic. You also need to deliver your client solutions in a way that is truly remarkable – and that requires personalised, engaging and memorable experiences.

The clinic down the road is delivering a similar health outcome for a similar client. If you're going to stand out, you need to evolve how you deliver your service and how you stage your client's care experience.

Again, your choice to go into private practice and grow your clinic allows you the commercial and creative opportunity to do what you love – help more people, help them more often and add more value. So overlooking the experience milestones in your client's journey doesn't make sense. You need to provide holistic and remarkable solutions that transform client experiences.

The client journey

You probably have a great base of clients who love you and really appreciate what you do for them. Your aim is now to create more of these fans in a way that encourages them to actively 'rave' about your clinic to others in their network and, in turn, leads to more clients choosing your clinic for their healthcare needs.

Imagine having your new patients arrive with a feeling that they're in the right place for their health from their first visit – instead of spending most of that first visit with a degree of uncertainty, or being sceptical about whether they've made the right choice. They'd be more open to following through on your recommendations and more committed to their journey with you from the start, making it easier to work together to get meaningful health outcomes.

Throughout your client's journey, certain milestones signify their health progression and transformation. You have the opportunity to identify those meaningful milestones for your clients so that you can craft moments around them so that they are memorable. Examples of these milestones include the following:

· welcome or registration to your priority list (or waitlist)
· new client assessment visit
· phone call follow up after the new client visit
· time-based milestones – such as reassessment at the end of the school term or after a 12-week rehabilitation program is completed
· appointment–based milestones – for example, the appointment to discuss and present the management or treatment plan for the coming weeks and months for a client, or the appointment for the final visit of a specific care program such as WorkCover compensation or a government-sponsored program such as chronic disease management
· therapy outcome–based milestones – for example, marking progress in a certain activity or exercise as measured by a standardised in-treatment assessment such as range of movement in a joint or ability to perform a certain task fully without restriction and/or pain
· meaningful outcomes (discussed more in the following key focus).

By clarifying your client's journey as a sequence of milestones (events) that represent progression in their timeline and therapy outcomes, you're able to pre-frame, anticipate, guide and respond to their needs in a timely way to help them make the meaningful progress they want. The subtle, yet significant action is to document the personalised journey in a resource that is shared with the client, called a patient progress plan. In this plan, you detail for your client your recommendations and a timeline for treatment and milestone achievement.

Relatable experience

Jasmine, a clinic owner with a team of physiotherapists, had struggled to get her therapists to adopt the appointment-based milestone of delivering patient management plans as one part of the milestones of a client's journey into their practice. Her team were apprehensive because they felt they couldn't predict the future with their plans (and so provide dates for milestone of progress or achievement for the client).

Following deeper training on how empathy mapping is at the heart of patient-centred care and our passion to help people, Jasmine was able to get engagement from the team. She overcame their apprehension by emphasising their clients' education and empowerment, and how these were improved through providing hope, a meaningful goal and some simple adjustable steps to keep them progressing. Her team needed to think about it from the client's perspective, not their own – and not get caught up in it not being perfect, or whether they can predict the future or already communicate well.

Jasmine was over the moon when she was able to turn the team around, passing on this feedback from a client:

> An employee with a non-work related injury saw Jeremy
> [Jasmine's team member] this week, for treatment and to get
> some written information regarding her injury (to assist with
> management onsite until she has recovered). Jeremy provided
> a written management/treatment plan which outlined her
> restriction recommendations and a timeline. This information
> is more thorough than we are used to receiving from offsite

physiotherapists, and it is extremely helpful to the site medical centre. So thank you Jeremy! We have already started recommending people with other injuries to visit Jeremy.

When Jasmine asked Jeremy what he did to get such amazing feedback, he replied, 'It was the client journey and patient progress plan'.

To learn more about how to create management plans for your clients, access your free training on our website at www.clinicmastery.com/grow-your-clinic/free-courses.

You can also scan the following QR code to access a free management plans video series on the Clinic Mastery website.

Key focus: Meaningful goals

Principle: Find a worthy pursuit

> Our job is improving the quality of life,
> not just delaying death.

Hunter Patch Adams (Robin Williams) in *Patch Adams* (1998)

Overservicing versus underservicing

Our primary role as health professionals is to provide the best recommendations to each client. Your plan when creating meaningful goals for your clients must outline what you know and believe to be the best way for the client to overcome their health concern or challenge and reach their meaningful outcome.

We are not financial planners or personal assistants for our clients. We must first deliver our best health recommendation and only after that should we consider any logistics regarding the resources of the clients (such as time and money). If your recommendation is compromised before the client has been engaged about what the treatment involves, you are compromising their health and your integrity to put their health first.

As health professionals, we can have the right intention and the wrong execution. In an attempt to show how much we care (consciously or subconsciously), our effort to embrace empathy can instead take the form of expectation. We include implicit or explicit expectations about what our clients can or cannot do when it comes to their healthcare. Expectations about what they can afford in time, money, commitment, dependence or independence in their journey and so much more. It's important to seek to understand the expectations of your client, rather than making those assumptions that form the basis of your expectations.

You don't need to come back

Are you in sick care or health and wellness? As health professionals, we love helping people to live their best life. Positioning ourselves as the trusted health advisor for our clients means that we are always looking for better ways to optimise the quality of their life. Remember – our clients don't need to come back to us. To help ensure they do, we should be aiming to provide our clients with constant and never-ending improvement. The reality is that we are always updating our knowledge and skills to help the human body, and our clients should reap the benefit of professional development.

We should be proactive and establish some level of care to review and contribute to our clients' progress on their original and ongoing meaningful goals. A lot of change happens within the body during one hour, let alone one day or one month, so your focus should be on how can you not only 'maintain' your clients' health and function, but also contribute to optimising their health and function so that they can do more with a strong, healthy and capable mind and body. This may mean identifying related health concerns and/or challenges, identifying new meaningful goals, offering different health products, programs or services, or connecting them with your network of professionals or services to build on your previous treatment success with them.

A meaningful outcome is something that resonates with the client and can be celebrated – no matter how big or small. It's an outcome that makes a difference to their world and is measurable. The outcome could be that they can now say they complete a certain task, or grade how well they can complete it – for example, a child now being able to speak in front of their classmates, or an older client being able to walk a certain distance with their partner on the beach as part of their evening routine and maintaining connection.

Sometimes therapy can take months or years, depending on the client and therapy, so it's important to track and highlight meaningful and measurable progress along the way – what we call milestones. We celebrate those milestones by crafting a moment around them, through some sort of celebration or acknowledgment.

Mentor session notes

Empathy mapping client milestones in a journey

A *fiduciary* is someone who acts in alignment with their client's needs and well above their own needs. The fiduciary relationship is built on trust. To simplify and guide how you get your therapists on board with understanding the importance of playing the fiduciary role and providing the best recommendations for your clients, we recommend using the *trusted health advisor triangle*.

The three parts of the triangle are physiology, philosophy and methodology. By working through each of these parts with your therapist team, you're able to role-play any client presentation in your clinic to outline the ideal recommendations. The challenge is when therapists compromise their recommendations based on their own beliefs or perceptions of what the patient can afford or can commit to. A better option is to present your best recommendation and then make any accommodations (not compromises) only once the client is aware of what you have outlined to be the best recommendation for them.

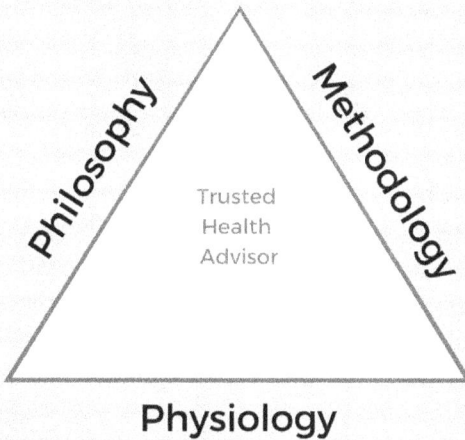

Physiology

Physiology

Grounded in the physiology of healing, transformation, form and function, our recommendations need to be based on the current evidence of the human body. Using physiological principles and evidence-based practices is an important first consideration when working towards achieving meaningful goals for your clients. An example would be mapping the expected healing, recovery or progression timelines of a certain clinical presentation based on the documented evidence of physiological adaptation, transformation and developmental progressions.

Philosophy

Philosophy is about connecting your experience, the client's perspective and the clinical evidence to form a paradigm for how you approach the delivery of your health and care.

Given that the evidence is continually being expanded (that is, it's not 'complete'), we are required to distil our clinical experience and education into a number of guiding principles (in other words, our philosophy) to be able to practise with a degree of consistency. Your philosophy relates to how you deliver client education, the vocabulary you use, how you integrate other therapists into the client's care, and how you deliver recommendations in the form of management plans.

Methodology

The client's plan will be backed by collaboration with the client on what needs to be done to create progress towards meaningful outcomes. The methodology will encompass what is done, when, by whom and where so key milestones are identified in the client's journey. Your methodology will outline techniques, sequences of therapy interventions, timelines for their delivery and milestones of a client journey to be delivered. Your methodology will be influenced by the additional education, workshops, facilities, equipment and resources you invest in on behalf of transforming client experiences.

In order for your team to follow through and deliver healthcare 'like you do', it's really important to clearly define, document and train on the physiology, philosophy and methodology in your clinic. This is why all clinics are so different in how they deliver their healthcare experiences. If you go to one physiotherapist, psychologist or speech pathologist in one suburb, you can then visit the same profession in another suburb for an entirely different experience. They might all say that they operate their clinics as evidence-based practices; however, this only contributes to some of the elements that make up the eventual client experience. Being clear on your trusted health advisor triangle will help your brand evolve to attract more ideal people – including team members (especially therapists), clients and partners.

Key focus: Measures

Principle: Track your impact

> You treat a disease, you win, you lose.
> You treat a person, I guarantee you, you'll win,
> no matter what the outcome.

Hunter Patch Adams (Robin Williams) in *Patch Adams* (1998)

Keep on helping people

On the other side of 'I love helping people' is the result of seeing your clients achieve their meaningful outcomes. This is not only meaningful, but can also be measurable. Where a client perhaps once couldn't perform a certain daily task, now they can. Or perhaps they're able to do something better than ever before. Seeing the progress we intended in our client's journey brings us great satisfaction as health professionals. It's why we do what we do as health professionals. It's even more fulfilling when you've faced adversity or setbacks along the way and still managed to make that progress. Setbacks are common – the human body and human experience are subject to many influences and forces that contribute to progression or regression of someone's health.

We know that the human body is never in a fixed state. It's always adjusting to the conditions, environment and stressors that it's exposed to. Tracking your impact allows you to know if you're making progress in a timely and meaningful way that aligns with the client's goals. While tracking your impact is the objective, given that the body is never fixed, we have the opportunity to continually make progress, and continually make measurable and meaningful change. The body and state of the human experience doesn't stop adapting to the biological, psychological, social or environmental forces, so why should we stop helping people make meaningful and measurable progress in their life? We need to keep on helping people.

Committing to your cause

Getting into a rhythm of *doing* in the client's journey – at the expense of time spent reflecting or analysing to track your progress – is easy. We have busy appointment schedules and several more people to see in a consulting day. It's not always easy to keep on helping people, perhaps because you're not able to find time in your appointment schedule, or they drop in and out of care. Whatever the reason, not having consistency in working the patient plan can limit the measurable progress.

You committed to the cause of helping people – it makes sense that the best version of you doing that is to be able to reflect, track, analyse and improve the progress plan at meaningful milestones along the way.

How will you measure up?

With factors such as increasing government regulations and third-party insurance requirements, perhaps you feel like we're progressing to a healthcare world where accountability is the cornerstone of accessibility – for you and your clients. Payers don't want to invest money without outcomes, so health professionals and clinics have an opportunity to lead the way with their commercial and creative ways to measure up. Create meaningful and measurable progress for clients now and continue to do it. As long as you're offering a valuable exchange that's accountable to progress, keep on helping people. We didn't get into healthcare to settle for client satisfaction; we want the fulfilment that comes from creating transformational change for our clients by delivering meaningful and measurable progress.

Aim to stand out based on making measurable and meaningful progress for your clients over their lifetime as their trusted health advisor – allow them to go from one meaningful milestone to the next. And hopefully those clients then connect you with more of your ideal clients (personas) so that you can continue to amplify your impact.

Reduce regression with reporting (what's it going to take)

As part of forming a patient–therapist alliance and achieving meaningful and measurable outcomes for a client's healthcare, it's valuable to review your progression. The intention is to prevent regression by tracking important measures that allow feedback loops to drive improvement in their healthcare journey. This can minimise client drop-off, enhance collaborative decision-making and improve client outcomes. Where possible, using the validated measurement tools specific to your profession or to the healthcare setting are ideal. Some of the reporting you can utilise include:

- **Patient-reported outcome measures (PROM):** Outcome is to identify the client's perception of their health status and/or progress; for example, quality of life, symptoms or functional ability.
- **Patient-reported experience measures (PREM):** Outcome is to identify the client's perception of their care and service; for example, net promoter score or quality of communication.
- **Therapist reported:** Outcome is to identify client's progress in subjective and objective assessments to gauge outcomes and experience.
- **Practice reported:** Outcome is to identify the client's progress in their client journey according to the ideals, standards and systems you've implemented; for example, new client checklist and follow up.

Core element: Moments

Moments allow you to go from low light to highlight in the client experience. Create remarkable healthcare experiences by delivering personalised, engaging and memorable moments.

Key focus: Personalised

Principle: Put the care in healthcare

> **They may forget what you said, but they will never forget how you made them feel.**
>
> Carl W Buehner

A connection opportunity

Healthcare is a deeply personal experience. Clients often share sensitive information about their life, and that can be a vulnerable experience for them. As health professionals, we're given a lot of trust based on an assumption (and regulations to back it) that we'll use those insights in confidence to personalise our care for clients. The trust is established from a personal connection and is the basis of us putting the care in healthcare.

Personalising client experiences allows you to:

- make clients feel valued
- deliver a best care approach
- offer sustainable solutions for clients
- impact clients' livelihood by focusing on their meaningful goals
- satisfy your team's professional desires through offering best practice
- gain fulfilment through making an impact
- gain trust and be positioned as a trusted health advisor
- create a more productive work environment through creating a positive culture
- create a clinic you are proud of
- explore your creative freedom to modernise healthcare.

Remember – your clinic success relies on adding more personalised value to your clients. You'll commercially be rewarded by creating more raving fans who refer more clients, partners and prospective team members to you.

Learning from a role model

We commonly hear clinic owners say, 'I wish my therapy team treated clients more like I would'. Whether it's to do with the attention to detail about the experience delivery, the progressive nature of therapy methods, or the communication clarity with which you guide clients through their care – or anything in between – you may have identified a skills gap that you need to close for greater consistency in the client experience at your clinic.

As your grow your clinic, add more therapists and increase the operational and business demands, your ability to train those skills and share those systems with your team can be limited. You can be and need to be their role model by defining, documenting and delivering the training to your team. Along the way, you can also facilitate other team leaders or therapists with experience to be able to do the same – actively transfer skills as a role model.

Care is always in demand

Being in high demand with clients is flattering at first, but then it becomes challenging as you navigate the demand for your clinical services while trying to empower other therapists to build their case load. If it's not you, then perhaps it is the senior therapist on your team who is in high demand and the juniors (or that 'thorn in the side' poor performer) who have too many spaces in their appointment calendar.

The bottleneck of the calendar that preferences the higher performers can be seen as an opportunity to personalise your training and development of your therapy team so they all are able to craft better connections with their client community. As a default, we believe every health professional cares about their clients. However, as a matter of design, you need to be able to demonstrate this care at all points – from the subtle to the significant interactions with clients in their care journey. That design is the result of good systems that allow you to show how much you care.

Bottle your blueprint

Capturing the acts of care to be able to teach your growing therapist team is possible. While some therapists will need development in their mindset and beliefs, others will need support in their capacity and confidence. All of these areas can be developed when you have a blueprint in place to show them the way.

You have an opportunity to bottle the actions and interactions you and your high-performing therapists do to create the connection with clients. Transferring the skills and training the systems takes careful observation through shadowing, detailed documentation of methods and real-world role-play. Success won't happen overnight. But for your therapists to deliver better care, you need to take better care of their training and development so that they can better care for their clients.

The 'Fred factor'

Fred Hollows was a prominent ophthalmologist who restored eyesight to thousands of people around the world. In one interview Fred said 'Every eye is an eye. When you are doing the surgery there [Cambodia], it is just as important as if you were doing it on the prime minister'. Fred embodied healthcare that was consistent with quality and connection to all. The 'Fred factor' is a representation of the idea that people will never forget how you made them feel through your care. The 'Fred approach' requires connection and consistency of physiology, philosophy and methodology.

Looking like you don't care

A 2008 study by John Gattorna for the Macquarie Graduate School of Management found that of all the reasons a business will lose a client, 68 per cent was attributed to perceived indifference – the feeling that you don't matter. You're just another number. It's challenging to think that a client could never return because they believe we don't care. We do care. We love helping people – it's why we do what we do.

However, failing to follow through on the things you say you're going to do, as subtle as they may be, can be significant – leading to a feeling of perceived indifference. At the heart of being a health professional is showing how much you care by connecting and communicating with clients to help them make meaningful progress in their life.

Put the care in healthcare

At every milestone in a client's journey, you're able to show how much you care by personalising an experience that empathetically maps to their journey. You can't leave it up to how your therapy team feels on the day; you've got to set some standards, and commit to the transfer of skills and the training in systems to deliver personalised care.

Key focus: Engaging

Principle: Elevate the experience

> Only a life lived for others is a life worthwhile.
>
> Albert Einstein

The extension of 'I love helping people'

The decision to go into private practice offers you a commercial and creative opportunity to deliver healthcare differently. The clients in your community have no shortage of healthcare options, so elevating the experience of your clients and delivering on your difference not only is important for creating more raving fans, but also facilitates engagement of your clients in their healthcare journey.

We all start our clinic with an inspiration to provide an engaging experience, a better quality experience and, most of all, a caring experience. Naturally the extension of 'I love helping people' is that we love helping people more often and adding more value to their lives. We love being in service of others. Elevating the health-care experience is an approach that allows you to continually find new and better ways to meet those objectives.

The reality of doing it

Whether it's lack of time or lack of inspiration or any other dis-traction that can come as you grow your clinic, actually bringing those elevated experiences to life for your clients can be an after-thought. Careful consideration, design, systems, training and people are needed to be able to integrate engagement into the experience. The reality of doing it is often much harder than the dime-a dozen ideas that are readily available. It's important to slow down, and remember you're here to grow your clinic as sustainably as possible. That means do one thing well and then move on to the next. It also means you need to consider the sustainability of what you implement – think of the time, resources, people, money and, most importantly, the contribution to meaningful outcomes that your elevated experiences will have.

Sacrificing substance for a superficial style

Perhaps another clinic in your area provides the kind of elevated and engaging experience you're aiming for. You might be able to copycat this clinic and aim for the same experience, but without much of the context on who the ideal client persona is and know-ing the details of the relevant empathy mapping journey, you're unlikely to be able to deliver the substance that your clients need and want. Instead, your efforts will likely come off as incoherent and superficial, causing the opposite effect of your intended out-come and having a negative impact on your clients' experience. Remember, you do you.

It's not particularly sustainable to copycat. What is sustainable is substance. Substance allows you to deliver cohesive, robust and elegant experiences that allow you to achieve meaningful results.

Your clients want solutions, in the form of meaningful progress. To do that you need to intelligently integrate in your elevated experiences.

Intelligent integration

Substance can be achieved when your engaging experience is created to 'help someone specifically'. Run ideas through the filter of your empathy mapping on your ideal client persona and ask yourself what you could do to create a moment and deliver an elevated experience around this specific milestone in their journey to contribute to meaningful progress.

A moment is an opportunity to engage your client in a way that elevates their experience at a specific milestone in their journey. Here are a few ways to create engaging moments:

· **Celebrate:** To praise and enjoy the moment.
· **Reinforce:** To use the moment to focus on a key message, instruction or piece of education as the client moves towards the next milestone.
· **Transition:** To use the moment to progress to different methods, exercises, therapists or routines.

Moments can be made memorable when they:

· elicit strong emotion
· are filled with meaning
· engage the five senses
· are shared with others.

Not a one-hit wonder

Remember your brand is a reflection of doing the thing you say you're going to do. Brand is about delivering your products, services and experiences consistently. Your clients expect consistency with what you say and do. Their experience is not a single moment delivered at a certain milestone, but rather the sum of their entire experience. Your opportunity is to build the systems for sustainably delivering engaging experiences for your clients to create more raving fans.

Key focus: Memorable

Principle: Be in the moment

> ### The opportunity is to create raving fans not just satisfied clients.
>
> Ben Lynch

Create the space for meaningful exchanges

Being in the moment is a great state to be in as a health professional and clinic owner. It's as if time slows down. You're connected to the client and the moment. You're the most resourceful version of yourself, finding solutions and doing it with ease. It's a great experience as a health professional because our presence in the moment cultivates a better experience for our clients.

Our clients need our full attention to get the best assessment, diagnosis, treatment and care. Having an awareness of where your attention is focused during your appointments – and encouraging the same awareness in your team – allows you to create meaningful exchanges with your clients.

Then start to dig a little deeper. We all want good word of mouth, but what memorable stories are you creating for your clients to share within their community?

We all love to tell our friends about good experiences we've had. How are you ensuring that your clinic comes up in these conversations, and not the clinic down the road? Always running on time is a good start. Giving the client your full attention is the next step. But what more can you do? Can you craft robust client journeys with meaningful milestones? Can you offer a carefully designed and fully integrated connection between physiology, philosophy and methodology for remarkable solutions?

You must deliver meaningful connections that people will remember and talk about. Presence allows you to make a meaningful connection to the moment, the person and their problem so that you can see the opportunity, and become memorable to each client.

Peak–end effect

Being memorable from the client's perspective can be explained by the peak–end effect, which is a cognitive bias that impacts how your clients will remember your connection, consultation or interaction. The bias relates to your clients giving a greater weighting to the delivery of the moments at each of their milestones. This means greater weighting is placed on the peaks of the experience and the end of the experience. The peaks include the most intense positive or negative moments. The end includes the final part of their experience.

The peak–end effect means certain moments in your clients' experiences are more important than others. Extra emphasis is placed on your initial interactions, such as new client assessments or the first appointment. If you don't get those experiences right, you might not have an opportunity for more in the future as clients seek alternative options.

The opportunity to create memorable experiences starts with the structure of your continuing professional development, and your onboarding and mentoring of your therapists to know how to lead a consultation. You need to put as much emphasis on this as on you and your team's technical knowledge. Remember – clients don't care how much you know until they know how much you care. So make space for that care through personalised connection and communication.

Relatable experience

Daniel, podiatrist and owner of a multidisciplinary clinic, shared with us some feedback they received from their newest practitioner – and their first ever psychologist in their practice – about the clinic's admin team and the systems it had in place to improve client experience. The feedback made Daniel's day and that of so many of his team members. The new practitioner passed the following on to the 'Awesome Admin Team':

> *I had a new client today who moved me to tears when she told me how amazing the reception team were with her. She told me she had never had such a good experience in regards to booking her appointment. Let me say this: that approach of making this person feel welcome at our service made the biggest of differences in this person's life. It meant that she did come to see me and now has a clear plan going forward for improving her life significantly. She is finally getting the support she needs. I am so very grateful that this is the first point of contact that our clients have. Tears in my eyes type of positive impact this has had! SERIOUSLY!*

Core element: Multipliers

Multipliers add more value to the moments you deliver at each of the milestones in a client's journey to transform a seemingly forgettable healthcare experience into a remarkable one.

Key focus: Staging

Principle: Design robust, cohesive experiences

> The secret of success is making your vocation your vacation.
>
> Mark Twain

Work is theatre

Joseph Pine is a best-selling author who coined the term 'experience economy'. In a recent *Grow Your Clinic* podcast with Pine, he emphasised that 'work is theatre and business is a stage', capturing perfectly the imagery that inspires the creation of truly remarkable healthcare experiences. When we start a consulting day, we are showing up and acting the part of the health professional. Acting isn't fake or phony; it's about being intentional as to which parts of ourselves to share in the appropriate context, knowing that our clients need us to be fundamentally human in our interaction, but that we can also play the character of the health professional trusted advisor at the same time.

The creative freedom to design robust, cohesive and on-brand experiences for a niche within our community is an impact and commercial opportunity. As Pine has highlighted, experiences in their truest form are distinct economic offerings. They add more value to clients and they add more value to your clinic.

Mentor session notes

Michael Rizk, co-founder of iMove Physiotherapy and Clinic Mastery mentor, created and offered a new world of experiences at his clinic – in the form of the tailor-made global running experience called iMove Explore. This experience is a leadership, running and adventure tour of the Arctic Circle and Iceland, and is a distinct economic offering for their ideal client personas at iMove Physiotherapy. The tour offers these clients the opportunity to see the mountains, beaches, volcanoes, glaciers, lakes and landscapes of some of the world's most picturesque places. They designed the experience for clients to go beyond their limits and expand their world by:

- running on thousand-year-old trails
- submerging themselves in the lakes that time forgot

- exploring the culture and immersing themselves in the food and local activities
- expanding their experience of the world, and growing their potential within it.

This experience offered more than just physical adventure. It engaged what Rizk called 'the awakening of the mind to allow you to use adventure and a sense of play in your day-to-day work, business and life'. In this offering, the iMove team moved beyond simply providing physical therapy health services and entered the realm of experiences. Joseph Pine, author of *The Experience Economy*, refers to experiences as 'time well spent' and services as 'time well saved'.

As clinic owners, you have the choice to go beyond simply providing health services and to explore a new world of experiences (distinct economic offerings). That's not to say health services are not important or valuable – they are still the cornerstone of healthcare and clinic ownership. However, the commercial and creative opportunity that is afforded to you as a clinic owner is that you don't have to follow the status quo. In a private practice, you are unlikely to be restricted by bureaucracy and you likely have a desire to 'help someone specifically'. The conditions are perfect when it comes to your freedom and ability to transform client experiences and deliver remarkable solutions for your community.

Time well spent

Attention. It's scarce. Everyone is trying to capture the attention of everyone else. And competition always exists for your attention – whether that be your kids asking what's for dinner, the advertisements on your social media, or the inbox full of requests from suppliers, team members and partners. The competition to capture attention goes beyond the clinic down the road that might be trying to capture the attention of the same client or community that you seek to serve. The competition is global, 24/7, 365 days a year.

You seek to capture the attention of your community to educate, engage and enrol them into a health journey that delivers meaningful and remarkable solutions. So what you offer and how you offer it needs to be worthy of their attention. The community is developing a more refined discernment about where they want to invest their attention and spend their time. However, don't discount the opportunity you have to provide that remarkable experience – to position time in your clinic as time well spent because of the experience you offer as a health professional. That experience can make people intentionally choose you to spend their time with.

Perhaps we can default to thinking that because clients come to us with a problem, they are somehow begrudgingly showing up to 'spend their time' with us until they get 'fixed'. The opportunity as described by Joseph Pine is to instead design robust, personal, transformative and cohesive experiences. The risk is to not focus on the proactive creation of these experiences so your clinic becomes a place where people believe their time is well spent – and instead create a place where people get compared, commoditised and overlooked by prospective team members, clients and partners.

Architect and experiential designer Jon Jerde, founder of The Jerde Partnership, proposed, 'Our purpose is to fabricate rich, experiential places that inspire and engage the human spirit … What we do is design time … the primary design focus is not an object, but time itself. It's designing what happens to people in time, in a place'.

What this requires is intentional design that has clear organising principles to transform and transcend the healthcare journey – from the education you actively engage in with your clients, through the aesthetic and physical environment of how they interact, to the connection with others in their journey through shared experiences that engage them in personal way. The starting point can be a simple mind shift: imagine if clients paid for the experience of 'time well spent' at your clinic (for example through an admission fee) and the service of 'time well saved' was simply one part of that. What would you do differently to deliver a personalised, engaging and memorable experience?

Key focus: Symbols

Principle: Connect purpose with processes

> ### If you don't stand for something, you will fall for anything.
>
> Alexander Hamilton

The legacy of an oak tree

Chris and Lauren are the founders of Eat Speak Learn Canberra, offering speech pathology and exercise physiology services. The following is their story.

We started a family tradition in 2013 of documenting important milestones in our life. It all started with the birth of our son, Flynn. We took Flynn to the arboretum in Canberra and captured a photo of him next to a baby oak tree. It's now become a tradition every year to get a photo with Flynn next to that same oak tree to document their growth and celebrate another milestone.

Not only was Flynn born, in 2013 the National Disability Insurance Scheme (NDIS) was started and we also decided to launch Eat Speak Learn from our spare room at home, with the intention to help families in our community to document and celebrate the milestones of growth.

We wanted to give our families something that they could be really proud of, and help them celebrate achievements no matter how big or small – because therapy outcomes don't happen overnight. We often compare a therapy journey to that of the oak tree. An oak tree starts as a small acorn. It battles storms, and relies on the generosity of its environment to grow. It takes years and years to build its strength and develop its potential, just like kids. The journey of growth is such a beautiful thing and it's when we reflect at those milestones that we celebrate the progress we've made.

For the families we work with, we set meaningful outcomes and take time to reflect on their growth and development at various milestones.

When our clients or one of our team members achieve one of the meaningful outcomes (milestones) they've set, we celebrate (moments) all the hard work that's gone into that by placing a paper-shaped leaf on our 'tree' (wall art) in the Eat Speak Learn clinic's welcome room (not our waiting room).

The tree provides us with a daily acknowledgement of what can be accomplished with hard work and dedication. It also demonstrates to other families that they're not alone in their journey. A whole community of people are sharing similar experiences.

Not only is the paper-shaped leaf added to the tree wall art in our clinic, we also acknowledge that accomplishment by sponsoring the plating of a real tree.

Eat Speak Learn has adopted a forest of oak trees at the National Arboretum in Canberra. We are recognising our clients' achievements each quarter by turning those leaves on the tree in our welcome room into living breathing oak trees in a very special place.

Not only do our kids have their own special trees up at the National Arboretum, but each and every client that we support at Eat Speak Learn also has the opportunity to have their very own tree there.

Wandering through that forest with our family has always been special to us and now it's going to mean so much more when we watch our community find their trees and celebrate their growth.

We look forward to giving our clients the coordinates to their tree, along with a number of symbols of their growth – for example, a pencil case, workbook, drink bottle or key ring (multipliers). The symbols we use will change over time through collaboration with our clients and team, keeping utility, sustainability and meaning at the forefront of our innovations.

Find your symbol

How can you symbolise meaningful outcomes to celebrate progress at milestones in your clients' healthcare journey?

Remember, at the core of our purpose as health professionals is the desire to help more people, help them more often and add more value to their life. The statement 'I love helping people' is the precursor to achieving meaningful outcomes for the community we seek to serve. Documenting the milestones of progress along the healthcare journey, celebrating the growth and creating the symbols for our clients to document the experience are central to creating raving fans and, in the process, amplifying your impact as a Clinic For Good.

Clinics that purposefully use symbols to enhance the client experience towards achieving meaningful outcomes while aligning their commitment to being a Clinic For Good will stand out as remarkable options within healthcare. It's the clinic owners bold enough to stand for something and bold enough to deliver on those promises who will grow their clinic and amplify their impact the most.

Key focus: Surprise

Principle: Do the subtle, yet significant thing

The only limit is your imagination.

Hiro, *Big Hero 6* (2014)

Joshie's adventure

Chris Hurn, CEO of Fountainhead Commercial Capital and author of *The Entrepreneur's Secret to Creating Wealth*, recently wrote in HuffPost about a customer experience that went above and beyond – and the experience came after Hurn had returned home. After returning from a family vacation at the Ritz-Carlton on Amelia Island (Florida), Hurn and his family realised that their son's beloved stuffed giraffe, named Joshie, did not make it home. So, like most parents would, he improvised, telling his distraught son as he put him to bed, 'Joshie is fine. He's just taking an extra-long vacation at the resort'. Luckily Joshie had been found in the laundry at the Ritz-Carlton and arrived back home safely a few days later. To the surprise and delight of Hurn's son (and the rest of the family), inside Joshie's 'travel cabin' (the parcel) were photos showing what Joshie got up to during his extended vacation. The photos showed Joshie:

- wearing shades by the pool
- getting a massage at the spa
- making friends with other real and stuffed animals
- driving a golf cart at the beach.

The team also issued Joshie with a Ritz-Carlton ID badge, as an honorary member of the loss prevention team.

The surprise was subtle, yet significant. This was a gesture from the laundry and loss prevention team. It wasn't a leadership enforced requirement.

The lesson here is that, as a clinic owner, you can facilitate surprise and delight through experiences like the Joshie story for your own clients. You can create raving fans, much like Chris Hurn now is, by providing the subtle yet significant extras for your clients as part of their client experience. When you create the space for surprise, the culture for your team to see an opportunity and act, or the client journey structure to go above and beyond the status quo, you create the possibility of stories like this being shared by your community. You truly become remarkable.

Imagine if ...

Imagine if you had unlimited budget to invest into your client's experience. Imagine if you had uncapped team members to contribute to your client's experience. Imagine if you asked this question of yourself and your team – 'Imagine if …' This is a great exercise to use with your team to collaborate on the possibilities about transforming client experiences with no limits. Where could it take you? How could it allow you to redefine healthcare experiences? What industries could you learn from? Who could help you deliver your client experience? This concept can take you from the subtle – 'Imagine if we could capture and celebrate every meaningful achievement in our clinic' – to the significant – 'Imagine if we could build a playground for our community and the kids that come for therapy at our clinic'. The possibilities are infinite. Imagine if you asked your team …

Assets in action

Have a think about whether you could incorporate some of the following simple client experience ideas at your clinic:

- Send a welcome video to a new client from the clinic when booking is made.
- Email new client expectations, clinic directions and paperwork prior to the initial consult.
- Offer a welcome pack with practical value for your client's health.
- Think about welcome room sensory experiences that include scent, touch, sight, taste and sound.
- Send regular communications via text message or email appointment reminders, or call clients.
- Book a follow-up appointment at the time of booking the initial appointment.
- Implement a 'first 20 seconds' procedure to smile, say welcome and engage new clients on arrival.
- Induct and orientate all new clients at their first visit.
- Create an appointment structure to run on time every time.
- Use scripts to deliver consistent messages between practitioners.

- Explain what you'll cover in your consultation at the beginning.
- Deliver printed management plans to every new client with their outcomes defined.
- Ensure the practitioner handover of client to reception at front desk reiterates the discussed plan.
- Integrate technology for seamless payment processing.
- Ensure the client can make forward bookings according to their management plan at convenient times.
- Capture client feedback using the net promoter score (NPS).
- Reward loyal clients with special offers to products, services or experiences.
- Acknowledge client referrals in a timely, personal and genuine manner.
- Offer welcome room services and refreshments (such as a footbath or beverages).
- Provide a follow-up phone call to new clients to check on their experience.
- Write reports to other health professionals in the client's care to help adopt a team approach.
- Hand over items such as credit cards and personal belongings to clients with two hands.
- Identify the significant meaning behind the client's health problem.
- Use a customised app such as Physitrack to deliver tailored home exercise rehabilitation and create independence for clients.
- Show the client home activities, exercises, routines and habits so they can help themselves.
- Include follow-up emails and text message reminders if clients don't have future bookings.
- Recommend the best products, services and therapists to get the client the quickest result.

- Celebrate your client's birthday with a message from your clinic.
- Implement a client journey checklist to ensure quality and consistency for all clients.

High-impact action

Consider the following key insights and actions as you build your client experiences:

- Use empathy mapping to design client journeys and show how much you care.
- Identify the meaningful goals of your clients to stay the course on a care journey that achieves great outcomes.
- Track your impact across patient outcomes, experiences, therapist observations and assessments to know how your client and clinic are progressing.
- Embrace the 'Fred factor' and bottle your blueprint for how you deliver care so that your team can consistently deliver the *care* in healthcare.
- Elevate the client experience by using your empathy mapping to create moments where you enhance the important milestones of progress.
- Be 'in the moment' to create raving fans, not just satisfied clients.
- Work is theatre, so be intentional in your designing of robust, cohesive experiences.
- Connect purpose with processes and leave your legacy, like Eat Speak Learn's oak tree.
- Joshie's adventure shows us that core values lived daily are the core ingredient to going above and beyond to create a client story worth sharing.

Experiences summary

In order to grow your clinic, you need to create raving fans by transforming client experiences. You can focus on multiplying the moments around meaningful milestones in a client's journey to create experiences worth remarking about and stories that are worth sharing. The opportunity is to follow through on your core reason for being a health professional – the fact that you 'love helping people' – by embracing the creative and commercial freedoms of private practice to deliver modern and progressive health experiences for 'someone specifically'.

Conclusion

DOING WHAT YOU KNOW

Dream big, start small. But most of all, start.

Simon Sinek

Good people

The binding thread that connects us as health professionals is a desire to serve the people in our local and global community. We love helping people. We believe that life is better with a stronger and healthier mind-body-spirit. As health professionals, we're committed to helping people experience better health so that they can do more of the things they love doing, with the people they love. We believe that helping people to be the best versions of themselves is a great contribution to society – a noble pursuit. As health professionals, we believe that being a clinic owner allows you, not owes you, the commercial and creative opportunity to transform the healthcare experience to help more people – including clients, team members, partners and the causes that matter to you. At their core, health professionals are Good People who want to amplify their impact and grow their Clinics For Good.

Clinics For Good

Two elements are central to being a Clinic For Good:

1. **You are a 'good' clinic:** You are sustainably growing your clinic by creating meaningful and measurable growth across each of the 7 Degrees outlined in this book. You need to grow your clinic in order for you to enable the second element.
2. **You do 'good':** You amplify your impact by aligning, integrating and contributing to the causes that matter to you.

Even with the best intentions, Good People creating Clinics For Good are faced with the hardships, adversities and realities of being a business owner. Whether it be navigating the stress of breaking even, losing team members, working insanely long hours, navigating the emotional roller-coaster of fluctuating passion for your work, juggling the work–life integration with family, dealing with overwhelming demands for your attention or anything else that happens to distract you from your big vision, being a clinic owner is a massive undertaking. It's perhaps bigger than other undertakings because you care so much about the people you work with (including your clients, team, partners and community), so you want to give it your best, uphold your commitment and follow through on what you say you're going to do so that you can bring to life your vision as a Clinic For Good. In order to overcome those hardships, adversities and realities, it's important to embrace the Grow Your Clinic experience with an approach that emphasises that you do it ASAP – as *sustainably* as possible.

ASAP

Wanting to progress to that next milestone in growing your clinic as soon as possible is natural. However, there's always another milestone to hit after that one, and another after that; the milestones keep coming. It's quite an adventure.

Juggling the 'needs of the moment' that demand you work 'in the business' and the desire to devote time to working 'on the business' to sustainably create a Clinic For Good requires clarity and commitment to *how* you will navigate the adventure. It can feel frustrating when you're constantly dealing with emails, calls, team member enquiries, client feedback and operational issues, when all you want to do is work on the 'big ideas' to bring your vision to life. Without any clarity or commitment to *how* you'll navigate the adventure of being a Clinic For Good, you'll find the juggle between taking care of business needs now and building your future business a real challenge.

In a subtle, yet significant adjustment, perhaps you can progress to that next milestone in growing your clinic by embracing the ASAP – as sustainable as possible – approach instead of as soon as possible.

Sustainable is:

- simple, not easy
- transformational, not transactional
- leaves a legacy, not a liability
- evidence-based practice, not compromise
- profitable, not just breaking even
- creates workflow, not workload
- meaningfully inspired, not motivational will-power
- fulfilling, not draining
- impact, not indifference
- infinite, not finite.

Doing what you know

At the start of this book, we explored the importance of knowing what to do so that you could grow your clinic as sustainably as possible. The reality is that learning how to run a business as a clinic owner was unlikely to have been part of your university training as a health professional. You need to learn on the job, through experience, from peers, from coaches and advisors, from books, podcasts and anything in between. While timeless principles can be applied to growing your clinic, the reality is that as new philosophies, methodologies and technologies emerge, the knowledge base of how to grow your clinic is ever-expanding.

In this book we've shared some of the best practices we've used to help grow clinics within our team and community of clients. However, learning without doing is useless. So it's valuable to ask yourself:

- Do you **know** what to do to grow your clinic?
  - If yes, then *action a fraction* every day.
  - If no, get guidance, ask for help, learn some of it yourself, and leverage the expertise of others so you don't need to do it all by yourself.
- Are you **doing** what you know to grow your clinic?
  - If yes, how well are you doing it? You should embrace mastery – a lifelong pursuit of improvement, and being 1 per cent better than you were yesterday. Mastery is not about just 'doing it once'.
  - If no, embrace progress over perfection; you don't need to know it all before you start and find the support network to help you.

Action a fraction

Those clinic owners who will get the most out of this book, who get the most out of the content, coaching and community at Clinic Mastery and who get the most out of themselves are action takers. They 'action a fraction'. They take action on a fraction of what they know, every day; they're not trying to do it all at once, and nor are they trying to be an 'overnight success'. They're simply and sustainably going beyond knowing what to do and doing what they know by practising the 'action a fraction' approach.

Every day is a new opportunity to make progress – the action might be small or it might be significant, but you're still moving towards your vision for the future when you take action. No matter how close or far away the next milestone in growing your clinic may seem, action a fraction every day. It will help you to grow your clinic as sustainably as possible and help you to amplify your impact as a Clinic For Good.

All the best in taking action by doing what you know.

If this book resonated with you, please pass it on to someone else who it might also resonate with.

ABOUT CLINIC MASTERY

Alone, we can do so little;
together, we can do so much.

Helen Keller

At Clinic Mastery, we believe that health professionals are good people, and that through their work they do good every day. We believe that those health professionals turned clinic owners want to be able to amplify their impact by helping more people in their local and global communities.

Every day we wake up to help these health professionals to Amplify their Impact™ by creating Clinics For Good® which are sustainable, successful clinics that have a positive and profound impact for the causes that matter to them. Let us be clear: we work with change makers – good people inspired to be a force for good in the world.

We work with progressives who want to shift the status quo in their profession. We work with clinic owners who want to lead inspired teams, transform client experiences and grow their clinics as sustainably as possible.

Clinic Mastery's influential growth can be attributed to our values-based approach to growing your clinic and our mission to support the most impactful community of health professionals in private practice. Some of the things we do to support this mission are:

- for every client we enrol, we provide a series of microfinance loans to businesswomen in developing countries through

Opportunity International, supporting Clinic Mastery's mission and helping to break the chain of poverty in a sustainable way

- for every progress report completed by our members each month, they acknowledge their growth by choosing a cause that we contribute to on their behalf – such as providing meals to people suffering from hunger, providing days of education for children or providing days of access to clean water for people around the world.

We make this impact happen through our Business Academy, where our members are provided with coaching, content and community support to implement Clinic Mastery's 7 Degrees framework.

Insights: Coaching

Making the right decisions at the right time is vital to growing your clinic sustainably. Through our coaching framework, you'll receive key insights from a team that have the experience and expertise to help you make those key decisions in alignment with your vision of the future. Clinic Mastery's Business Academy is the ultimate co-pilot for a clinic owner who is navigating the stages of business growth.

Intelligence: Content

You don't need to start from scratch when documenting and collating the systems to sustainably grow your clinic. Clinic Mastery's Business Academy provides you with a massive and ever increasing content library of systems, policies, procedures, templates and plug and play assets used by clinics in the real world. This content library provides you with the operating intelligence to help you grow your clinic in alignment with the key insights you've gained through coaching.

Implementation: Community

Clinic Mastery is the community for progressive, purpose-driven health professionals who want to further ignite and integrate their passion for helping people as they grow their clinic. We use our innovative methodology to help clinic owners think differently and collaborate better. Through our extensive private community forum, alongside industry leaders, specialist consultants and our mastery partners, you're able to get answers on any topic about growing your clinic.

Your next step

To learn more about whether we can help you, the best place to start is the Assess Your Clinic scorecard. This will help us to diagnose the biggest opportunities for you, and the steps that you can practically implement to continue on the journey of growing your clinic. If you feel like there is scope for us to help you with the implementation and you'd like to work with us – of course, you can explore that.

To learn more about Clinic Mastery, and to access the Assess Your Clinic scorecard, simply scan the following QR code or head to www.clinicmastery.com/assess-your-clinic.

KEEP IN TOUCH

You can contact us via the Clinic Mastery website (www. clinicmastery.com) or one of our social handles:

- facebook.com/clinicmastery
- instagram.com/clinicmastery
- twitter.com/clinicmastery
- youtube.com/clinicmastery
- pinterest.com/clinicmastery
- linkedin.com/company/clinicmastery.